JUDGMENT AFTER ARENDT

Judgment After Arendt

MAX DEUTSCHER
Macquarie University, Australia

ASHGATE

Published by
Ashgate Publishing Limited
Gower House
Croft Road
Aldershot
Hampshire GU11 3HR
England

Ashgate Publishing Company
Suite 420
101 Cherry Street
Burlington, VT 05401-4405
USA

Ashgate website: http://www.ashgate.com

British Library Cataloguing in Publication Data
Deutscher, Max, 1937-
Judgment after Arendt
1. Arendt, Hannah 2. Judgment (Ethics)
I. Title
170

Library of Congress Cataloging-in-Publication Data
Deutscher, Max, 1937-
Judgment after Arendt / Max Deutscher.
p. cm.
Includes bibliographical references (p.) and index.
ISBN-13: 978-0-7546-5688-3 (hardcover : alk. paper)
1. Arendt, Hannah. Life of the mind. 2. Philosophy. 3. Thought and thinking. 4. Will. 5. Judgment. I. Title.

B29.D428 2007
191--dc22

2006021580

ISBN 978-0-7546-5688-3

Printed and bound in Great Britain by Antony Rowe Ltd, Chippenham, Wiltshire.

Contents

Acknowledgements

I have written this book as a direct response to Arendt's own work, referring only occasionally to other writers on Arendt, and then mostly to mark a point of difference from their approach. But what I have written has been made possible by the wealth of material on Arendt that has appeared recently – especially in the last two decades. I would like to mention in particular the work of Ronald Beiner, Richard Bernstein, Margaret Canovan, Agnes Heller, Jerome Kohn, Julia Kristeva, Andrea Nye, Jacques Taminiaux, Dana Villa and Elizabeth Young-Bruehl. I also should mention some challenging discussions with George Markus on Kant's theory of judgment and its relation to Arendt's ideas. Errors in interpreting Kant that have remained would be my own.

I owe a great deal to the spirit of experimentation in new ideas and methods in philosophy that has marked the life of the Australian Association of Phenomenology and Social Philosophy. I made my first venture into writing about Arendt *qua* philosopher at the annual conference of that association in 1991, and thus met Agnes Heller and Ferenc Feher, the principal visiting speakers, who had been, of course, closely involved with Arendt and her work. They were encouraging and helpful in their advice and criticism. I was invited to speak (in 2002 and then again in 2003) at the annual conferences of the Association (then reconstituted as the Australian Association for Continental Philosophy). Those papers on philosophical themes in Arendt ('In the Blink of an Eye' and 'Being Willing') have become Chapters 3 and 7 in this work. I am grateful to the Association, and to those members of it who questioned me so thoroughly, and spoke encouragingly. Also, I developed the ideas on metaphor in describing mental activity that has become Chapter 4 while a visiting scholar in 2003 in the department of philosophy and the School of European Studies at the University of Queensland. I thank those departments for their scholarly and financial support.

Phyllis Perlstone, Isabel Karpin, Zoë Karpin, David Ellison, Penelope Deutscher, Marguerite La Caze and Daniel Nicholls have given vital encouragement and critical advice about various chapters. Paul Crittenden read the penultimate draft in its entirety and I thank him for his probing questions and constructive suggestions. Macquarie University has generously supported my work, first in terms of study leave and then by expediting my early retirement, to take up writing full time.

Abbreviations

LM	*The Life of the Mind*, Hannah Arendt: Book One, 'Thinking'
LMW	*The Life of the Mind*, Hannah Arendt: Book Two, 'Willing'

Introduction

Hannah Arendt describes thinking, willing and judging as within historical events and moral pressures. The meaning of thinking places in relief the sometimes destructive and sometimes beneficial 'wind' of thought (LM, 178). Arendt tells us of her 'preoccupation with mental activities' as arising most immediately from having attended the trial of Eichmann in Jerusalem in 1961. She observed the way Eichmann spoke of what he did as an official taking a direct role in the state policy of total extermination of Jewish people in Germany and the countries under its control. He was responsible for the official murder of innumerable Jewish people – indiscriminately – and yet what Arendt was struck by was 'a manifest shallowness in the doer that made it impossible to trace the uncontestable evil of his deeds to any deeper level of roots or motives.' Arendt finds writing about thinking 'awesome' (LM, 3), and the title *The Life of the Mind* 'presumptuous' in its promise to reveal the nature of thought and the mind. She disclaims the position of 'philosopher' as 'professional thinker' but (like Simone de Beauvoir) only so as to be free to develop the kind of philosophy that she needed.

Neither a 'demonic Evil' nor some 'stupidity' that might have explained his actions as due to incomprehension appeared in Eichmann when Arendt observed him at his trial. When confronted with his role in administering mass murder, Eichmann did not appear to have believed that he had committed any crime. He can 'function under the Nazi regime', Arendt observed, and he can even 'function well enough within the Israeli court and prison procedures', but 'when confronted with situations for which such routine procedures did not exist',[1] he is 'utterly helpless' and his 'cliché-ridden language' is a 'kind of macabre comedy'. It is the 'absence of thinking' – the absence of the preparedness to 'stop and think' which awakened Arendt's interest in thinking.

For all that, Arendt does not imagine that thinking will directly produce good deeds out of bad feelings and motives. Like Socrates in Plato's *Meno* she doubts that 'virtue can be taught'. 'Moral habits and customs can be unlearned and forgotten … [at an] alarming speed [when] new circumstances demand a change in manners and patterns of behaviour', as Arendt learned to her cost in her Germany of the 1930s. It was not some lack of moral education that Eichmann lacked – as if he had 'not learned or had forgotten his lessons' when he signed orders with the effect that the victims of Nazi prejudice be transported to be killed. She observed a negative quality that she described as 'thought-lessness',[2] a lack that pervaded everything Eichmann

---

1 In particular, when he had to speak for himself – explain why he had been prepared to be involved in murder.

2 Her friend Mary McCarthy, editor of the manuscript for *The Life of the Mind* tried to tell her that 'thoughtless' was inadequate as an English idiom. I hyphenate the word, interrupting our over-familiarity with it, and to suggest something of the gravity of the superficiality that she wished to convey.

said and every account he made of himself and his actions. This lack seemed to pervade a whole life. While observing the trial she was caused to wonder whether the activity of thinking itself might help to condition us to refuse to collude with evil.

In order to pursue this idea, Arendt marks a change within a long tradition of philosophy that contrasted the *vita activa* ('active life') with the *vita contemplativa* ('contemplative life'). Contemplation was reckoned to be 'the highest state of the mind' and Arendt remains friendly towards thinking as a contemplative withdrawal, good simply in and of itself. But the reader must take care, for she brings a critical eye to bear upon how we use that withdrawal, and upon debased versions of it. It is as one more thoughtless cliché that we declare 'If only people would stop and think!' Furthermore, while thinking may condition us against conforming with evil that has become conventional, to deploy thinking with the express purpose of guaranteeing good behaviour would devalue it as a mere means to other ends. Thinking is part of living well and is a (fragile) bulwark against evil. (At least it supplants the time we would have spent in conformity.) So it would be precious to maintain that it had no bearing upon our motives, feelings, intentions and actions. It can moderate what we do in that *vita activa* – the public, noisy, busy, urgent sphere where resolve must swiftly follow thought, and that resolve must find its place in prompt action.

The life and concept of mind

In *The Life of the Mind* Arendt writes philosophy so as to displace metaphysical theories of mind. Arendt attacks the 'two worlds' theories of mind. She shares Gilbert Ryle's historical understanding of dualism,[3] tracing it from 'scholastic and reformation theology … Stoic-Augustinian theories of the will, Platonic and Aristotelian theories of … the immortality of the soul [and] in Descartes [who] was reformulating already prevalent theological doctrines of the soul in the new syntax of Galileo' (Ryle 1949, 23). Arendt means to write philosophy without creating a new metaphysics, and to this end, examines the resources of metaphor. Her method involves investigating the history of the illusion of dualism.[4] For Arendt, 'there are not two worlds, because metaphor unites them':

> I have clearly joined the ranks of those who for some time now have been attempting to dismantle metaphysics, and philosophy with all its categories, as we have known them from their beginning in Greece until today. Such dismantling is possible only on the assumption that the thread of tradition is broken and that we shall not be able to renew it. … The loss of the [continuity of the past as it seemed to be handed down from generation to generation] does not destroy the past, and the dismantling process itself is not destructive; it only draws conclusions from a loss which is a fact (LM, 212).

3 I mention Ryle in the same sentence as Arendt. She signals her attention to his methods. Influenced by phenomenology, each created a new genre of philosophy, 'post metaphysics', but historically informed.

4 By investigating the role of metaphor, she avoids the category confusions that Ryle exposes.

In 'dismantling' metaphysics, Arendt understands the impulses towards dualism, and treats her predecessors generously. She recognises the force of their thought even as she criticises them. In history they come before her; as thinkers they *are* 'before' her, in her presence.[5] For Ryle, we can apply our concepts of mind, as we can name local features of a landscape:

> It is, however, one thing to know how to apply … concepts [of mind], quite another to know how to correlate them with one another and with concepts of other sorts. Many people can talk sense with concepts but cannot talk sense about them; they know by practice how to operate … inside familiar fields … They are like people who know their way about their own parish, but cannot construct or read a map of it, much less a map of the region or continent in which their parish lies (Ryle 1949, 8).

It is Arendt's hypothesis that a dualism of thought and behaviour can be understood as a *metaphor* that is grounded in our experience of withdrawal from the world when we think, resolve our will, and take time for judgment. The business of metaphor is to present the facts of one category of discourse in those of another. How alike to Ryle's observation of 'dualism [as] the presentation of facts belonging to one category in the idioms appropriate to another'. That is precisely what metaphor and myth achieve.

Arendt finds the origins of her questions in classical Greek (and Roman) philosophy, along with the medievals' development of that tradition. In the precise sense of the word that carries no insult, Arendt's philosophical writing was to its times, ec-centric.[6] These days we are asked to admit the *decentric*.[7] We revalue the de-centring of the subject, the author, and so on. Arendt was already involved in *re*-centricity. That requires taking another centre, offset from the established point, and then (if you have the drive, knowledge and genius) subtending traditional discourse from this shifted point. The newly demarcated field, with its offset boundaries, then registers as 'eccentric'. In learning to read Arendt as a philosopher as well as a social and political thinker and critic, we must, then, place her work amongst its near contemporaries such as Jean-Paul Sartre, who went to Germany in the 1930s to attend lectures by Edmund Husserl. He was bent upon re-forming into a phenomenology of perception, the abstract formulations of the *intentionality* of language made by Brentano and Meinong.[8] Ryle, too, was eccentric in going to Germany then, for the same purpose.[9]

5 See Daniel Nicholls's 'The Vision of Morality' (Deutscher, 2000, 147–62) who recognises this rewarding ambiguity in the way an historical figure should be 'before us'.

6 The hyphen disturbs the slur and reminds us of the inflexion. Complex machinery involves ec-centric systems.

7 Author's neologism.

8 Husserl's final version of this was written in the late 1930s. Because he was Jewish, with all that implies, his *Crisis of European Sciences and Transcendental Phenomenology* (!) was not published until the 1950s – along with its remake in Technicolor by Merleau-Ponty as *The Phenomenology of Perception*, in 1945.

9 Back in Oxford, planning lectures on Bolzano, Brentano, Husserl and Meinong, he was mocked – 'Ryle now talks about three Austrian railway stations and a Chinese game of chance!' (Small 2001, 54).

The Second World War, and Arendt's role in it as a Jewish intellectual forced to escape from Germany during the 1930s, resulted in a break with the principal 'philosopher' in Germany, her teacher, colleague and sometime lover, Martin Heidegger. Heidegger himself distrusted the tendency for thinking to be taken over by 'professional' philosophers. Arendt's mocking of the pretensions of 'professional' thinkers is part of her undertaking the responsibility of being trained within the tradition of philosophy. She displays an easy familiarity with the whole range of philosophy that stems from the pre-Socratics, through the Greeks, then the medieval philosophers, through to the 'modern' philosophers from Descartes to Husserl. But, as with Sartre (and Ryle), Arendt learned new possibilities for philosophical writing from this new phenomenological tradition in German philosophy that arose with Husserl in the late nineteenth century.[10] In his final work, *Crisis of European Sciences and Transcendental Phenomenology*, Husserl wrote of philosophy and consciousness within the social and political crisis in Europe. He had a vision of philosophy as articulating the consciousness within which we encounter things and each other, so as to understand the differences that cause conflict and destruction. There is more than an echo of this concern in the way that Arendt approaches theories of mind and the business of thinking.

Thinking

Reviving Plato's idea of thinking as a conversation with oneself, Arendt reconsiders its 'invisibility' and 'inaudibility'. The 'privacy' of thought is enacted; this has implications for dualism's fallacy of 'two worlds' of mind and matter. Thinking 'stands in need of outward criteria', as Wittgenstein put it. Thinking has its autonomy, and maintains our integrity and power of judgment. Nevertheless, Arendt says, the 'privacy' of thought is a privation – of public discourse. Thinking presents to us what is absent from the senses; thinking readies us for active imagination. Thinking dismantles and recreates our concepts. It requires no special realm of truth beyond empirical methods of enquiry.

When thinking takes imagery in hand, it compresses experience to make recall possible. Arendt invokes the myth of Orpheus and Eurydice. The gods permit Orpheus, grieving for Eurydice, to descend into Hades to bring her back. He breaks his promise not to look back at her until they have crossed the border; she vanishes back into the underworld. Arendt uses this story as an allegory for the relation between 'subterranean' thought to its expression above ground. There is a crevasse between thought and writing (or social conversation) that must be respected. To speak or write (thoughtfully), we leave thought behind. Finally, drawing upon Kafka's vision of a 'He' who bears the pressures of what has happened, what will happen and what will have to be done, Arendt disturbs the Augustinian picture of past, present and future. In so doing she begins to locate the power and limitations of thought.

10 The most famous developments are by Heidegger in 1927 (*Being and Time*), Sartre in 1943 (*Being and Nothingness*) and Merleau-Ponty in 1945 (*The Phenomenology of Perception*).

Arendt contrasts emotion with thinking in terms of its relationship to bodily expression. We do not *learn* to blush with embarrassment but we must learn a language in which to express thought – whether to ourselves or to others. Since, unlike emotion, thought does not *appear* in one's body, it is by metaphor that we can describe thinking. Arendt's ideas of how metaphor is grounded in experience, lead her to suggest that the metaphors we use in describing thinking reveal it as virtually 'ineffable'. I modify her ideas here. We must learn to dismantle 'ineffability', just as she would dismantle dualism.

The reflexivity that thinking involves requires plurality within the self. We form and strengthen a sense of self in thinking things through,[11] but (as Arendt observes) it is a plurality in the self rather than a simple identity that we discover. Engaging this plurality, we can enjoy our own company, conversing in solitude. In contrast, it is when we have lost or repressed this reflexive plurality that we are cast out of solitude into loneliness – a state that Arendt describes as one of 'unbearable and unutterable horror'. Thought requires moments of privacy in order to strengthen the thinker's autonomy, to enrich their inner life and to prepare for the challenge of public encounters. But thought without public expression and response loses its way. To think is also to be prepared to think things through with others. Our need, as thinkers, for a public life will lead Arendt into the business of *willing* and *judging*.

Arendt marks what is peculiar to thinking by attending to the imperative, 'Stop and think!' What I have to do may be to *not* do something. To wait is to *not walk* off, to forbear is to *not say* what is on the tip of my tongue. In this, I am engaged in *negative* actions. Arendt's description of thinking as a 'stop and think' reminds us that to think is to be *not doing* something that otherwise we would have gone ahead with. Thinking turns out to be a negative action akin to *waiting*; thinking shares the ambiguity of *waiting*. It is action by inaction.[12] In these and other ways the mind (and thinking) seems to be marked by a kind of 'absence' or 'negativity'. Arendt alludes to this elusiveness in explaining our natural attraction to a dualism that imagines mind and body as separate entities. It is to expose the fallacy of dualism that she makes such close observations about thinking (and willing and judging) as a withdrawal from the world of perception and action.

Willing

Willing is part of the 'life of the mind', in dealing with what is not present to our senses. We think of what *has happened*, then form a will about how things *shall be*. Arendt explores the origins of the modern reader's scepticism about the Will, and exposes the conflicts of mind that gave rise to the various doctrines about it. Whereas thinking is marked by a mood of calm, and its needs are satisfied by thought itself, willing is marked by tension. When we call upon the will, something needs to be done. Resolution of the will's tension is achieved only by appropriate action – by directly solving the problem or by dismantling its components. Considered as an

11 A point made to me by Zoë Karpin, to counterbalance Arendt's claim.

12 Arendt's ideas will be developed explicitly in relation to Ryle's (on *Negative Actions*) at this point.

activity, willing is a superstition. ('From the tarmac, I was willing the plane to land safely.'[13]) I interpret it, rather, as a *mode* – that of *being willing*.[14]

Despite the troubled history of the Will, Arendt works to restore confidence in a concept and practice of willing. In a critique of the Will as an inner Command, she displaces the 'I' that is bent on dominance over its very own desires, habits and obduracy. In this renewal of 'willing', she demonstrates the need for something more than thinking, desiring, and then acting. We recognise the business of willing in free action. In releasing ourselves from conformist conduct, we 'set ourselves' towards our project. Such resolution has involved thinking and judgment. As against a long tradition of regarding the will as a force virtually transcendent of our nature, we find our willing (not surprisingly when all is said and done) in our expressive and performative utterances of the form 'I will …' or 'This shall be done …'.

Willing is elusive. It is neither an action[15] nor a *telling* of myself what I am to do. Arendt links willing and being free in a significant and particular way that derives in part from Augustine's realisation that it is *counter will*, not conflicting desires, that pose the response and problem for willing. More exactly, as Kant declares, it is in the will that we discover the possibility of freedom. But this discovery appears as something other than the answer to the weary old problem of how we tip the balance between given alternatives. The freedom we have in virtue of being capable of willing is that of *originating a new series of events*. The problem of *free will* had been misconceived as a force, inevitably quasi-supernatural, that intervened *ex machina* to oppose nature. Or else, thus tainted by association with such models, the will itself is rejected as an illusion. It is accepted merely as 'the strongest desire', or some quality of 'decisiveness' in one's temperament. Arendt develops a line of thought that makes an allegory of Kant's association of *thought* with *phenomenon* and *will* with *noumenon*. Thought's province is experience and concept. In *willing* we go beyond thinking. Nevertheless, far from claiming success in some novel solution to Kant's problems, Arendt declares herself (in the concluding pages of *Willing*) frustrated in her attempts to resolve the differences between thinking and willing. Her aim had been to understand how, although so different and even opposed in their priorities and demands upon our time and psyche, they could coherently work together and support each other.

Judging

> If judgment deal[s] with the past, the historian is the inquiring man who by relating it sits in judgment over it. If that is so, we may reclaim our human dignity … from the pseudo-divinity named History … Old Cato … sums up the political principle implied in the reclamation: '*The victorious cause pleased the gods, but the defeated one pleases Cato*' (LM, 216).

---

13 An example given me by Isabel Karpin.

14 'The will is "Will" when a concept and "will" when acting in a human subject' (Mary McCarthy, LM, 253).

15 To say that willing is an action generates a regression. One undertakes actions either willing or unwillingly, or even listlessly, as when there is nothing that I *am* going to do.

Mary McCarthy, friend of Arendt and editor of *The Life of the Mind* writes, 'Hannah Arendt died suddenly on December 4, 1975. It was a Thursday evening; she was entertaining friends. The Saturday before she had finished "Willing"' (LM, 241). In fact, Arendt had deferred writing on judgment, touching on the issue many times, but keeping other concepts in the foreground. Part III of this book is therefore an elaboration of what her writing suggests, and the development of my own ideas in co-ordination with these fragments. The elusiveness of *judging* recalls the elusiveness of thinking, and to discuss judgment requires a renewed examination of thinking in relation to willing. As a disturbance of ideas, Socratic thought uses the pursuit of definition as a pretext for a disruption of the habits of thought. For Arendt, too, philosophy renews our understanding of meaning by disturbing our familiarity with words. To *mean* something by our words and actions requires us to 'differ' – from each other and from our settled use of words and mores. This 'differing' is the system of deferral that Socrates called his 'ignorance' of meaning. In disturbing our habits, thinking begins to free us up for hitherto unconceived resolutions. And in becoming willing with a renewed mind we discover thought and will as precursors of judgment. When only action can still 'the will's worrying disquiet … [to think] produces [only] a paralysis of the will' (LM, 37). To break out of the impasse by will is violence – by judgment we bring thought and will to a head.

In beginning to deal with the need for judgment, and to recognise its autonomy in relation to both thinking and the will, Arendt had detoured back behind the origins of the problem in Kant. For Kant, it is by judgment that we bridge the gulf between the phenomenal world and the 'noumenal' order of being that lies beyond the range of established concepts. (It is in this 'noumenal' order that Kant locates our moral freedom.) He recognises the gulf in his process of dividing *reason* from *intellect*. It is by *reason* that we can recognise the experiential conditions of knowledge. It is by *intellect* that we grasp this 'noumenal' order. It is within this 'noumenal' order that we are free to act within a moral constraint, able to recognise issues of principle even while subject to natural causality.

For Arendt, these 'mythical constructions' (as Husserl called them) are an allegory of the gulf between thought and will. She wants something from them that is consistent with that re-establishment of the 'value of the surface' with which she opened *The Life of the Mind*. A dualism of mind and matter can be undone only as part of the dismantling of 'appearance' as against 'reality'. Within Kant's way of thinking, judgment has to work 'magic' if it is to traverse the divide between the phenomenal and the noumenal. Arendt uses *natality* to disrupt Kant's metaphysical problem of 'causality in the empirical order and freedom in the realm of pure understanding'. The arrival of a new being as from nowhere, with no previous history, becomes a metaphor for a freedom that is part of the natural order and yet autonomous. After this disruption of metaphysics by the newborn, we can lay hold of Kant's difference between 'phenomenal' causality and 'noumenal' freedom in our own way, in our own allegories.

In Kant, this distinction of 'phenomenal' and 'noumenal' runs parallel with 'what we can think' and 'what we must will'. In the second book ('Willing'), Arendt recognised how 'thought' is at odds with 'will' in mood. Following this lead, I describe how the competing demands of thought and will are brought to a head by the need for judgment. Judgment enters the scene as we move towards active involvement and, equally, when we 'stop and think'. Judgment is confined neither to the role of spectator, nor to that of the involved party, but it must involve a thinking will. It requires a willing thought to resolve the tension between thought and will. (Arendt's epigram, 'The only outward manifestation of the mind is absent-mindedness' reminds us how judgment must take in hand both thought's 'absence' and the will's wrench from thought.) I describe how there is a real, though indeterminate effect of thought upon action. There is a reserve of detachment that judgment carries with it from thinking's withdrawal. As to freedom – what we do may have its natural causes while being subject to moral and rational principle. In judgment, we return from thought, willing to bring under a concept or principle (or under a new concept or principle) what we experience and observe.

Dismantled metaphysics

To dismantle metaphysics requires me to take it in hand. Inevitably some sticks to my fingers. Some language of mind must survive dualism's hold on the imagination of what is involved in thinking, willing and judging. In attacking dualism's exaggeration of each individual's *privacy* of consciousness, Ryle stressed our dispositions and capacities as the non-visible and yet non-occult categories that structure a being as 'mindful'. Arendt did much the same with her revival of Kant's talk of our various 'faculties'. In their reference to dispositions and capacities, to 'faculties', they both continue the ('broken') tradition of Aristotle's appeal to powers in explaining a thing's 'soul'. The 'hidden' soul is what something or someone *can* do, even when it does not display its inclinations and possibilities. Arendt (with Ryle) reads Aristotle's attribution of a 'soul' to all living things in a fashion that deconstructs rather than supports dualism. Aristotle attempts to slip out from under the weight of the ideas about the 'soul', which had been so valued and inscribed by the talking Socrates and the writing Plato: 'Enough has been said of the views about the soul that have been handed down by our predecessors. Let us start again, as it were from the beginning.'

For the Greeks, the soul that left the body persisted (like Eurydice in Hades) as a ghost – a wraith, a remnant of the body, whose doom was to be aware of what was going on in the world, but incapable of acting within it. Given their adulation of heroism and of defining oneself in public action, any 'soul' would be unhappy to find itself in such a situation. Plato corrected this denigration of the soul as an impotent shadow, only to adulate the soul as present in the body to ready itself for a finer and more 'rational' life, freed from the needs and confusions of bodily existence. Plato permits his Socrates to state the risk in this view. Freed from bodily restriction, this ideal life of the soul might be illusory. Rather than being freed by death, the soul might simply die with the body (*Phaedo* para. 70). Informed by these problems, Aristotle makes the soul intrinsic to the body of which it is a form.[16] One's 'soul'

16 True, Christian theology beats up his talk of the 'soul' in an effort to found its need for something to survive the body and to meet its Maker. But Aristotle's 'soul' is distorted beyond recognition in this co-option.

could no more exist without one's body than could a banksia tree's robustness exist without the banksia tree. Plants, earthworms, and us, we all have souls, for these are the ways that what composes us goes together so that we function. Aristotle was himself inclined to imagine immortality for the soul as the 'form' of the body. But the form of the body is the *way* it forms. After its body's decay a 'soul' continues only as the 'form' of another body.

If, in our twenty-first century, philosophy has been set free of a dualism of soul (or mind) and body, our challenge is to reconsider the concepts and phenomena of the thinking, willing and judging body. To give centre stage to thinking, willing and judging as autonomous (even while framed socially and physically) might appear to readmit that old 'ghost' in the machine. Working with Arendt (and others), however, in attending to our allegories of surpassing time when we think, will and judge might allay that fear. I would argue that we are held captive by the opposing images of dualism and of reductive materialism. We are still inclined to remain willing victims of the illusion that we judge as from nowhere and no-when. Instead, we might learn to validate the materiality of mind even as we vindicate the power of thought to disturb each solution it constructs.

PART I
Appearances of Thought

Chapter 1

Appearances

Restoring appearances

Arendt approaches thinking by a detour around the rift of 'appearance' and 'reality' that is called the dualism of mind and body. The 'things of the world' are what can appear:

> In this world which we enter, appearing from a nowhere and from which we disappear into a nowhere, *Being and Appearing coincide* (LM, 19).

Epigrammatically – 'Nothing could appear … if recipients of appearances did not exist.' Reality does not reduce to its appearing, though. Just to the extent that *being* can appear (sometimes *via* specialised instruments), what *does* appear appears *as being* – as something that *exists*. A dualism of *appearance* and *being* is further undermined by the fact that the humans and other animals to which things appear are themselves things that appear. As much as we are the ones to which the world appears, we are numbered amongst the things of the world:[1]

> The worldliness of living things means that there is no subject that is not also an object and appears as such to somebody else, who guarantees its 'objective' reality (LM, 19).

Consciousness itself is within the 'worldly' order. From the pure fact 'that I am aware of myself and … can appear to myself', the reality of what I seem to be conscious of is 'never guaranteed'. As part of the world, each thinking 'I' loses its central position – 'to be alive means to live in a world that preceded one's own arrival and will survive one's departure.'

That 'world' in which every conscious being lives transcends the consciousness of any being to whom it appears. Still, it is marked out by the time spans of those who live in it, along with the natural recurrences of day and night, and the seasons that it presents to them:

> On this level of sheer being alive, appearance and disappearance … are the primordial events (that) mark out time, the time span between birth and death … Thus the lived experience of the length of a year changes radically throughout our life (LM, 20).

This temporal 'appearance and disappearance' structures our experience of time – 'a year is the fifth of the whole life of a five-year-old'. Against these relativities we

---

1 See Sartre on the phenomenon (Sartre 1976, 'Introduction'), and Heidegger's nuanced treatment of appearing (Heidegger 1962, 'Introduction'). 'Each writes in the spirit of Nietzsche's attack on Being as lying *behind* appearance'.

construct an idea of an invariant length of a year 'that never changes', set against a concept of a world without beginning or end.

Arendt begins to differentiate 'the inorganic thereness of lifeless matter' from 'living beings' in terms of *appearing* and *appearance* rather than of *mind* and *body*. These 'living beings … are possessed by an urge toward self-display which answers the fact of (their) own appearingness' (LM, 21). This idea of self-display is introduced by a twist on the philosopher's standard picture of the 'richness' of the world of appearance in contrast with the bare, spare world of the physicist: What is 'hardly ever mentioned by the thinkers and philosophers … [is] the sheer entertainment value of its views, sounds and smells.' There is a theatrical side to this. The appeal of 'being' itself is the appeal of the 'world in its appearances' as the entertainment value of the world as the bearer of beauty. This value of things beyond their usefulness is matched by the value that the viewer of them places upon themself in the desire to display their *own* appearance(s):

> Living things *make their appearance* like actors on a stage set for them. … To appear always means to seem to others, and this seeming varies according to the standpoint … of the spectators. [E]very appearing thing acquires … a kind of disguise that may … hide or disfigure it (LM, 21).

The scudding beauty of the world along with this plasticity of roles of those who behold it all underlines the stable solidity of the world, in fact. This stability is presupposed by these appearances and is the stage for our own display of them.[2]

If 'all the world's a stage' on which we can display ourselves, this world is all the ways it appears to us. This fact makes it possible to displace the 'natural straightforward attitude'[3] of my experience as a translucent medium that carries me directly to its relatively opaque object. Instead, I 'withdraw from the world as it appears and … bend back toward the self' (LM, 22), to experience as (to use my own expression) 'its seeming to me that …' rather than as 'the world's appearing (to me) thus and so.' Arendt points out the fallacy in inferring from this shift in attention, that 'really' we experience only our own experiences. She analyses the fallacy while recognising its plausibility:

> [This fallacy] would never have been able to survive … if it had not so plausibly corresponded to some basic experiences. As Merleau-Ponty put it, 'I can flee being only into being' (LM, 23).

I can reject the reality of what presents itself, but then can turn only to reality in some other guise. Arendt remarks pithily that 'since Being and Appearing coincide for men, this means that I can flee appearance only into appearance.' Arendt's theme of thinking is that it appears as a *withdrawal* from the world of action. Though the world must *appear* in order to *appear real*, to treat the world as only *its appearing to*

---

2 See *On Beauty and Being Just* for a consonant investigation of beauty and display (Scarry 1999).

3 A phrase Husserl creates and constantly uses in his final work in 1937 (Husserl 1970).

me signals an attitude of withdrawal from it. The world does not have to be known (impossibly) as a *being in itself*, in order that it, *itself*, be known, but a withdrawal from the world of action is made possible by thought. The withdrawal can be described only in terms of what it is not – and in terms of what is foregone in order that thinking take the power of pre-eminence. In the existentialist terms of Sartre and Beauvoir, in *being for myself* I take cognisance of a world that has being for me. I do not, in that same act, take cognisance of my *being for another*. That mode can take me by surprise when I discover myself as the object of another's scrutiny. In Arendt's terms:

> [To treat the world only as it '*seems to me*'] would cause no great problem if we were mere spectators … thrown into the world to look after it … and be entertained by it. … However, *we are of the world and not merely in it* … While we come from a nowhere, we arrive well equipped to deal with whatever appears to us and to take part in the play of the world (LM, 22).

Other things appear and disappear as we open and close our eyes, but our own appearing and disappearing does not thus appear and disappear. I cannot hold sway over this appearance of myself. This shows that the 'two worlds' picture is a radical distortion of my experience that I have in *being for myself* (Deutscher 2002, Chapter 7). Since that *being* that I take to be so privately 'my own' can appear to another, it is in the very realm of *being in itself*. It is not *another* being, but a differing mode of the same being. But we are not at once out of dualism into the uplands of patent physicality:

> [That I can flee appearance only into appearance] does not solve the problem [that] concerns the fitness of thought to appear at all, and the question is whether thinking … can [ever] find an adequate home in the world (LM, 23).

Dichotomies of mind and body

Restoring the surface

In this opening section, entitled 'Appearance', having set out from the 'phenomenal nature' of the world, Arendt is about to deconstruct ('true') *being* as against ('false') *appearance* by a 'reversal' of that 'hierarchy' so as to privilege the 'surface'. This leads her to reconsider the relation of body and mind, and to put '*appearance* and *semblance*' in place of the old dichotomy of '*being* and *appearing*'. She moves forwards from the critique of any dichotomy of *being* and *appearing* established by Nietzsche and taken up by the phenomenological tradition.[4] In fact she 'find(s) a first consoling hint regarding this subject … (in) … the old metaphysical dichotomy of (true) Being and (mere) Appearance.' Things do appear. In the attempt to establish the dichotomy, to privilege 'being' over 'appearing', the metaphysician relied on

4 Principally, Husserl, Heidegger, Sartre, Beauvoir and Merleau-Ponty.

'the primacy … of appearance' (LM, 23). *Appearing* is the only clue we have about this *being* as 'behind' the appearing.

The difference between the images of the world presented by the sciences and those thrown up within our 'everyday' dealings with things and people has revived the old metaphysical distinction. This difference does not, however, overtake the distinction of *being* and *appearing*. The object that is studied and described scientifically is known *as it appears* to the scientific investigator by measuring instruments and within speculative theory. The scientist works within the logic of *appearing* and *being* in the continual revision of experiment and theory. In Kant's philosophy, the bifurcation of *phenomenon* and *Ding an sich* ('thing in itself') places *appearance* in the textual foreground, just as Heidegger's division of *being* and *beings* places perceptible and lived *modes of being* in the philosopher's spotlight. Observing this inevitable primacy of appearance, Arendt ponders:

> Could it not be that appearances are there not for the sake of the life process but … that the life process is there for the sake of appearances? … [I]t should be obvious to the naked eye that the enormous variety of animal and plant life, the very richness in display in its sheer functional *superfluity*, cannot be accounted for by the common theories that understand life in terms of functionality (LM, 27–8).

When Arendt speculates that this urge for self-display cannot be explained in terms of 'functionality' (presumably a reference to any form of evolutionary mechanism), she sees the urge for display – the phenomenon of its luxuriant excess – as making no calculation of its practical benefits. The urge to display might have become entrenched in our species because of its role in attracting a mate and as a mode of competition with rivals. Nevertheless, whatever 'functionality' might explain its origin, our present use of that urge may have only a vanishing resemblance to what originated it. Intelligence has been of an evolutionary advantage to our species and having become intelligent we can philosophise. But one cannot infer that we are following some obscure 'evolutionary imperative' in making this particular use of our intelligence. There is, in that sense, no such thing as an 'evolutionary imperative'. To think so is to reinvest the process with a kind of hidden purpose – of 'ensuring the survival of the species'. Since evolutionary theory is constructed to *counter* an appeal to any over-arching Designer, an adaptive mechanism itself has no *purpose* of ensuring survival – whether (depending on one's version), of individuals, species, or genes. Such an idea would mirror the old theology in which a Creator imbues us with just that darkling intelligence by whose use we shall, after long travail, finally recognise that True Creator of our nature.

From evolution, via the surface, to mind and body

Our desires for self-display that attract Arendt's attention involve aesthetic judgment and are proto-political in intent. Arendt is not reducing the concepts of conscious behaviour to those of an evolutionary mechanism. Her language, though not reductionist in style, sustains an anti-dualist strategy nonetheless. The findings of 'modern science' as such, but also the socially interactive spirit of enquiry required by the sciences (as by philosophy and by literary creation) have dislodged Descartes' 'esprit' from its separate and controlling function over his 'corps'. Arendt's 'value of the surface' includes what anatomical investigation and ingenious experiments can discover. These strategies disclose worlds of new 'surfaces' – of the liver, heart and brain inside the body – of the interface between orbiting electrons and more or less stable nuclei of atoms, and so on. And, consider again the difference between the 'surface' as the sensible, expressive and legible human body as against its inner organs, bones, blood and sinews. It is the 'appearance' that these inner organs make possible that constitutes us essentially as ourselves. Even the brain, the repository of our memories and organ of our intelligence has its importance in enabling us to display our appearances – as worker, comedian, lover, speech-maker, dancer or philosopher.

All the same, Arendt is sensitive to the increasing role of physical theory in explaining these appearances. She is about to discuss a theme she calls *Body and soul*; *soul and mind* and the contemporary reader will be aware of a controversy about a possible *identity* of thought with functions and processes of the brain. Arendt is well aware of the work of Wittgenstein, Ryle and Strawson on the analytical side, and of Valéry and of Merleau-Ponty in Europe. While she works within a shared problematic of 'mind' 'soul' and 'body', she has her own version of the problem of the 'inner' and the 'outer'. She draws upon Heidegger's *displacement* of 'mind' and its 'objects' by *modes* – of *being in the world* – and cites Merleau-Ponty's treatment of 'inner' and 'outer' in terms of the 'visible' and the 'invisible'. Arendt suggests that the (metaphorical) divide of 'inner' and 'outer' is not the same for *soul* and body as it is for *mind* and body. It is not that the soul is somehow more 'spiritual'. Neither soul nor mind is an *entity*. They are capacities and skills, proneness and inclination. 'Soul' collects different capacities and inclinations than does 'mind'. As our capacities and inclinations towards feeling, the soul is more directly revealed in the body than is the mind. As the activation of our capacities and inclinations towards thinking, the life of the mind makes its 'outward sensible appearance' only in metaphorical language. As the activation of our propensity to feel, the life of the soul includes unlearned bodily expressions. While expressions of emotion may be conscious and deliberate, bodily gestures articulate them:

> [I]n its very intensity [this life of the soul] is much more adequately expressed in a glance, a sound a gesture, than in speech. … The emotions are no more *meant* to be shown in their unadulterated state than the inner organs by which we live. … The way they become manifest without the intervention of reflection and transference into speech – by glance, gesture, inarticulate sound – is no different from the way the higher animal species communicate very similar emotions to each other as well as to men (LM, 31–2).

In contrast, there are no standard natural signs of thinking. Unlike emotion and other feelings, thinking is rescued from inaccessibility only by language:

> Our mental activities … are conceived in speech even before being communicated, but speech is meant to be heard and words are meant to be understood by others who also have the ability to speak, just as a creature endowed with the sense of vision is meant to see and to be seen (LM, 32).

Thus, when we speak our thoughts, it is the thought itself that becomes manifest. Feelings stand in contrast with thoughts in this respect:

> [W]hat becomes manifest when we speak about psychic experiences [feelings] is never the experience itself but whatever we *think* about it when we reflect upon it. ... Every *show* of anger ... already contains a reflection on it and ...this gives the emotion the highly individualised form which is meaningful for all surface phenomena. To show one's anger is one form of self-presentation: I decide what is fit for appearance (LM, 31).

Arendt is developing a central role for *phenomena*, *appearing*, and *self-presentation* in her account of the life of the mind. The kind of non-dualism that Arendt describes – and performs – has its centre in her image of the person as a being *to whom things appear* and, equally, *who itself appears in the world of appearance*. (This resonates with Beauvoir and Sartre's *being for itself* that turns out to be, equally, a *being for others*.)

Displacing dualism

Although the spirit of her writing is not that of a reductive materialist, Arendt is resolute in her non-dualism. Nevertheless, we can recognise the problems faced by physicalist theories of mind within her theorising. Thinking may *happen* to me – I catch myself thinking about the first house I owned. Thinking is also something I *do*. Although under the sign of the negative, that I *stop* to think implies an action. I *stop* and think. Arendt observes how Merleau-Ponty attempts to soften dualism without falling into an extreme materialism, but his gesture does not satisfy her understanding of how 'mind' and 'soul' appear in the body:

> Merleau-Ponty ... (who) tried in all earnest to embark upon a 'philosophy of the flesh', was still misled by the old identification of mind and soul when he defined 'the mind as the *other side* of the body' (on the ground that) 'there is a body of the mind, and mind of the body and a chiasm between them.' Precisely the lack of such chiasmata or crossings over is the crux of mental phenomena (LM, 33).

Merleau-Ponty partially corrects this idea of a 'chiasm' between mind and body. An activity of 'mind', thought, is an abyss 'without foundation'. The soul, our propensity to feel, stands in marked contrast with the mind:

> [The soul] is not bottomless; it does indeed 'overflow' into the body; it 'encroaches' upon it, is hidden in it – and at the same time needs it, terminates in it, is *anchored* in it (LM, 33).

What Arendt makes of the distinction goes beyond what Merleau-Ponty has articulated. Evidently, as our propensity to feel, the soul involves the dispositions of the body – in 'anger, courage, appetite and sensation generally' (Arendt citing Aristotle, LM, 33). But Aristotle says in a 'rather tentative and uncharacteristic way' that insofar as the mind (the propensity to think) involves the use of imagination, which employs the afterglow of sensory experience, it could not exist or function without the body. In contrast, Arendt's 'mind' effects a metaphorical displacement of what we experience in sensation and feeling. She will develop her idea of the mind as manifest in metaphor, but here it is 'self-display' that takes centre stage. The distance and control that metaphor's power of displacement from sensation and feeling gives us, works in co-ordination with the need for *display*:

> A mindless creature cannot possess anything like an experience of self-identity; it is at the mercy of its … moods and emotions, (each of which) is a somatic experience; my heart aches when I am grieved, gets warm with sympathy … and similar physical sensations take possession of me with anger, wrath, envy (LM, 33).

This is a 'mere expressive stage, prior to its transformation' by thought's power of metaphor. We gain some power of choice over how we *appear*, and this enables us to construct an identity. Neither a feeling nor an emotion, courage is more than a propensity for certain behaviour, too. Arendt installs a proto-post-modern innovation. Courage is a kind of performance. We make ourselves courageous in our choice of what we display. Courage is the decision not to display one's fear:[5]

> The courageous man is not one whose soul lacks this emotion (of fear) or who can overcome it once and for all, but one who has decided that fear is not what he wants to show. Courage can then become second nature or a habit, but not in the sense that fearlessness replaces fear, as though it, too, could become an emotion (LM, 36).

Arendt's *Life of the Mind*, in 1971, like Ryle's *Concept of Mind* a little earlier, in 1949, places itself in an uneasy position with respect to a *science* of psychology. She complains about the 'monotonous sameness and pervasive ugliness so highly characteristic of the findings of modern psychology', compared with the 'enormous variety and richness of overt human conduct'. Arendt objects to lending any psychology that cannot respect individuality the status of a fundamental explanation of behaviour, feeling and thought. Even a psychology like Freud's that seeks to interpret thought, feeling and intention still reduces life to a few general categories, and has to be supplemented by common discourse, literature and phenomenology.

Semblance and hypocrisy

Thought and feeling involve our capacity for pretence. That we may pretend to have thoughts, feelings and intentions is a common source of commonsense dualism. Within the picture conjured up by pretence, *I* become 'one thing on the outside' not matched by my (true) inner self. Arendt disturbs this picture by use of a new notion of 'willing'[6] that she connects with her theme of our desire for display, gaining a new angle on the old problem of 'mind' and body', 'inner' and 'outer', 'private' and 'public'. The classical dualist model meshes with the Christian obsession with the

---

5 One cannot ignore the resonance between Arendt's and Sartre and Beauvoir's ideas of freedom and consciousness as formed by 'nihilation'.

6 This 'willing' is a theme of the second volume of her *Life of the Mind*, and of Part II of this work.

'whited sepulchre' who shows a good public face but who does not feel within, what they evince.

Arendt, however, points out that one who acts boldly is not a 'hypocrite' though they feel sickening fear all the while. They would not be more 'honest' if they declared their fear. Certainly, that 'pretense and wilful deception on the part of the performer (along with) error and illusion on the part of the spectator are … among (our) inherent potentialities' (LM, 36). But in Arendt's thought, these old 'sins and failings' appear only as inadequate forms of our virtues.[7] We live a decent and admirable life because we choose *not to appear*, in certain respects. Whether with numbed feelings or while feeling almost unconquerable exasperation, a parent, woken from deep sleep, acts towards their child with tender care. Their truth lies in the conduct. And since there is, also, offensive and misleading pretence, Arendt distinguishes between *self-display* and *self-presentation*:

> Self-display has no choice but to show whatever properties a living being possesses. Self-presentation [in contrast] would not be possible without a degree of self-awareness. … Only self-presentation is open to hypocrisy and pretense, … and the only way to tell pretense and make-believe from reality and truth is the former's failure to endure and remain consistent (LM, 36).

It is not so much, Arendt points out, that 'hypocrisy is the compliment vice pays to virtue', but that 'virtue begins with (my) compliment to it, by which I express my being pleased with it.' The hypocrite is the one who is not true to their social promise to act according to that special pleasure. But this is not to say that 'man … has created himself.'[8]

Appearance and semblance

Arendt distinguishes *appearance* from *semblance*. This is meant to replace both Locke's way of distinguishing between *appearance* and the 'substance' that we think of as *lying behind* it and the Kantian distinction of *phenomenon* and *thing in itself*. For Locke, there are on the one hand the impressions formed in us – our sensory 'ideas' as of a world presented directly. On the other hand there is the world as described in physics – something postulated to satisfy the conditions of theory, and not presented, as such, within our sensations. The 'world' of colour, sound, taste, smell and touch is then partially salvaged as the powers of things (as described within physics) to bring about those sensations within us. If the world is *only* as described within the elementary terms of physics, then in it nothing is coloured.[9] A sensation as *of* colour could not, if physics is descriptively complete, be *of* anything that physically exists. If sensations *are* red, and nothing in the physical world is red, then sensations are not in the physical world! Radical physicalism may end up in a still more severe version of dualism.

---

7 I have discussed this matter in detail elsewhere (Deutscher 1983, Chapter 7).

8 Sartre does recognise the facticity of feelings that I may nonetheless '*nihilate*' so as to frame or modify them.

9 A 'power' in things to produce sensations of colour in us is a colourless.

Moral ontology

The intelligible division between *appearing* and *being* is one that we negotiate in practice. Arendt draws a moral lesson from the failure to draw a viable metaphysical division between the two. We avoid hypocrisy – 'not being as one appears' – by taking up strategies of appearing that we can sustain.[10] I am as 'sincere' as any fragmented human being can be when I 'appear always as [I] wish to appear to others even if it happens that [I] … appear to no one but [my]self' (LM, 37). In contrast, as a hypocrite I let my manner of appearing to others drop away when I am sure I am alone. To appear 'as I am', I accept the task of making a visible, assessable object of myself. I need to get to know myself – to discover what behaviour and commitment to action I can, in fact, sustain. This includes the thoughts and feelings I can sustain along with that behaviour. *That* we think (and *what* we think) sets the ethos of our lives, but it is not what truly we are. We can think terrible things and then do the right thing the instant that the occasion demands it. We can have fine feelings and then proceed to act unscrupulously, cruelly. Arendt expresses the thought provisionally here:

> Because of the gap between inside and outside, between the ground of appearance and appearance, … no matter how different and individualised we appear and how deliberately we have chosen this individuality, it remains true that 'inside we are all alike', unchangeable except at the cost of the very functioning of our inner psychic and bodily organs (LM, 38).

We should not be afraid of 'mere semblance'. Distinctions can be made between semblance and appearance, and between 'authentic' and 'inauthentic' appearance. Mirages 'dissolve of their own accord' and despite our study of astronomy the sun appears to 'rise'. We have to deal critically with semblance and with appearance while dispelling the illusion that we are on the way to uncovering pure being behind the appearance: 'the uncovering destroys a deception; it does not discover anything authentically appearing' (LM, 39).

Arendt plays a skilful game with the grave tradition of *being* and *appearing*; she shifts us from regarding it as a dichotomy about which we can only theorise, remote from it. She relocates the rift between appearing ('semblance') and 'being' (how something is), setting out from the way in which organisms display a 'semblance' in order to confuse or delude their would-be predators:

> [Q]uite a number of [animals] are also able to produce semblances – [to] … counterfeit a physical appearance – and men and animals both possess an innate ability to manipulate appearance for the sake of deception. To unmask the 'true' identity of an animal behind its adaptive temporary color is not unlike the unmasking of a hypocrite (LM, 39).

Hypocrisy, no simple matter of 'appearing as one is not', is the production of an image that one cannot sustain in public, under stress. An image one would not bother

10 Like Sartre, she is claiming that we do not achieve 'sincerity' by aiming at some essential 'given' in oneself.

to maintain in private. In this rift between *appearing* and *being* the difference between what actually occurs and what is empirically discernible gives some plausibility to the metaphysics of being and appearance. Arendt comments thus on the division between an inner self and an outer one of 'mere public appearance:

> [An inside self] never appears to either the inner or the outward sense, since none of the inner data possess stable, relatively permanent features which, being recognizable and identifiable, characterize individual appearance … It is precisely the absence of form and hence of any possibility of intuition that characterizes our experience of inner sensations (LM, 39–40).

Thought objects

Calling on Kant as exemplar, Arendt draws a distinction between what she calls the 'thinking ego', and the 'self'.[11] Kant's '*Ding an sich*' ('thing in itself'), like the traditional 'God', is 'not nothing' and yet cannot 'appear'. It cannot have being 'for us'. She observes that for Kant, these things are indeed not 'given'. They exist as if for us 'in the emphatic sense that reason cannot help thinking them and that they are of the greatest interest to men' (LM, 41). But Kant is mistaken in what he concludes from this interest:

> [He is wrong] to conclude … that there exist 'things in themselves' which, in their own intelligible sphere, *are* as we 'are' in a world of appearances. [Such a conclusion] belongs among the metaphysical fallacies, or semblances of reason, whose very existence Kant was the first to discover, to clarify and dispel (LM, 44–5).

Kant inclines towards the thought that our mind moves in an 'immaterial' sphere when we deal with what we understand rather than what we sense. To be in deep thought is like being in a deep sleep, he suggests, and this may be to the advantage of thought. The ideas in sleep 'may be clearer and broader than the very clearest in the waking state' just because we do not sense the body during sound sleep (LM, 44). Although she scorns these ideas about dreaming Arendt is interested in his idea of a kind of 'withdrawal' that is characteristic of deep thought, in which we feel no 'resistance of matter'. (The 'swiftness' of thought.) Arendt points out the fallacy of concluding that in thought we deal with immaterial realities, but she is not content with P.F. Strawson's trivialising of the error.[12] It did *appear* (to the ancients) that only a timeless being could 'grasp' a timeless truth. We have to uncover and correct a mere 'semblance' here, not expose an error of inference. This line of criticism is more productive. The 'semblance' of immateriality in thought is a real phenomenon. Considerations of time and of one's embodiment seem to fall away. This is not a *fallacy*, nor even a simple *illusion* – a mirage that vanishes as we approach. A state of creative concentration must have this semblance of immateriality. This

11 Her treatment strongly recalls the way Gilbert Ryle discusses the self's 'elusiveness' (Ryle 1949, 186–98).

12 For Strawson the fallacy is to infer from our grasp of timeless truths that we, as thinking beings, are timeless.

creative concentration need not be a neglect of the body. A musician's absorption in performance requires total bodily involvement. Nevertheless, they remain only subliminally aware of that. As Arendt puts it, 'thinking permits the mind to withdraw from the world without ever being able to leave it or transcend it' (LM, 45).

In a manner more outright than Heidegger's and very like Sartre's (in his introduction to *Being and Nothingness*) Arendt borrows directly from Husserl in making the crossing between subjectivity and objectivity:

> Though the seen tree may be an illusion, for the act of seeing, it is an object nevertheless. … Objectivity is built into the very subjectivity of consciousness by virtue of intentionality. Conversely and with the same justness, one may speak of the intentionality of appearances and of their built-in subjectivity (LM, 46).

It is this 'intentionality of appearance' along with its 'built-in subjectivity' that makes a solipsistic stance possible. Perception and thought is given the stress of 'It seems to me that', rather than leaning on the signifying clause that follows: – 'the lion looks hungry and menacing'. Those words that warn of such an *objectity* for perception become a mere sentential 'filler' that defines my private state of 'seeming'.

Arendt proceeds to draw a perhaps too extreme distinction between thinking and sensing. Employing her idea that thinking achieves its character and mode by 'de-sensing' what has been sensed, Arendt moves to secure the difference by reminding us of the most abstract thinking, contrasting that with the everyday particularities of perception. I can expect only to *think* of the (Parmenidean) 'One'. I could never hope to sense it. I would remark though, that not all thinking has such an abstract object. After all, Descartes (whose doubts Arendt herself is here examining) contrasts specific perceptions ('I am here sitting by the fire in my dressing gown') with specific thoughts ('Perhaps I am merely dreaming that I am sitting by the fire') (Descartes 1954, 62). Such thinking does not strip his sensing of its content. Rather (as Husserl expresses it for our previous [twentieth] century), Descartes's doubt 'brackets out' the entire sensory content, leaving it in place within thought's domain.

In fact, the radical division between the objects of thought and of perception recurs only when Descartes's 'radical subjectivism' declines into the old demarcation between the 'true world as described by physics' and 'the merely illusory qualities discovered by the sense'. Arendt's other side of this coin bears the mark of better currency, it seems to me. In speaking of Descartes's 'doubts' concerning what he senses, she remarks 'how strong was the experience of the thinking activity itself', and how 'passionate was his desire to find certainty' by means of thought, since it could not be gained simply by sensing what came to him (LM, 48). She has made her own observation about the 'self' and a 'thinking ego':

> To the philosopher, speaking out of the experience of the thinking ego,[13] man is quite naturally not just word but *thought made flesh*, the always mysterious, never fully elucidated incarnation of the thinking ability. … [T]his fictitious being … is neither the

---

13 Husserl places all natural objects of perception within brackets; Heidegger abandons the 'I think' in favour of 'modes of being'.

> product of a diseased brain nor one of the easily dispelled 'errors of the past', but the entirely authentic semblance of the thinking activity itself (LM, 47). [14]

Arendt's approach accepts the semblance of a pure thinking ego, even as she exposes its illusory character as a stable object in itself.

Thought in common sense

Arendt's exposure of the illusion of a 'pure thinking ego' arrives in a parcel along with her ideas about thinking as a 'de-sensing' of what we perceive, and as a withdrawal from the world. It is the 'unworldliness' of thinking that gives content to the illusion of a pure thinking ego. In so doing, she plays with the idea of a 'common sense' that rescues us from this 'useless' otherworldliness. As she says (following Aquinas), I need a 'kind of' common sense to 'keep my five senses together and guarantee that it is the same object that I see, touch, taste, smell, and hear' (LM, 50) – the sense that others may see, touch, taste, smell and hear what I do. There is no organ of such a sense, nor any specific qualities that it reveals. For Arendt it is what rescues sensation from its privacy – an attitude of resolution – an 'accomplishment' (as Husserl calls it) to perceive something in sensing it. This involves the realisation that 'though each single object appears in a different perspective for each individual[15] the context in which they appear is the same for the whole species' (LM, 50).

> [T]he five senses, utterly different from each other, have the same object in common, members of the same species have the context in common, members of the same species have the context in common that endows every single object with its particular meaning (LM, 50).

Arendt dares to say that a 'sensation' of reality arises from this *threefold* 'commonness'. It is 'sensational'! In dreaminess or exhaustion I can lapse into 'sensing sensations' rather than taking in and assessing a 'real world'. It is a 'sensation' when I 'come to'. The objects of sensation again stand out – over and against my experience and myself.

This common 'natural' ability of ours to perceive within the flux of experience a common object – common to the senses, and held and perceived in common between members of a species – is a prime part of what we call 'intelligence':

> To equate this 'inner sense' ['common sense'] … which cannot be physically localized with the faculty of thought is tempting indeed, because among the chief characteristics of thinking, occurring in a world of appearances and performed by an appearing being, is that it is itself invisible (LM, 51).

At the same time, Arendt wants to make a strong separation between *thought* and *common-sense reasoning*. Common-sense reasoning, including both practical

---

14 This analysis is elaborated in Le Dœuff's studies of the 'transcendental' attitude exhibited by various Shakespearean characters (Le Dœuff 1986, 26–8).

15 And the same point applies to the variety of senses that provide the one world for one individual.

calculation and scientific theorising and testing, does deal with things and involves no 'withdrawal' from the world. According to Arendt, what 'remains forever beyond [the] grasp [of thought]' is 'precisely reality as given to common sense, in its sheer thereness' (LM, 51–2):

> Thinking, however, which subjects everything it gets hold of to doubt, has no such natural, matter-of-fact relation to reality. … Descartes' … error … was to hope he could overcome his doubt by insisting on withdrawing from the world altogether. … But thinking can neither prove nor disprove the *feeling* of realness arising out of … *le bon sens*; when thinking withdraws from the world of appearances, it withdraws from the sensorily given and hence also from the feeling of realness, given by common sense (LM, 52).

Husserl's phenomenology of bracketing off perception's natural objects arises from the legacy of Cartesian doubt and dualism, and Husserl is ambivalent. Is his 'transcendence' a revolutionary new attitude or does it rescue a common practice from 'anonymity'?[16] Arendt herself places Husserl's (transcendental) method as 'the quite ordinary phenomenon of absent-mindedness, to be observed in anyone who happens to be absorbed in no matter what sort of thought'. In this reverse normalisation of Husserl's hyperbolic stance, Arendt has naturalised philosophising itself. Philosophy is natural to us, like breathing. A breath of fresh air that becomes a 'wind' of thought.

Intellect as science: reason as thought

By reference to physical theory we understand how a familiar everyday world, available to the senses, arises for us:

> Thinking … plays an enormous role in scientific enterprise, but it is the role of a means to [the end of] knowledge which … belongs to the world of appearances.[17] Cognition … never leave(s) the world of appearances altogether; if the scientists withdraw from it in order to 'think', it is only in order to find … more promising … methods [to use] towards it (LM, 54).

This attitude is part of a concept of *unlimited progress* – as if, even if science were to come to the ultimate truths about nature, it would develop new theories since 'the very continuity of the research implied something merely provisional'. Thus, Arendt argues that 'the scientist remains bound to the common sense by which we find our bearings in a world of appearances' (LM, 55–6). Lacking the power of thought to undo its own basis, science can find ways of making some progress, though its 'chief weakness … is that it lacks the safeguards inherent in sheer thinking, namely, thought's critical capacity (LM, 56).

Arendt refers us to Kant's distinction of 'Intellect [*Verstand*] whose concepts serve us to apprehend perceptions', and 'Reason [*Vernunft*], whose concepts serve us to conceive, or comprehend' (*Begreifen*). Intellect desires to grasp what is given

16 See my 'Husserl's Transcendental Subjectivity' (Small 2001, 3–24).

17 The new phenomena revealed by instruments and interpreted by theory are, themselves, 'phenomena'.

to the senses, and constructs the sciences. Reason wishes to understand *meaning* and becomes involved in 'thought'. It is best to set out from the metaphors that fall so naturally to Arendt's hand. *Verstand*'s desire is to 'grasp'. Thus, truth may come within its 'reach'. In contrast, not satisfied with the 'truth' grasped by *Verstand*, the desire of *Vernunft* is to 'search'. Within these metaphors of the manual labourer and the knight-errant, the distinction is consistent. *Vernunft* can establish *meaning* while on the quest, and this establishment is its special business – a capacity denied to the *Verstand* of science and of common sense. It is the business of common sense and science to determine 'what something is, and whether it exists'. But in asking, not 'Who is just?' but 'What is it to be just?' Socrates established a 'search for meaning' at the heart of thought. This 'search for meaning' is the affront to common sense:

> It is the sixth sense's function to fit us into the world of appearances and make us at home in the world given by our five senses; there we are and no questions asked (LM, 59).

Arendt describes Leibniz's distinction between truths of reason and truths of fact[18] to show that this is not her distinction between *Verstand* and *Vernunft* – Leibniz's 'intellect, the organ of knowledge and cognition, is still of this world; … it falls under the sway of nature' (LM, 60). Making the distinction is risky, inviting a return to the dualism she opposes. Certainly, 'the source of mathematical truth is the human brain, and brain power is no less natural … than our senses plus common sense' (LM, 60). This remark, however, implies that our ability to think is something beyond mere 'brain power'. Arendt's quotation from Yeats suggests a magnified comparison of computing and thinking that imagines the power of thought as a *deus ex machina*. This is not her position. There are no 'spiritualist or dualist truths' that run in parallel with 'scientific fact'. No sooner has Arendt answered the scientific idea of one's conception and birth as a 'random event' with Yeats's avowal 'A true miracle, say I / for who is not certain that he was meant to be' than she withdraws this 'meaning' from the arena of cause and effect. That one's life is 'meant to be' is not a *truth*.

Thinking meaning: from appearance to thought

There is the meaning of words and there is the meaning of intentions. I may be conceived and born with an intention – that of my parents that I become heir to their ideas, property and way of life. Or, born into a vacuum of expectations about what I should do with my existence, I may come to *mean* my existence to be *this* rather than *that*. These meanings are consistent with the degree of randomness in outcome that attends biological conception. Our *meanings*, culturally evolved and personally modified, are consistent with the chanciness of life – that human life should have appeared on the scene at all. Arendt's language is evocative of these hoary issues, but they are not her real concern. The meaning that can be lent to existence is what

18 A distinction taken over without question by Hume in his attack on the 'rationalism' typified by Leibniz.

comes by thought. This meaning is not a 'truth', whether of science or of any other 'realm':

> To expect truth to come from thinking signifies that we mistake the need to think with the urge to know. … The proposition that everybody who is 'was meant to be' can easily be refuted; but the certainty of the 'I was meant to be'[19] … is inherent in every thinking reflection on the I-am (LM, 61).

Although thinking must be employed in the attempt to know, a division between truth and meaning goes hand in hand with knowing and thinking. Truth is what can be known; what has meaning is what can be thought. Truth can be attained; it is a matter of fact. Questions of meaning have responses but not definitive answers. Thinking about meaning has no result beyond its own production. It is part of our life. Philosophers ('professional thinkers') have the vice of trying to rescue thinking from itself. They think that they can regularise and improve the reputation of thinking by making it subject to 'the criterion of truth'. They will to obtain positive results – philosophy is to be built upon a 'growing treasure of knowledge … retained and kept in store by civilization' (LM, 62). Even Kant, having sought only 'to eliminate the obstacles by which reason hinders itself … could not part altogether with the conviction that the final aim of thinking, as of knowledge, is truth and cognition' (LM, 62–3).

Arendt's distinction between thinking and acquiring knowledge means that thinking does not share science's aim of finding truth as verifiable fact – something that then remains useful as permanent data. Her explanation of this difference by appeal to a 'search for meaning' risks a relapse into a search for truth, nevertheless. Why should there not be truths about meaning? And is the scientific endeavour so different? All facts, even if verifiable in principle, are liable to revision. This meaning of Arendt's operates as an elusive quarry rather than as a description of thought's aim. Also, is thinking inevitably about *meaning*? If I find myself thinking about the first room I rented, what comes to me is my living in it, who was invited there, and so on. To say that my thinking was a 'quest for the meaning' casts a strange light upon it. This thinking about the room does reveal a meaning of one's life then – the desire to study, the need to establish privacy and all that might have meant. Such thoughts take on their own momentum. But the question of the 'meaning' of those experiences seems academic. As uncovering meaning, thought's aim must remain at the edge of awareness – an edgy business. It begins to emerge why any meaning that is revealed must remain elusive. Otherwise, it will appear as specific and intellectual knowledge – merely of the meaning of words, or of a guru's spurious knowledge of some 'meaning of life'.

In the midst of these difficult questions about her own quarry, it is a relief to find Arendt discovering Kant's difficulties about *Vernunft* – thought's 'reason' as against what is gained by the knowing intellect, *Verstand*. *Vernunft* does not deceive, since it does not offer truth. It falls to *Verstand* to do that. In consequence, Kant's own 'ideas of pure reason' are not truths, ultimate or not. Rather, they 'have the reality

19 The text actually reads: 'the *certainty of the I* "*was meant to be*"' … Perhaps this is a deliberate flouting of syntax, or it may be a slip on the part of Arendt or of her translator.

of a schema … [and] should be regarded only as analoga of real things' (LM, 64). As such, these 'ideas of reason' cannot represent 'the realness given by the senses playing together, kept in tune by common sense' (LM, 64). But neither can they (truly or falsely) *represent* some otherworldly realm. Kant does not wish to face this limiting fact without at once veiling it. If the objects of 'pure reason' were pure 'thought things' then it would appear that he has succeeded only in re-introducing the realm of pure speculative metaphysics that he meant to place as beyond the limits of critical inquiry.

Kant sometimes traduces his own distinction between *Vernunft* and *Verstand*. To claim that in thought, in 'pure reason', we find it 'necessary to regard all order in the world as if it had originated in the (intention) of a supreme reason' is to draw positive conclusions, as if of fact, from the pure ruminations of thought. But Arendt points out how Kant recants this error. He admits that the speculative interest of reason in freedom, immortality and God – these special objects of thought – cannot warrant his 'transcendental investigations'. So he backs away from those earlier 'positive' conclusions of transcendental investigations, relinquishing the appeal to 'purpose' and 'intention' as providing the meaning of the meaning of thinking. Arendt cites Kant with finality: 'Pure reason [thought] is in fact occupied with nothing but itself. It can have no other vocation' (Kant 1998, 610). Relief from the high-tone of a 'search for meaning'. Re-life for thinking.

Chapter 2

Thinking

Invisible, inaudible

> [A]mong the chief characteristics of thinking … is that it is itself invisible … Peirce … ignor[ed] the fact that thinking is not only invisible but also deals with invisibles, with things not *present* to the senses though they … mostly are also sense objects … collected in … memory (LM, 51).

> Plato concluded that the soul is invisible because it is made for the cognition of the invisible within a world of visible things (LM, 73).

> The life of the mind in which I keep myself company may be soundless; it is never silent and it can never be altogether oblivious of itself because of the reflexive nature of its activities (LM, 75).

Nothing seems more evident than that thinking is invisible. I look at someone writing. Fingers flash over the computer keys, then mark passages of a book with a 'high light' pen. For a moment the writer looks thoughtful. She turns to someone beside her, says something. He makes some reply. I go to look, as if to see the very thinking they're engaged in. I catch myself in the absurdity of the attempt. I am content to observe they're thinking.[1] I begin to reason meditatively like Descartes before me: 'Thinking must be a non-physical process occurring in a mind – a special place distinct from body.' More recent thoughts obtrude: 'The activities of the brain and the rest of the nervous system in co-ordination with the hormonal and other bodily systems are quite remarkable. They might amount to thinking.' Still, the very *thinking* of that 'system' – the human being – does not appear as such to the scrutinising eye.

Arendt is struck equally by the *in-audibility* of thinking, reminding us of Socrates whose 'thinking' is the silent conversation he has with himself. This extension of *conversation* to a process between me and myself, as 'two in one', evokes what we do when we think. Bent on keeping it to myself, what I am thinking seems so loud in my head that I have a tremor of fear. Someone might overhear it. Finding ourselves far from the city on a longed-for holiday, we are moved to the cliché – 'It's so quiet you can hear yourself think'.

Internal dialogue is a conversation dress rehearsal. Thinking stands to conversation as stage dialogue does to talking about the play after the event. One's thinking is sometimes a quite articulated conversation with oneself. At other times it is more a process of snatches of images associated with certain feelings, brief

---

1 A slight inflexion returns us to the problem of invisible/inaudible. Can I observe *their thinking*?

shorthand symbols whose meaning only the person knows, or perhaps understood by no one – something to be interpreted by a friend or analyst. As such, thinking is like a conversation between people who know each other well. Intimate friends may use few, if any, words in parts of their conversations. A nod, a gesture, a responsive expression, a burst of bodily miming in response to that expression add up to an exchange of views and feelings, efficient in its use of the immediacies of intimacy.

The likeness of thinking to a conversational internal dialogue intensifies the question whether *invisibility* should characterise it so centrally. I imagine that in thinking, if profoundly deaf, I might visualise the movements of my hands in 'signing', and then the gestures of a response. If deprived of sights as well as sounds, like Helen Keller, and having learned to converse by using touch to reveal another's gestures and lip movements, my inner discourse might take the form of kinaesthetic images.

In alighting first upon the *invisibility* of thinking Arendt thus reminds us, inadvertently, of the outlook of the sighted deaf. Perhaps the 'invisibility' of thought comes first to the mind of someone who both sees and hears because, in its gestures and facial expressions conversation is visible no less than audible. Furthermore, these thoughts we read are those of a philosopher – Arendt's in this case. They are the thoughts of a *writer*, whose thoughts are signified first as *visible*. The writer's 'inner' or 'invisible' thinking first emerges[2] as words glitter onto a computer screen.[3] But whether imagined as in-visible or as in-audible, thought is described by a curious kind of negation of what we do. For the thinker and for thought's recipient, thought is present as an absence of what is made available to public witness and assessment.

Private thought: public privation

Arendt quotes Epicurus the Stoic's injunction to be a philosopher by 'living in hiding.' From earliest childhood, in learning to speak we learn of its dangers.[4] So thinking is part of our privacy – we *learn* to keep our thoughts to ourselves. Until we learn this trick, we voice thoughts without first thinking them as a separate activity. Thought is there 'in' our utterance. The subsequent adult dreams of a child's mind as a state prior to innocence itself. Thinking becomes inaudible out of our need for a profound privacy – like voicing a conversation aloud in our car as we drive to work, trialing it for an encounter. (The car – a capsule of privacy moving in the interstices of public ways.) If thinking is a form of privacy we choose as a social strategy then thinking may be only as 'invisible' or 'inaudible' as we make it.

Arendt explains her notion of the 'invisibility' of thinking in contrast with the invisibility of latency or potentiality. Of someone who *can* tap dance there is nothing to be seen as they go about any other business. It is, in Aristotle's words,

2 Although the writer is 'setting down their thought', what appears may emerge quite to the writer's surprise.

3 For Arendt, cut off from her origins in Europe, written correspondence continued her 'conversations'.

4 '… from the moment I could talk, I was ordered to listen …' ('Father and Son', Cat Stevens, 1970).

a 'potentiality'. So there is no mystery in the fact that our *thoughtful-ness* is not visible. Any power is visible only in its realisation. What marks out the in-sensible character of thinking is that the activity itself remains, in Arendt's words, 'non-manifest in full actuality' (LM, 72). One has actualised one's power and still, others cannot see or hear it.

Arendt releases revealing metaphors. 'Being manifest' means 'being in hand', 'ready to hand'. Thinking is 'grasped' by metaphor. To think is to 'stop and think' – the activity is characterised as an abstention from doing or saying something. Arendt has used a social metaphor of *withdrawal* to characterise this abstention.[5]

Arendt is now able to make more of the distinction of 'mind' and 'soul'. The soul is 'a more or less chaotic welter of happenings which we do not enact but suffer and which … may overwhelm us'.[6] The 'invisibility' of feeling as the actualisation of the soul is not so profound as that of that of the 'mind' when thinking. Our passions, feelings and emotions, Arendt suggests, are 'hidden' merely as are our bodily organs. When I keep my emotions 'to myself' I suppress a tremor, curl of the lip, a blush. I bring these back barely within the body. The actuality of feelings may be apparent to another's eye or ear, while I have chosen no manner of expression of them:

> [T]he passions … have an expressiveness of their own: we blush with shame or embarrassment, we grow pale with fear or anger, we can shine with happiness or look dejected. [And] we need a considerable training in self-control in order to prevent the passions from showing (LM, 72).

In contrast, thinking won't occur unless we *do* it; if we don't want it to *show*, then we needn't engage in it in the first place. The other contrast between feeling and thinking is that we have to *learn* ways of making 'manifest' what we think. We just blush when embarrassed, but we have to learn to speak, write, and to choose expressive uses of the body in order to convey our thoughts. Contrary to what Arendt says at one point (LM, 72), it is not always under our control whether we think – or cease from thinking. Nevertheless, thinking does not appear in us like a flush of blood to the face or a tremor in the hand:

> The only outward manifestation of the mind is absent-mindedness, an obvious disregard of the surrounding world, something entirely negative which in no way hints at what is actually happening within us (LM, 72).

This 'outward manifestation of mind' that exhibits itself in 'absent-mindedness' will receive more attention as the work progresses.[7]

---

5 Gilbert Ryle ('Negative Actions', Ryle, 1973, 81–93) explores the connection between what we do in *not* doing something, as when we wait for someone, and the activity of thinking. We examine this in the next chapter.

6 Aristotle (and Ryle after him) would have stressed our *capacity* and *proclivity* for these responses.

7 See Chapter 6 of this work.

The gravity of thought

When Arendt writes about thinking she makes us think of what we do when a great deal is at stake. From the outset, she found the origins of her concern with thinking in the *thought-less* actions of Eichmann. Her question about him concerns what is *lacking* in someone who, not consumed by hatred, could take charge of the administration of the murder of millions of people. Such actions seem to be empty of meaning. To construct a meaning out of it would be to raise up 'orderliness' as worth more than life itself. *Order-liness* as a *holy-ness* – a sense of order that reifies the *following* of orders. The person who commits evil of a magnitude beyond comprehension is revealed as 'lacking', having lost touch with the possibility of his own thought. In reaction to this phenomenon that 'defies moral reason', thinking becomes, itself, an icon of some quality possible in human life. That horrendous evil can be done by a banal conformist raises up thinking, fragile and of breathtakingly slight effect, as infinite in value.

Reading Arendt about thinking can produce a variable feeling, sometimes uneasy. She recognises this unease about the value of thought, warning us of the 'professional' thinker's co-option of it. Thinking itself can be emptied of significance by promoting it above all else in the life of the mind – and the body. Arendt hovers between a sense of dealing with thinking as our most familiar activity, and confronting something rare and precious. This ambivalence derives from the origin of her enquiry. It is Eichmann's *lack* of thinking that is exhibited in the banality of his evil. It is the *absence* of a common and ordinary thing rather than the *presence* of some profound or demonic quality that typifies his administration of mass murder.

Thinking and solitude

Withdrawal and death

Arendt makes intricate connections between *solitude*, *representation* and *death*:

> No mental act is content with its object as it is given to it. It always transcends the sheer given-ness of whatever may have aroused its attention and transforms it into … an experiment of the self with itself (LM, 73–80).

Summoning up a Roman tradition, Arendt makes play with the notion that to be amongst others is 'the sign of being alive, aware of the realness of the world and self'. To think is to be alone:

> [To think] is to cease to be among men, a synonym for dying – to be by myself and to have intercourse with myself is the outstanding characteristic of the life of the mind (LM, 74).

Arendt connects this metaphor of the 'withdrawal' into thinking as being 'dead to the world' with a distinction between loneliness and solitude. In forsaking involvement with others, still we carry with us that 'plurality [which] is one of the basic existential conditions of human life' (LM, 74). In thinking, we are *conscious* without being conscious of another interlocutor. Nevertheless, to be conscious does imply a *duality*. In thinking I am *con*-scious – I am in a state of knowing-*with*. With whom? With myself. Thus, in thinking, I *keep myself company*. I may be deserted by others, or have deserted them, but it is 'only in loneliness that I feel deprived of human company, and it is only in the awareness of such deprivation that men every exist really in the singular, … [a state of] unbearable and unutterable horror' (LM, 74).

The inner imaginary theatre of discourse with oneself as if with another interlocutor is, according to Arendt, a chief source of the tendency towards dualistic theories of mind and body. Before one can exist steadily in solitude, one is aware only *that* one exists. Kant is famous for his claim that there is an 'I think' which accompanies 'all other representations', but at most, this awareness 'guarantee(s) the identical continuity of a self through the manifold representations, experiences and memories of a lifetime' (LM, 74). She makes another revealing description of Kant's notion of an 'I think, that accompanies all perceptions', declaring that Kant's 'I' is 'altogether silent' – merely an 'I am I'. The 'silence' here is not just the silence of all thinking. I am 'silent' before myself since I have not achieved the '*reflexivity*' involved in any 'thoughtful' activity. The plurality needed for thought – that one can converse with oneself – requires more than being consciously the same throughout my various experiences.

The *reflexivity* achieved through plurality is 'one of the basic existential conditions of human life on earth' (LM, 74). A conscious living being is only one of many interacting others of the same kind. Arendt takes up again the Roman tradition that 'to cease to be among men is a synonym for dying.' The life of the mind, though contrasted with that of the public citizen, must map that plurality within itself:

> The mind can be said to have a life of its own only to the extent to which … existentially speaking, (this social) plurality is reduced to the duality … implied in … the word 'consciousness' (LM, 74).

Through the 'reflexivity' of this 'consciousness' I recognise that 'I keep myself company' when I think. Solitude is thus proof against loneliness.

The thinking by which I keep myself company is 'invisible' – 'inaudible' to others unless I speak my thought. Still, this 'life of the mind' is 'never silent'. It is full of one's own incessant conversation – one's *chatter* to oneself. This 'reflexivity' is the fact that one's thinking or recalling is always a *thinking-to-oneself* or a *recalling-to-oneself*. It speaks to Arendt of the 'inwardness' of the mind. This reflexivity creates the apparent dualist perception of mind and body as separate. But no such 'special site' – the 'mind' as distinct from the 'body' – is established simply by our power to withdraw from the world of public affairs – to '*stop and think*':

> I am aware of the faculties of mind only as long as the activity lasts … the thinking ego of which I am perfectly conscious so long as the thinking activity lasts will disappear as though it were a mere mirage when the real world asserts itself again (LM, 75).

Sensing and thinking

Withdrawal is connected with our power of thought also because it is part of our capacity to 'present to (ourselves) what is absent from the senses.' In hearing or seeing (and so on) we are not thereby thinking. Afterwards, we are left with after-images of what we had sensed, but this does not yet amount to thought. Nevertheless, it enables us to imagine what we have not seen, and to recall what we perceived. Now we are on the threshold of thinking. Remembering what we saw goes beyond the storing of images. Arendt calls upon Augustine:[8] 'What is hidden and retained in memory is one thing, and what is impressed by it in the thought of the one remembering is another' (LM, 77). To remember is to begin to think. It is not merely a drift of images left from the past. In any case, images are not always centrally involved in remembering. You can remember various things you did yesterday without much imagery of it. You're asked what you did and you talk about it. Images may flash before your mind, but the business of conversation is in the foreground – it is 'imagination … [that] transforms a visible object into an invisible image' (LM, 77). Such an 'object of thought' omits a limitless array of images while yet remaining a spur for their revival – we actively recollect concrete events. An event of complex impressions and perceptions is retained as one single thing.

This process is often called *abstraction*, and yet its simple wrapped package yields so much that we might call it *concretion.* Arendt's approach to memory's condensation of experience models a thing's 'presence' in perception. This 'presence' would be not the myth of perfectly translucent consciousness that Derrida exposes, but the workable fact that *when you see things, they are 'presented' to you.* When you get a present you get the whole thing, all at once, yes. But when someone does make a new present by making their present to you, then, long after the wrapping paper has gone out for recycling you are unwrapping what has been given you. What I see is thus 'present' – the things I see are the 'presents' the world makes to me. I choose to accept the gift. I open my eyes and ears. Later when I think of them, I re-'present' these things. This is not a repetition of the world as present to me. That would be hallucinatory. Rather, in re-'presentation' what I sensed becomes compacted. I then have it available as a unit and can to proceed to think about it.[9]

Thanks, memory thinks

There is this compression of the past that recall makes possible – and requires. At the same time we get another present from Arendt – Heidegger's play upon 'thank' and 'think'. If, in perception, in our most direct involvement with 'things themselves' (Husserl) the world is made 'present', then it is made 'a present'. And if it is made a 'present' then when we *think* this present we can thank *being* ('*that there is*') for such largesse.

---

8 Arendt wrote her doctoral thesis on this North African philosopher and theologian (354–430 A.D.).

9 To take this further would be to enter a perhaps-technical territory of thought, meaning and perception.

Yes, it was of *being* that Heidegger thought of thinking as being a sort of thanking – for just *being*. Thanking *being* is that thoughtful sense of wellbeing when, for a long moment, you can welcome whatever comes. Yes, *being* appears as in individuals rather than as a 'particular' of some dreary universal. You're delighted by those brilliant lights through the slight mist of evening – by the pure movement of your vehicle – how your view extends and contracts as you move. In that mood of 'thanking being' these individual things and events are simply, themselves, metaphorical vehicles for 'being itself' – for there being anything, something, at all. This 'thanking being' is not the reckless universal quantification, 'for any *x*, whatever it is, well, thank you!' The gladness about *being* would be cancelled by the intrusion of something obnoxious or cruel. The thinking (of) *being* that thanks it *is* one's being glad at the very fact of it. In its delight individuals sustain this thoughtfulness.

Thinking and meaning

Does the world have a meaning? Does human life in general or one's own life in particular have a meaning? Does the universe itself mean anything? Arendt says that these questions are 'contrary to the human condition'. That 'human condition' means having to labour to stay alive, having to work to be at home in the world and having to act to take our place amongst our fellows:[10]

> *Thinking as such is* not only the raising of unanswerable 'ultimate questions' but every reflection that does not serve knowledge and is not guided by practical needs and aims, is, as Heidegger once observed, 'out of order'. It interrupts any doing, any ordinary activities, no matter what they happen to be (LM, 78).

Despite her rejection of dualism Arendt's approach to thinking respects Descartes's attention to it. Her 'two worlds' are those of the world of thought and the world of one's active engagement. Descartes discovered the 'one thing you cannot doubt'. Necessarily, when you utter 'I think' or 'I exist', what you say is true. Since Descartes can doubt he has a body and cannot doubt his existence, he concludes that his thinking self is separate from his body. But the self with which he had begun his search for certainty had involved his body intimately. He was *born*[11] in 1596 in Le Havre, went to school, studied law, joined the army and wrote philosophy – his cumulative identity as a bodily being.

So, in discovering a brilliant certainty of himself as purely a 'thinking being' it is as if he had *ceased to exist*. Paul Valéry's remark satirises '*Je pense donc je suis*' (I think therefore I am') as '*Tantôt je pense et tantôt je suis*' ('Sometimes I think and sometimes I am'). Arendt relates this idea of a conflict between thought and

---

10 In her earlier work *The Human Condition* Arendt fully outlines, historically and philosophically, the nature and development of these three basic conditions of human existence.

11 'Nothing speaks more urgently of our existence as a bodily condition than … our *natality*' (Arendt 1958, 178). Also the theme of *Of Woman Born*, a book of social criticism by the poet Adrienne Rich (Rich 1977).

existence to a traditional 'affinity' of death with philosophy. She recalls Plato's saying that it looks to outsiders that the philosopher is pursuing death. Later, the Romans, too, would say that the use of philosophy was for the old – to teach us how to die. In the nineteenth century, Schopenhauer wrote that 'death is the inspiring genius of philosophy'. In the twentieth, Heidegger was famous for his '*Sein zum Tode*' ('being-towards-death'). Death is already remembered as a limit of our being. These reflections carry Arendt to open her next Section (10) with 'Take on the colour of the dead'. The antagonism between *thinking* and *common sense* is a misunderstanding. The tension between thought and common sense is a battle within the thinker. The *warfare* between thought and common sense is '*intramural*'. The one who thinks is none other than the one who acts. The battle is between the thinker's own understanding of the rigorous conditions of what 'pure' thinking achieves, and their awareness that this *thinking*, like all human activity, has its existential conditions.

Thinking corporeal being

About halfway through 'The intra-mural warfare between thought and common-sense', Arendt works more intensively on the 'withdrawal' from the world that makes thinking possible.[12] The withdrawal surrounds it with an aura of paradox. The common experience that 'while you are thinking, you tend to be unaware of your own corporeality' helps to explain how Descartes was pulled in two directions:

> The soul can think without the body except that so long as the soul is attached to the body it may be bothered in its operations by the bad dispositions of the body's organs (Descartes 1954, 7–124).

Arendt has already opened the theme of memory, imagination and thought.[13] In memory, we 'bring back' what we have experienced, but in a different mode of 'presence'. Otherwise, when we recalled things it would be 'as though remembrance were a kind of witchcraft' – as if what I had seen were now happening. Hallucination rather than recall. So, thought depends on a 'de-sensing' of the raw materials that we gain by the use of sight, hearing, and the rest. Yet, we express the fact that we can recall something vividly by saying that 'it is as if I were seeing it again'. This expression has the force of a simile, whose corresponding metaphor is 'I saw it in my mind's eye'. Simile and metaphor can describe thinking, as invisible and inaudible. Arendt argues that since thinking itself is 'invisible' on account of the 'withdrawal' from the world that is involved in the process, to say what we are *doing in* thinking is conveyed in metaphor.[14] Thus we *can* express and enact *what* we think, making it precise to others.

The invisibility and inaudibility of thought is not simply the fact that at best one sees or hears *that* someone is thinking. (One does not see or hear their thinking.) Thought's absence from view is to be understood by what the thinker has in view,

---

12 From this beginning, she will exhibit the roles of willing and judgment.

13 Note her earlier discussion of Augustine on sense, imagination and memory (LM, 77).

14 See Chapter 4 of this work.

not by a bifurcation between mind and body. One is 'lost to the world', absorbed in the nature of time, difference and similarity, what it is for something to *be*, what it was. And these absorbing objects of thought drop out of one's intellectual sight in the instant of involvement in everyday business. This sublimation[15] generates the sense of the two worlds – of mind and matter.

'Where is fancy bred?'[16]

Arendt wants to locate the attractions and pitfalls of *philosophical* thinking itself: 'No experience yields any meaning ... without undergoing the operations of imagining and thinking'. The philosopher lives in the '*land of thought*', and tends to regard the immediacy of the world given in sense as without meaning: 'Seen from the perspective of thinking, life in its sheer 'there-ness' is meaningless'. For Hegel, it is as if the world 'outside' thought has a deep lack[17] – a '*withdrawal of being*'. '*Only the Ideal is Real*' he says, finally. In *Being and Time*, Heidegger, too, senses an '*oblivion of being*' in the world apart from thought. Only in thought is there a true '*presence of being*', an '*opening up* of being', Heidegger declares (LM, 88).[18] Heidegger thus associates the recovery of truth with *a-lethia* – an awakening from the forgetfulness ('Lethe') that flows between the world of the living and the spectres in Hades. Arendt does not rely much on Heidegger's language of 'being' but she is inspired by the underworld as a figure for philosophy. She will use it to recast the problem of thought and its disassociation from the world, along with its tenuous but negotiable relation to the normal involved activity of daily life.[19]

Arendt finds here a distortion that appears within the mode of perception intrinsic to a withdrawal into thought. Lacking awareness of its peculiar position of withdrawal, the thinking ego deludes itself in sensing an absence or loss of meaning in the world itself. Then the withdrawal from the world involved in thought can produce a reversal of perspective – an apprehension of the vacuity of thought: 'Seen from the perspective of the immediacy of life and the world given to the senses, thinking is, as Plato indicated, a living death'. No sooner has the philosopher found security and truth within thought than they become aware of its fragility and the instability when removed from the world of sense and social interaction. Arendt finds Kant embracing this instability. His predilection is for unsettling questioning rather than for results established once and for all:[20]

---

15 A change from gaseous to solid state, bypassing the 'intelligible intermediary' of the liquid form.

16 'Tell me where is fancy bred / Or in the heart or in the head.' (Shakespeare, *The Merchant of Venice*, Act III, Scene 2.)

17 Arendt is considering the Hegel of *The Phenomenology of Spirit* (Hegel 1967).

18 There is something of this in Sartre when he observes, 'Only in absence, when the Other becomes my object of thought, can I think of him as a true subjectivity' (Sartre 1976, 286–7; Deutscher 2003, 153–6).

19 This theme is to be explored in Chapter 6 of this work.

20 Kant is relevant here as the philosopher who, before Hegel, attempted to set limits to any possible metaphysics.

> I do not share the opinion that one should not doubt once one has convinced oneself of something. In pure philosophy this is impossible. Our mind has a natural aversion to it. (LM, 88).

The business of thinking is thus likened by Arendt to the tale of another figure from Homer's *Odyssey* – that of Penelope. Each evening she must undo her day's weaving. Each day we must let go of the thinking we have achieved, to start tomorrow with a fresh mind.

Arendt depicts thought as a departure from the world, and the re-entry to the world as forsaking thought. There is no chasm here between philosophers of the 'European' and the 'Anglo-American' persuasion. Rather than marking such a division, Arendt draws a distinction between those who sense the de-stabilising power of philosophy and the 'professional' thinkers who would establish results and conclusions. The succinct words of David Hume (an iconic figure for analytical philosophy) sharpen the sense of how the world is 'blown away' by the wind of thought – and how social life then prevails over those arguments that disturb everything one could take for granted in life:

> Where am I or what? From what causes do I derive my existence? … What beings surround me, and on whom have I any influence, or who have any influence on me. I am confounded with all these questions. … (N)ature herself …cures me of this philosophical melancholy. … I dine, I play a game of backgammon, … and when I wou'd return to these speculations they appear so cold and strain'd that I cannot find it in my heart to enter into them any farther (Hume 269).

Chapter 3

Recall

Thinking of what we live through

De-sensing experience for thinking

Arendt follows Augustine's description of a refinement of perception in which 'the vision which was without[1] when the sense was formed by a sensible body, is succeeded by a similar vision within' (LM, 77). 'Vision without' is the observed scene, as in 'She was a vision of delight', not the *process*, as in 'Vision involves the stimulus of the retina'. How is this 'vision' internalised, and in what sense? A mental image as a *vision* of delight is a metaphor like 'seeing in the mind's eye'. It is an apt description of a *result*, not some mental counterpart of an ore-refining process. To push 'seeing in the mind's eye' from metaphor towards literalness reifies 'inner vision'. By what inner organ would we discern it?[2]

In the compression of the past involved in recall we 'de-sense' what we experience, says Arendt. She writes of this 'de-sensing' as a familiar process:

> [E]ven the simple *telling* of what has happened, whether the story then tells it as it was or fails to do so, is *preceded* by the de-sensing operation.[3] Greek has this time element in its very vocabulary: 'to know' … is a derivative of 'to see'. To see is *idein*, to know is *eidenai*, that is, to *have* seen. First you see, then you know (LM, 87).

Imagine. I'm on a picnic in the park, senses flooded – grass, conversation, birds, sun, grass. Next morning the event comes back. Momentary images, like snapshots. *Images*, de-sensed are already prompts for thought. They flicker on what I am now looking at like images cast onto objects by a film projector running in daylight. The scenes bend and jitter around and over them. Then the images fade, replaced by the economy of words and symbols. What I had had only images of, I now recall as events. In a few words I tell all that happened. 'Yes, he was there and, yes, she … and the dog … and the children of course. They went for a walk in the bird sanctuary. We ate … you know …'.[4] Thought, 'de-sensed', exceeds the rate of perceptions, images and the spoken word.

Arendt writes so naturally of memory as de-sensing what we have experienced that she forestalls scepticism about its mechanism. Her aim is to reveal a power

---

1 'Without' – that is, focussed externally.

2 See Ryle 1949, 246–7.

3 It is that operation that saves imagination and thought from being the madness of hallucination.

4 Arendt does not venture into a psychology or semantics of this 'de-sensing'.

in thought, and de-sensing is part of the 'withdrawal from the world' that thought needs in order to compress sensation, and to deal with its own objects. Thought's 'de-sensing' is needed not only for the power of recall to surpass sporadic images. 'De-sensing' might revive unhappy memories of the 'abstract image' as a bogus explanation of how we think about things in their absence. Arendt simply observes and uses these facts in themselves. In being freed of the immediacy of what we sense, thinking gains a certain quiet power when my situation requires me to go beyond mores, customs and habits. In the 'de-sensing' of what I have perceived, by thinking, I gain some autonomy, liberty within my situation.

A darkness about thinking as 'de-sensing' crosses my mind. Thinking may desensitise us when we fail to 're-sense' what we deal with. Insensitive to what people live through, planners of cities and of wars fail to respond to the distress they countenance. Speaking 'in control of their words', always of 'reasonable demeanour', they seem unassailable. Our very own Phillip Ruddock[5] can 'wait out' the refugees who, even behind the razor-wire, mutilate themselves to attract public sympathy. 'How dare they cast themselves on our mercy and then rebel?' he thinks. 'And how thoughtless are the protestors …', he ponders. 'They think nothing of the consequences of not having my firm policies', he so carefully considers.

We want to 're-sense' him and his 'thinking'. We want him to stop 'thinking' – to suffer with the asylum seekers, the refugees, those who risk their lives and their children's in un-seaworthy vessels skippered by criminals. We want him to feel, to care, to react, and to respond to the sights and sounds of his prisoners in their distress. His perpetual thinking in his groove disgusts us. Sense might prevail if his senses derailed him. Arendt contrasts thinking with planning and calculation of ways and means, but we cannot forget a Ruddock by defining Arendtian thought, instead, as a concentration only on ultimate ends. What are they, and how often do we find them? Arendt's 'thinking' is, rather, a *dwelling upon* what has been discovered rather than a discovery of facts and therefore includes in its objects our ways and means of doing things. To pay attention to ways and means may be a sign of serious thought, showing how we mean what we say. Not to calculate means not to care whether you can provide. It is not because Eichmann pays attention to ways and means that we are disgusted that he so steadily and methodically proceeds with them. He doesn't think what he's doing. Our final hope is that if he were to think, deeply, reflectively, hard and long then he might be weakened in his course: Hamlet lamented how his 'resolution was sicklied o'er by the pale cast of thought'!

Past to present; thought to expression

Arendt herself continues in the tradition of the phenomenology of Husserl and its adaptation by Merleau-Ponty.[6] There is also an Aristotelian legacy in her various 'powers' of mind:

---

5 The minister for immigration in the Australian Federal Government, 1996–2004.

6 It would appear that Arendt was reading Merleau-Ponty's *The Visible and the Invisible* (Merleau-Ponty 1968).

> Imagination, therefore, which transforms a visible object into an invisible image … is the condition *sine qua non* for providing the mind with suitable thought-objects; but these thought-objects come into being only when the mind actively and deliberately … recollects and selects from the storehouse of memory whatever arouses its interest sufficiently to induce concentration (LM, 77).

Gilbert Ryle might mock this as 'para-mechanics' – this story of refining visible objects into invisible images and then into wispy 'thought-objects', only to find that the power of memory is required to bring into being the very thing it is selecting from its storehouse. For Arendt, though, the description of a mental 'process' is bound to be a matter of metaphor.

Like Ryle, Arendt emerges from a long dip in the phenomenological tradition to write in direct and simple prose[7] whose historical texture, richer than his, provokes her thought. She is confident that philosophical history does not displace philosophy. Being formed by the writing of Augustine, Kant, Husserl, Jaspers, Heidegger and Merleau-Ponty, her language of thought (unlike Ryle's) is placed within general figures of temporality. As traditionally conceived, thinking attempts to get ahead of time – to regard the world from the position of one already dead. To be unaffected by public issues, to regard death with equanimity as if already on intimate terms with it marks the tradition from Stoicism to Thomas Nagel's *View from Nowhere*. To break with this tradition of objectivity[8] Arendt speaks hyperbolically:

> While thinking I am not where I actually am; I am surrounded not by sense-objects but by images that are invisible to everyone else. It is as though I had withdrawn into … the land of invisibles, of which I would know nothing had I not this faculty of remembering and imagining. Thinking annihilates temporal as well as spatial distances. I can anticipate the future … as though it were already present, and I can remember the past as though it had not disappeared (LM, 85).

Arendt is modifying a classical tradition. In dealing with objects of thought, as when I remember the dead, I make present to myself what I had known. Arendt revives a myth of disappearance, of Orpheus, whose Eurydice relapses into Hades when he turns back to look at her (LM, 86). One turns to look back at one's thought, to write it down. It is gone in the blink of an eye. Arendt has begun to critique the image of time that recurs in the philosophy of 'a continuum that stretches from the nearby into the distant … past or future' (LM, 85). Only thought can traverse these indefinitely extended temporal distances. But it is only thought, in the first place, that converted the 'no longer' and the 'not yet' into the 'far distant'.

Time and space take turns, each as a metonymy for the other. In recalling Orpheus who travels as if in space to an underworld far off from any dwelling, Arendt pursues her theme of the 'un-worldly' character of thought.[9] Orpheus has to cross 'Lethe' – sleep or death figured as flowing between life and thought, living and dead, present and past. If truth is '*a-lethia*' then it is the absence of sleep or death

7 One would have to except some Germanic textual manners, for which Mary McCarthy used to chide her.

8 I would argue that it is a spurious objectivity (Deutscher 1983, Chapter 1).

9 I embroider Arendt's brief and provoking remarks.

– an absence of an absence of wakefulness. It is an absence of 'truth' that has to be endured in the crossing. A strangely double absence, if truth itself is rightly figured as the absence of deathly sleep. In this very absence of absence, place acts as a trope for time, allowing imagination to throw the impossible before us. Orpheus must travel back in time to find Eurydice alive. Space is made temporal in the figure of a river – matter in the category of continuous change. And, in conjunction, the river as symbol of the negative activity of sleep (or death) constructs a bridging metaphor for the impossible time travail. Like an actor's stage, Hades frames Orpheus, permitting him to *charm Pluto and persuade Eurydice*. The frame elides his transgression of time and of categories.

We know about Pluto's rule that Orpheus must not look back at Eurydice; she must follow behind until both have achieved the land of the living, which is to be their new *present*. Orpheus must not look back because *space* has been made metonymy for *time*. 'Not looking back' is no mere edict. She cannot be presented to him until they *are* in the present. Textually, it is to spare the narrative the contradictions endemic to placing past events amongst the present that Orpheus *must* look back and Eurydice *must* vanish. The reader overlooks this because the story has Orpheus at its centre – as if it is only his tragedy. To create tension, Eurydice *insists* that Orpheus look back and he feels he must acquiesce. Still, it is Orpheus's tragic error to agree. Within the story, it is simply his weakness to cast that glance. She is still within Hades while he is the space-time traveller from one land to the other. He knows the rules, but does he understand them? *Don't look back when you leave what is about to be past* is a constant theme of legends. Lot's wife looks back to the world of sensuality and is at once dead to pleasure and to the promise of the new austere life. Lohengrin's wife must break her husband's command, must hold him until the morning loses him, day for knight. Bluebeard's last wife chooses to disobey the edict and 'looks back' into the enclosures of her husband's past. Some are born to risk bringing images of the dead out of the closet. Eurydice falls beyond retrieval because Orpheus looks back at his dead past; Bluebeard's wife dies unless she looks back at Bluebeard's past dead.

Thinking as a little death

Arendt adapts Orpheus and Eurydice as figures for the life of the mind. Thinking is a 'little death' within the everyday. Understood through myth, thought is actual nonetheless. Arendt's 'objects' of thought as 'invisibles of which I would know nothing had I not this faculty of remembering and imagining', project what I had to leave behind in order to think. The negative of the film shows what I have to leave behind, even as I speak or write. Not only to conduct business or play sport must I forego thinking. If I think what I say when I say what I think (if I speak thoughtfully), then I allow the Plato's 'breeze' of thought to leave its quiet unspoken mark on what I say.

Thought lingers unspoken in what I then write, as a holiday lingers when I return to work. Can I bring a holiday back with me? I can tell you, I can show you pictures. I can but allude to a period whose significance is scarcely commensurable with the rest of the year. I leave a holiday behind just as I relinquish a 'land of thought'.

'Philosophy is what happens when language goes on holiday' (Wittgenstein). I grieve for its loss; pictures commemorate its passing as they would a death. To write a diary while away is to write already in expectation of this loss – a preparatory mourning. To be reminded by my diary of the events of the holiday is to value them again in feeling what I have lost – the comfort that those things did occur. Thinking is, then, a mental diary that presages its own death when the mind vacates its vacation and returns to speech and writing. 'Wonder is a mourning for the self as an autarchic entity ... The beginning of a new story?' (Irigaray 1993, 75). As writing and speaking is a mourning for lost thought?

The myth of Orpheus and Eurydice tells us that to force thought into the open is to mortify it. It is to exploit one's own thinking, as if to plagiarise oneself. Both Ryle and Sartre recognise this when they distinguish prior thought from the meaning of what we do in the moment for action. One would say only in self-deceit, 'I must do this because this is what I have deliberated to do.'[10] If I *were* to broach an issue only because I had deliberated and decided to do that, I would be engaged in something other than what I had decided upon. For if I broach the issue only to *keep faith with my deliberation* I have modified the meaning of my previous concern. Self-concern is now central – *keeping faith with myself.*

Orpheus failed to be true to his *Eurydice of the underworld* when he looked back at her as she was about to emerge into the world of every day. His loss was not a whim of the gods but a logical consequence of his looking back. In crossing the border he re-entered the present: to have *seen* Eurydice on the other side of the border would have been to *see* her in recollecting her. Approximate to hallucination. She *has* to vanish when he goes to *look* across the abyss of time. In going to look he ceases to recall her. Since he cannot *see* her (she exists at an earlier time), he is left with nothing. He has not been true to her memory, as we say. They were on a level footing while he remained in Hades – both in the past, the land of thought and recollection. But, as with thought, so with the dead whom we leave behind as we 'get on with our lives' (as the blustering jock says on talk-back radio.) That is to say, we have to choose, amongst the periods of our days, when we will devote ourselves to thought, to them, to the dead. Always bearing them in mind, we devote ourselves again to the *vita activa.*

Evanescent meaning

Thought supplies meaning rather than truth, claims Arendt, notoriously. Hers is not a sentimental 'search for the meaning of life' though, since not much value accrues to life from the side of thought: 'From the perspective of thinking, life in its sheer thereness is meaningless' (LM, 87).[11] Arendt explains the philosopher's intuition that

10 Similarly, '*I say this because it is what I thought yesterday*' is not now to speak thoughtfully.

11 Julia Kristeva brings such claims to the fore in the chapter 'Life as a Narrative' (Arendt 2001).

in common sense there lies an 'oblivion of Being'.[12] What the thinker has in view (*the nature of time*, *difference and similarity*, *being itself*) drops out of sight when everyday business takes over from thought. Thinking is never 'established', Arendt argues, because memory cannot bridge the crevasse between the engaged bodily self and the 'thinking ego' taken up by questions of *being*:

> I know of the mind's faculties only so long as the activity lasts, which means that thinking can never be solidly established as [a] … property of the human species (LM, 88).

Like Penelope's web, philosophical work is undone when the philosopher 'wakes up' to everyday demands. Vital to thought and intelligence, memory protects philosophical thought and everyday life by refusing to cross the crevasse between them. This secures Arendt's reading of Orpheus and Eurydice.[13] If the objects of thought are as if in the realm of the dead, of which we can be conscious only in a kind of dream, then to attempt to bring them across Lethe is to reify a shadow. To plant the objects of thought within everyday life is to think incoherently. The principal traits of thought are these: its withdrawal from appearance, its self-destructive tendency, its reflexivity and its 'sheer activity' that leaves no trace when we return to 'appearances'. In consequence, thought cannot establish itself (LM, 88). (It is Arendt's 'professional' thinker who attempts to prevent this evanescence of meaning.[14])

Arendt can shock us: 'In thinking we search for meaning, not for truth'. This is epigrammatic. What we think *can* be true, but to assign to thought the purpose of *discovering* truth would concoct a special realm in which claims of fact are free of empirical constraint. It falls to 'science' (in a general sense) to establish the facts of an issue. In narrative, thought can bring home what an event amounts to. Arendt was seized by a certain moment in the *Odyssey*. Odysseus is wandering *incognito*; people don't know whether he is alive or dead. A guest in some great hall, cloaked, he hears a scrap of his own life as legend:

> The bard sings some story of Odysseus' own life, his quarrel with Achilles: Odysseus covers his face and weeps, though he has never wept before, and certainly not when what he is now hearing actually happened … Homer himself says: The bard sings for men and gods what Mnemosyne … has put into his mind, [who] deprived him of eyesight and gave him sweet song (LM, 132).[15]

The 'sweet song' is more than just a recollection. As narrative and as musical art, thought is involved. The events of Odysseus and Achilles create their images. The images are 'de-sensed' in their co-option into a lyric. This 'compression of the past' brings Odysseus to tears. He weeps at what did occur. The song that works the art of

12 Plato, Augustine, Kant, Husserl and Heidegger and Sartre are archetypal in this regard.

13 My own ideas, formed in developing Arendt's text.

14 Even Kant would establish 'once and for all' the limits of metaphysics.

15 Odysseus is moved by unexpected beauty ('I have never seen a face so lovely'); his past returns to correct him. The 'unprecedented' moves him because precedence is already implicit in the comparison (Scarry 1999, 21–4).

recall truly relates the events. But the point of art is to give meaning about truths we have discovered already. We get nowhere by peering at this meaning. We must roam around it.[16] Thought, story or painting brings home what has occurred, intensifying our subjectivity. In subjecting us more acutely to the events we know, thought gives us objectivity about what we go through. Art makes us laugh, weep, ponder and smile at what we already know 'all too well'. It gives us objectivity 'up close', in contrast with an objectivity of repetition and detachment. After the work of thought, meaning appears in the disappearance of the event in rituals of remembrance. For Arendt's Greeks and Romans, deeds were meaningless if overlooked. In remembrance they come to have an enduring meaning that could not grasped by those who performed them.

Thought – lost and blind

Arendt moves from 'What makes us think?' to 'Where are we when we think?'. She might have written 'When are we where we think?'. Thinking relates in a peculiar way to time because it is 'out of order' – internally disordered and out of phase with the order of events 'in the world'. The time of thought relates to the time of worldly events in the way that the time frame of a play relates to the clock at which I might glance to check I will not miss the last train home:

> [T]he everywhere of the thinking ego … summoning into its presence whatever it pleases from any distance in time and space … – is a *nowhere*. (A) nowhere … by no means identical with the twofold nowhere from which we suddenly appear at birth and into which … we disappear at death (LM, 200).

Arendt reads this figure of the 'thinking ego' into Valéry's epigram '*Tantôt je pense et tantôt je suis*', which places us when we think as anywhere and thus nowhere. In the same figure, the thinking ego travels instantly to whatever region it thinks of – the ego is *no-when*. In Kant's 'time [as] the form of inner sense – of the intuition of ourselves and of our inner state' is our apprehension of events as 'in the future', happening now', and as 'long ago'. There is no immediate sensory intuition of the unchangeable historical relations of 'earlier' and 'later', but the old issue between a flow of time from future towards the past and a fixed relation of all events ordered by 'earlier than' and 'later than' takes on a different slant within Arendt's frame. One's changing relation to an event as future, then dealt with and finally recalled, is itself a series of events ordered as earlier or later than each other. One does not 'step out' of a time order in finding one's freedom. Rather, one's freedom is the power of temporal thinking, ordered as an event like any other, to bring 'before the mind' events from any location in time and space. This freedom involves a figurative dualism of 'thinking ego' and 'human body' – a phenomenology, not a figure outside the physical time order:

---

16 This idea recalls Ryle's image of philosophy as 'conceptual geography' (Ryle 1949, Introduction).

> [I]n order to create a line of thought (of time as ordered in a strict sequence) we must transform the *juxtaposition* in which experiences are given to us into a *succession* of soundless words – the only medium in which we can think – which means we not only de-sense but de-spatialize the original experience (LM, 202).

Holding sway over future and past

In 'finding out where the thinking ego is located in time, and whether its relentless activity can be temporally determined', Arendt reconsiders the 'thinking ego' in relation to past and future, avoiding the traditional spectator's image of the self as watching from a river bank on no-man's land. As if events floated down like leaves from the upper reaches of the future, flitted past in the present, and receded out of sight downstream into the past. She turns from Augustine's future as an expectation and past as a recall to Kafka's agonistic image of a 'HE' (her 'thinking ego') who struggles with the opposing forces of past and future. Arendt's use of Kafka's fiction expands her notion of a *life* of the mind. We *think* as well as act; we *stop and think*, creating a space-time volume of free movement; we think *under pressure*. Eichmann's failure to think is the failure to bear all of this and to succumb to one or other pressure. The one who does not think abdicates from judgement; they skedaddle from the threshold between past and future. This figure bridges Arendt's first volume, *Thinking*, to its successor, *Willing*. In its connection with willing, thinking turns to open up the space of the time called living in time.

Kafka's protagonist, situated at the intersection of opposing forces from past and from future, uses the future's possibilities against the conservative power of the past. In the same act, he uses the force of the past to drive him towards the future. Kafka's '*He*' is a force to be reckoned with, though his own intentions are partly hidden in his past and future. In withdrawing from appearances, the ego's 'time sensation' is of its mental activities recoiling upon themselves – past and present are 'equally present' because 'equally absent from sense'. As an object of thought, the 'no-longer' of the past is transformed into something at a distance – to approach or from which to depart. Kafka's character who struggles with a 'what is to be' that challenges him, and a 'what is no longer' that shoves him, is a fiction no less than the figures with which he struggles. They do not exist as adversaries unless *He* is placed between them. Yet, like his opponents, *He* is only ambiguously fictional. As free in space and time he is a fiction, but *He* is assumed by the mortal human being in its sporadic function of 'thinking ego'.[17] Arendt calls upon the ego's thinking and its material side. This 'ego' disrupts an otherwise 'continuously flowing stream of sheer change' (LM, 203) by reanimating what is 'no longer', and presenting what is 'not yet' as if a reality. And yet, only because this 'ego' is a function of a material being, subject to natality and to death can it disrupt a 'stream of change' that otherwise knows nothing of the arrival and departure of new and irreplaceable beings.

Kafka's allegory has the structure of Nietzsche's in *Zarathustra* where the 'paths' of past and future, meeting at a 'gateway', 'contradict each other … offend each other

17 A 'transcendental ego' as expounded by Husserl in 1937 (Husserl 1970).

face to face. [T]he name of the gateway is … "*Augenblick*"'[18] (LM, 204). This 'blink' permits action – the blink at the blank canvas of action that obliges, and permits, a response to demands of past and future. Arendt cites Heidegger on Nietzsche – this '*Augenblick*' is 'not the futile Now which it is only for the onlooker, but the clash of Past and Future' (LM, 204). For the onlooker who sees the succession of events but not the significant moment, there is no moment of blindness. They too 'see' this only in the retrospect of history.

These times of intense involvement when we deal in new ways with the pressures of past and of future are curiously difficult to recall; they remain with us as truncated phrases that record an upshot: 'That was when I refused conscription'. 'That was when she took time from her family and recommenced her studies'. An epiphenomenon of energy in the aftermath of the struggle commonly energises writing. Changes for which one is unprepared ensue. Setting down the detail of what has gone on draws on past skills in heading towards a future not yet comprehended. The blindness of the *Augenblick* persists through the record.

Living in time and thinking under pressure would be trivialised by reducing the present to a vanishing cut between periods. To think of the 'now' as only 'dividing' past from future would force it to approach, asymptotically, a cut rather than a brief period, so as to avoid the paradox that the 'now' contains both past and future. (This is Augustine's manoeuvre in the *Confessions*, by which he turns the whole of time into an illusion.) Arendt writes of the *Augenblick* as no mere vanishing point:

> Man lives in this in-between, and what he calls the present is a life-long fight against the dead weight of the past, driving him forward with hope, and the fear of a future … driving him backward toward 'the quiet of the past' with nostalgia for … the only reality he can be sure of (LM, 205).

Because we live in this present as the blink of an eye, the 'gap between past and future opens only in reflection, whose subject matter is what is absent – what has disappeared or has not yet appeared' (LM, 206). Within the fictional life of the 'thinking ego', this 'now', this timeless gap in time, is as if real. Arendt hunts down the vain illusion of Kafka's 'dreaming' ego who hopes for 'the unguarded moment when … quiet will settle down … long enough to give 'him' the … chance to be umpire, spectator and judge outside the game of life' (LM, 207). The resultant vector of the forces of past and of future might head in a new direction, she suggests, still *within* life's arena. Thought might act, not with a velocity that takes me beyond the world's gravity but to leave me on its surface, within its atmosphere.[19] This might be 'a perfect metaphor for thought' that recognises how thought has freedom in time and space while existing under the pressure of circumstance.

Arendt insists that Kafka's parable 'does not apply to man in his everyday occupations', but records the disturbance of the usual flow of events – their surface ruffled by the need for serious choice. She explains the parable:

---

18 Translated as 'now' or 'the now', '*Augenblick*' loses the kinaesthetic force of its 'blink of an eye'.

19 Note Arendt's metaphysics of the 'surface' in the first chapter of this work.

> [I]t does not apply to man in his everyday occupations but only to the thinking ego … withdrawn from everyday life … It is only because 'he' … is no longer carried along by the continuity of everyday life in a world of appearances that past and future manifest themselves as … a no-longer that pushes him forward and a not-yet that drives him back' (LM, 206).

If the 'thinking ego' imagined itself as 'ageless' and 'past and future as manifest to it, emptied of concrete content and liberated from spatial categories', the processes in which the thinker is actually involved would appear, willy-nilly, as the 'thinking ego's greatest enemy':

> Time inexorably and regularly interrupts the immobile quiet in which the mind is active without doing anything (LM, 206).

Thus, Arendt is taking Kafka's story 'a step further', varying the dream of 'jumping out of the fighting line between past and future.' The resultant vector of the pressures upon thought from past and from future need not project 'out of this world'. In her parallelogram of forces, 'the fighter would not … have to jump out of the fighting line in order to find the quiet … necessary for thinking' (LM, 208). The 'battleground' is a space he has created in his struggle, and in so doing he can find himself, in the blink of an eye, calm but not becalmed:

> [He is at] the quiet in the center of a storm which … still belongs to it … (where) we find our place in time when we think, that is, when we are sufficiently removed from past and future to be relied on to find out their meaning, to assume the position of … judge over the manifold, never-ending affairs of human existence in the world (LM, 209).

Arendt develops her metaphor for Kafka's *Augenblick* of the present: 'the small inconspicuous track of non-time beaten by the activity of thought within the time-space given to natal and mortal men' (LM, 210). The 'images' Arendt uses to locate thought make no sense with regard to 'historical or biographical time' where there can be no 'gaps'. To think of oneself as beset by forces of what is no longer, and of what is not yet, is already to cease to be 'a "somebody" in the full actuality of his concrete being' (LM, 210). Arendt does not accept the classical *nunc stans* (the 'standing now') of metaphysics. It is not an 'historical datum'. The challenge for her is to explain how thought 'beats' this 'inconspicuous track' within the everyday. How does thought have a bearing upon socially and politically framed decisions?[20]

Conservative classicists love to speak of the 'timeless' quality of the great works of a Shakespeare or Dante. Arendt is reinventing a sense for this dead language. 'This timelessness … is not eternity', she says at once. Thought is not beyond the forces of history and culture. Like Heidegger, she writes of how this 'timelessness' (within time) of thought 'springs … from the clash of past and future … and gathers the absent tenses, the not-yet and the no-more together in its own presence'

---

20 This possibility will be vital to the sense of the *willing* that she is to take as the theme of the next book of the trilogy, and to the possibility of an account of judgment.

(LM, 211). Like the post-modernists of whom she is a precursor, Arendt accepts the fragmentation of the tradition while treating the fragments with great care:[21]

> I have clearly joined the ranks of those who … have been attempting to dismantle metaphysics, and philosophy with all its categories, … [a] dismantling [that] is possible only on the assumption that the thread of tradition is broken and that we shall not be able to renew it … The loss … does not destroy the past … but is a fact and as such no longer a part of the 'history of ideas' but of our political history, the history of our world … What you are left with is still the past, but a *fragmented* past It is with such fragments of the past, after their sea-change, that I have dealt here (LM, 212).

Arendt's method is historical, fictional, poetic and analytical. As Arendt presents them, metaphysical doctrines encode modes of experience, elevated to the status of universal necessities. By dealing with metaphysics by fictional devices such as Kafka's *He*, one gains a critical distance from metaphysics without falling into its snare by a simple negation of it.

The site of thought is a precious place where the 'ungraspable whole' of one's existence from birth to death can be pondered. This site has to be occupied, she says, as if by 'an enduring presence in the midst of the world's ever-changing transitoriness'. Yet in dwelling in these lands of intellectual dreams (territories and dwellings not to be despised), we need the fiction of a 'sheer continuity of the I-am'. This 'ever-present' *I think* is itself but an *Augenblick.* Still, in that blink I position myself with respect to past and future. And that position itself disappears when, in the moment of blindness necessary to my use of past and future, I turn to do whatever it is that falls to me at this moment.

21 Like Michèle Le Dœuff, Arendt retrieves a transcendental ego even as she exposes it as a fictional category, and like Le Dœuff, Arendt finds a metaphysics of the transcendental ego in Shakespeare's *Richard III.*

PART II
Thinking with Others

Chapter 4

By Metaphor

The soul's body language

So, Arendt has distinguished the 'mind' as the capacity for thought, from the 'soul'[1] as a manifold of capacities and liabilities for feeling (needs, aims, attractions). She maintains, next, that showing our 'feelings' (even in this broad sense) does not involve the whole complex apparatus of language. After all, animals communicate their needs without intricate speech. There are, Arendt observes,[2] more or less unconscious and non-deliberate bodily signs of needs, feelings and sensations. One does not learn to wince in pain, to blush with embarrassment or to tremble in fear. There are, however, no such unlearned bodily signs of what we are thinking. You notice my trembling fear but cannot see or hear the thought makes me tremble. I tremble with fear at the thought that someone will be injured, because I love them. If that person is my mortal enemy, I breathe a sigh of relief that they might cease to be a threat. So, of course, as the capacity for thought, the 'mind' is intimately tied to our 'soul'. They are simply our inter-related capacities for intelligent, emotional, retentive, and projective actions and passions.

As a child I learn to 'read' these bodily signs of feeling and sensation, but I am not driven to metaphor in describing what I 'read'. Nor do I argue by analogy (the traditional theory) that since 'I' winced in pain, when I see someone wince I can conclude that they are in pain. Such a theory leaves me detached from any sympathy (or schadenfreude) at another's distress. Wittgenstein argues that the argument from analogy places my sensation as a 'beetle in a box' at which I peer, while you can never peek. Sartre, too, exposes the myth of one's sensation as in the 'hollow box' of one's soul. On Wittgenstein's argument, 'I' would have only a 'private' language regarding my own sensation, which would tell you nothing – and would, equally, lack content for me. In terms of Sartre's phenomenology, this attitude towards my sensations as essentially private is a refusal to relate to others; a self-protective attitude dressed up as theory. Wittgenstein makes the same point. To conjecture about someone's pain when they groan is to refuse them sympathy. Our responses to the bodily 'language' of a feeling are our modes of being in relation to another; we are no more distanced by thought from what we feel than we are set apart from our own amusement when we laugh. There are these platitudes about how sensations and feelings connect with bodily expressions and behaviour; our ideas of states of mind are expressed in a cluster of such platitudes: 'Sharp pain makes one wince' or 'when happy, we

---

1 Recall her distinction between 'mind' and 'soul' as the capacities for thinking and for feeling.

2 Chapter 1 of this work, pages 9–10.

are ready to laugh, to join in with others', but there are no such 'platitudes' about the signs of what we are thinking.[3] If there are no natural expressions of thinking how does language convey it? Sensation and feeling intimately involve thought, too. We need to explain the rich and subtle language of sensation and feeling that is connected with our thought about it.

The mind's metaphors

Thinking may be 'invisible' and 'inaudible' but we need to communicate this *thinking*. We cannot think *well* without the confirmation and criticism of others. Yet even in communication, *thinking*, which was performed at the cost of withdrawal, remains in its underworld. '*Tell me what you think about the invasion of Iraq*.' I tell you, but this 'telling' is not the *thinking* that I had engaged in privately – as if I then encoded and beamed it to you on the carrier wave of sound or script. I expect you to take in and understand what I say, but not therefore to decode my utterance and download my *thinking* into your private repository. Such a double absurdity would defeat the purpose of expressing what I think. To 'say what I think' is to form my thought – to *have a thought* about the issue. Thinking and speaking[4] go 'hand in hand':

> 'The need of reason' could never be adequately met without discursive thought, and discursive thought is inconceivable without words already meaningful, before a mind travels, as it were, through them (LM, 99).

Conversation is a social contract. One expects the other to say what they think, and is required to respond with open confirmation or criticism. Thought exists here *as* linguistic acts – thoughtful, considered, passionate, venturesome in gesture, expressive in tone and significant in silence. Then thought continues, complicated, in my waiting, listening and working to understand what I hear in response. It is hard enough to keep up with the demands of this interchange. I do not need the distraction of attending to private thoughts at the same time. Within its continuous process, conversation requires one's mind and soul – emotions, hearing irony as such, judging matters of logic and alleged fact. In the midst of this I hold on to what I want to say while the other holds forth. I think how to back out of a wrong path without losing command of my part of the discourse. Ready to modify what I have to say when it becomes my turn to speak, and taking into account what has just been said. I have to think what I am doing. This means not withdrawing into thought.

In saying 'man exists in the plural' Arendt explains this need to think with others. We are '*likely to go astray*' if deprived of communication. *Thinking*, 'conversing with oneself', is a limiting case of communication. That we can think privately has

---

3 David Lewis elaborates this idea: 'The concepts of belief, desire and meaning are common property. The theory that defines them … must amount to nothing more than a mass of platitudes of common sense, though these may be reorganized in perspicuous and unfamiliar ways' (Lewis 1983, 111–12).

4 We have noted earlier that the 'deaf-mute' also speak – 'sign' or a code of vocal and written language.

distinct advantages, though. Reasoning, considering various sides of a question, pondering on the meaning of what has been said and done are all possible when I am alone. (On the Cartesian model of thought as essentially private, thought can *only* be conducted alone.) The fact that in one sense my *thinking* cannot be placed on the public stage explains the moments of attraction to the Cartesian model. Free from dualism, we need not blink at the reality and the importance of private *thinking*. But it ought not to be reified or idolised. For all the urgency of her '*Stop and think!*' Arendt recognises that thoughtful conversation with others is the primordial event.

After all, conversation with myself contains only one person's expression of the various sides of a question. Although thought as conversation with oneself divides discourse into various currents, it is only according to the thinker's leanings that these are expressed. The 'duality' of thought is liberating, but still, I conduct the dialogue only with myself. I hear only what I imagine others would say. Even when I recall distinctly what another has said, it is a partial illusion that I have considered what they think. I have had to 'de-sense' what others have said, how they have said it, with what tones and in what context. It is a salutary shock when the voice I had converted into an object (voice) of my thought breaks in upon my 'so rigorous' consideration of what that voice *would* say within my thoughtful colloquy.

Arendt (following Aristotle) takes a further step. The urge that exists in thought to give an account of thing is '*prompted not by the thirst for knowledge*'. This is not so strange. First, remember that we think about what we know well. The urge of thought has a different goal from the acquisition of knowledge. That it is driven by '*the quest for meaning*' is Arendt's first risky try.[5] Perhaps her better question is why, even when we know what is the case, we bother to think. Thinking makes solitude possible in what would otherwise be loneliness:

> [It] is only in loneliness that I feel *deprived* of human company, and it is only in the awareness of such deprivation that men ever exist really in the singular (LM, 74).

Because meaning has been established (socially), significant solitude can be borne:

> [T]he sheer naming of things, the creation of words … is the human way of appropriating and … disalienating the world into which … each of us is born as a newcomer and a stranger (LM, 100).

Force of metaphor

If the formation of words for things dis-alienates the world, what are words? How can they achieve so much? As a metaphor transfers meaning to what cannot possess it, words acquire meaning by their connection with objects and events (and so on) that they cannot resemble. Some languages contain symbols with a pictorial resemblance to things, and the structures of words can map structures of things, but this does

5 David Ellison drew my attention to Arendt's metaphors of an (involuntary) *thirst* for knowledge as against an (intentional) *quest* for meaning. The 'thirst' can be 'slaked', but thinking only takes us further in our 'quest'.

not change the principle of language. Arendt looks to Chinese as an ideographic language, and observes that the schema for 'dog' is really no less de-sensed than the *word* 'dog'. All languages, 'ideographic' or alphabetical 'share … the unquestioned priority of vision for mental activities' (LM, 100–1).

Arendt had emphasised thought's de-sensing of what we experience so that it can take over from perceiving. In so doing, she exhibited a close connection between metaphors of vision and our expressions for thinking (LM, 101–2). In describing how thinking relates to the world, we are driven back to metaphors of vision. However, whereas vision presents us with at least one dimension of how the world is, thinking does not represent adequately what we mean to think about. Arendt is aiming to describe how language and metaphor connect with the possibility of thought:

> Language, by lending itself to metaphorical usage, enables us to think, that is, to have traffic with non-sensory matters, because it permits a carrying over … of our sense experiences' and thus that 'there are not two worlds because metaphor unites them' (LM, 110).

How *does* metaphor unite the two 'worlds'? Metaphors are extended possibilities of language in expressing thought and describing things. Arendt exposes Aristotle's useful account of metaphor as too simple for her main purposes. His 'metaphor' is a 'similarity of relations as in an *analogy* which always needs four terms'. The contraction of metaphor tends to hide this. *Old age is a twilight* suggests a weird but essential *similarity* between an aged person and the setting sun. Analysing the metaphor releases us from the cliché, exposing the similarity as between two *relationships. Old age* is to *life*, as *the setting sun* is to the *day*. Aristotle's *the wine cup … is the shield of Dionysus* (LM, 103) is indecipherable as a transferred resemblance between the two. The resemblance is between relationships. '*A wine cup is to Dionysus* (the god of wine) *what a shield is to Ares* (the god of war).' Each is their emblematic object of use.

Arendt points out the limitation of this attractively simple theory, which depends on all four terms being available to us in sense perception. There is no inherent *need* for metaphor here. The metaphor is stylised and superficial – one could reverse it without loss – *Ares' shield is a Dionysian cup*. Thinking stands in more radical need of metaphor. In his attempt to define the limits to any possible metaphysics, Kant needs metaphors that, although drawn from what directly appears, deal with what cannot be presented to an observer. Kant has set up a dichotomy between the *phenomenon* (the world of mind and sense in appearance) and the *noumenon* (the *Ding an sich* – 'thing in itself'). This *Ding an sich* is a reality underlying *phenomena*. Arendt, who would dismantle metaphysics, is interested from a different motive in the possibility of *radical metaphor*.[6] By metaphor, Kant summons up this *noumenon* of what we can only *appear* to us – that we cannot describe literally. Arendt says we need radical metaphor to summon up thinking, invisible and inaudible as it is. It is only by metaphor that thinking can be made public in speech, writing and action.

Arendt has 'reinstated the primacy of the surface' and yet must deal with this invisible, inaudible *thinking*. So she is interested to learn how Kant could appear

6 By 'radical', I mean *irreplaceable and irreversible* metaphor.

to include both *phenomenon* and *noumenon*, though no literal description of the *noumenon* is possible. Kant's *noumenon* is beyond experience. In contrast, each of us is immediately involved in this activity she calls *thinking*. It is part of 'the secret life of us'[7] – part of our shared understanding of what we can keep to ourselves. To augment Aristotle's analysis Arendt draws on the account of metaphor Kant used for the *noumenon*. A despotic state is described as a handmill (a 'machine') not because of any hidden similarity but because of the '*perfect resemblance of two relations between totally dissimilar things*' says Kant, echoing Aristotle's analysis. A *despot* is to the *citizens who obey unthinkingly*, what the *handmill's operator* is to the '*co-operating*' *parts of the machine*.[8] Arendt has to take a step beyond this model. She detours behind Aristotle to Plato for something closer to the ineradicable metaphor she needs. The psyche, that breath of life exhaled by the dying, stands to its corpse as the *soul*[9] does to the living body. Plato calls upon the metaphor we call his theory of Forms. On Arendt's reading it is an observable process invoked by his language of *Forms* that thus explains Plato's new idea of *soul*. The blueprint (*eidos*) that guides the craftsman's eye stands to the craftsman's finished product as Plato's new *Form* stands to the 'empirical specificities'[10] of what is *formed by* the *Form*. Though thinking cannot be transported into visibility we can use metaphor that can 'undo, as it were, the withdrawal from the world of appearances that is the precondition of mental activities' (LM, 103).

Radical metaphor

Such a complex comparative analogy might appear to move merely from one obscurity to another, but Arendt is interested, not in Plato's theory of Forms but the structure of the analogies upon which profound metaphors rely. Plato's example appears to include Aristotle's account of metaphor and then to surpass it. The *eye* as an organ of sight cannot resemble the *nous* as an organ of thinking. It is the *relation* between *eye* and the *object we see* that can resemble the *relation* between *nous* and the *object we think*.

Arendt describes the linguistic innovations necessary for the success of these new metaphors. To install his theory of ideal realities Plato co-opted the ordinary word for an artisan's blueprint (*eidos*). In achieving his metaphysical aims Aristotle too has to co-opt the ordinary word *energos*. This word simply described someone as busy or at work, but he 'frame[s] *energeia* [to denote] actuality in opposition to *dynamis*, mere potentiality' (LM, 105).[11] Arendt points out that '*kategoria*', meaning 'what was asserted in court about the defendant' comes to be our notion of a predicate (LM, 105). As an indictment 'hands down' something to a defendant, so

---

7 A phrase borrowed from the title of a 2003 Australian TV show.

8 The image recalls Arendt's opening the discussion of thinking by calling upon Eichmann's 'thoughtlessness'.

9 'Soul' must be established without observation of a soul – the 'soul' is unobservable within the world of sense.

10 An expressive term I have from Michèle Le Dœuff's 'Du Sujet' (Le Dœuff 1984).

11 Ryle co-opts Aristotle's theory of categories for his own new use (Ryle 1949, 7–22).

the predicate 'hands down' a quality to a subject. The direct and familiar language of the courts displaces Plato's Forms, which theorise this idea of a quality.

Arendt has raised the stakes. She needs metaphor in which not all of the four terms in the classical structure of metaphor are secured by what can be sensed. For a moment she disparages the profound metaphors she has found in philosophy. Embedded in philosophical speculation they are 'poetic rather than philosophical in origin' (LM, 105). Certainly there is a poetic quality vital to their sense. Is 'being poetic' a disparagement of philosophy? Has she agreed with Plato, if only for a moment, that poetry and philosophy are enemies? That they must keep strictly to their separate domains?

Once this issue is broached we are in for a bumpy ride. One reaction to an enforced dichotomy of philosophy and poetry is to idealise poetry. In combating the derogation of women the first pitfall is to idealise the *feminine* – a new and wonderful source of sensibility and insight. So, in resisting the philosophers' disparagement of poetry one is liable to set it up as a wondrous solution to philosophy's difficulties.[12] What poets praise and use openly, philosophers use covertly, suspicious that metaphor might displace reason. But suppose that metaphor assisted it. Suppose, with Arendt, that to describe thought we must rely upon radical metaphor in which one term – *thinking* – cannot be secured by observation. If the terms secured by observation did explain it by metaphor, metaphor would be distinctly philosophical precisely in being poetic.

Deconstructing radical metaphor

When Arendt says something provocative and paradoxical she then dismantles it rather than defending it at all costs. After flashing a dichotomy between philosophy and poetry she finds a 'deeper meaning' in Homer's metaphors that helps us understand how metaphor can serve philosophy. She invites us to search once more the metaphors put to work by Homer. Odysseus, on his return home (unrecognised) tells Penelope that he has seen Odysseus alive – 'he entertained him on Crete'. At this news her 'tears ran', and 'her body was melted, as the South wind melts the snow'. The metaphor generates repetition – we ourselves 'melt' in thinking of Penelope being melted by the story coming from the very one at whose memory she melts. The success of this series of metaphors that bring a narrative to life enables Arendt to show how metaphor can connect visibles (audibles, tangibles) with what cannot be seen. The power of the metaphor in representing feeling arises from one's sensation of returning warmth as snow melts – a sensation transferred to the body (as if in cold storage) being warmed by a 'South wind' of welcome news. The physical likeness of tears running and water drops starting to stream from snow buttresses the metaphor of the body as having been of ice. Arendt is suggesting this: because it is 'visibles' that lend metaphors their power, we can remain blind to the fact that the metaphor moves us because it evokes and helps us understand 'invisibles'. The

12 In *Three Guineas*, Virginia Woolf remarks acidly how, in times of crisis, women are given the role of saviors of society – as if their having been excluded from public life would now amount to a special wisdom.

language conveys to us how Penelope feels because Odysseus makes a metaphor of himself – an anonymous traveller. So, in giving Penelope good news, *his* being the agent of her returning warmth is inadvertent, like the rays of the sun. The series of metaphors is at once physically observable and emotionally charged – the invisibility of an absence – an absence made real in metaphor by Arendt – 'the invisible made visible is the long winter of Odysseus' absence – that lifeless frigidity of the years'.

This is a description, not a technical definition of metaphor. Arendt avoids the fold of the 'professional philosophers'. They would require a theory of metaphor that did not crucially involve metaphor. In explaining metaphor she had cited Homer's 'liken[ing] the tearing onslaught of fear and grief in our hearts, to the onslaught from several directions of winds on the sea' (LM, 106). Such analogies 'work only in one direction'. Storms explain emotions, not vice versa. But that is not quite correct, and makes it harder to understand how metaphor can convey what is invisible. We are as prone to describe storms as emotional as to describe emotions as storms. To describe a wind as 'vicious' and the ocean as 'pitiless' is to understand emotions better, even as we invest them in the elements.

Arendt is alive to the fact that a rock in the sea that 'endures' the winds and waves is a metaphor for endurance in battle. She remarks, dryly, 'The rock is not being viewed anthropomorphically – unless we add that we look at ourselves petromorphically'! We attribute rock-hardness to a human in the same breath as we attribute being stalwart to a rock. As she says, specific use of a metaphor is unidirectional – courage in battle is described by reference to an immovable rock. On another occasion, however, the choice may be reversed. Arendt's examples make this plain. 'Tears expressed simple sorrow, whereas melting snow metaphorically expressed thought.' This comparison may exaggerate the physicality of 'tears' and understate the thinking by which we take 'melting snow' as meaning a warming change. A novelist writes 'In tears, she turned away' rather than 'Sadly, she turned away'; they ask the reader to see tears of *sadness*. Tears are still a metaphor though they do flow naturally.[13]

So, how does 'language bridge the gulf between the invisible and the world of appearances' (LM, 108)? Gaining its force from sensations and observations, metaphor conveys to us something of what cannot be seen by summoning up a familiar relation with what can be sensed. Arendt closes this section with a memorable line: 'There are not two worlds because metaphor unites them'. In fact, language unites the worlds of thinking and appearances because the idea of two 'worlds' is itself a metaphor. Metaphor can unite the worlds because it is by metaphor that they were separated.

Thinking and speaking

Arendt pursues the idea of a *likeness* between thinking and speaking. A 'conversation with oneself', thinking already calls upon language for its existence, and its activation.

13 Our tacit contract of sensibility is mocked if the next chapter opens: 'Having finished slicing the onions …'.

We can take thinking and speaking as 'having the same source' says Arendt, inflecting Aristotle's 'language is a meaningful sounding out of words, sounds that *resemble* thoughts'. She develops this: 'Thinking actualises a product of mind inherent in speech and for which language found a provisional home in the world' (109). She borrows from Kant for a bridge between Aristotle's and her position. Kant's *land des denkens* (land of thought) is manifest not only to the mind but to bodily ears – inaudible thought and audible speech can each deal with what cannot be seen or heard. Both speech and thought concern what is absent from perception: the objects of scientific theory and of mathematics, and *meanings* – as what a philosopher investigates as *justice*, *friendship* or *memory*.

Also, no less than inaudible thought, audible speech must deal in 'analogies, metaphors and emblems' by which 'the mind holds on to the world even when absent from it'. These tropes 'give us bearings lest we stagger blindly' in dealing with what we cannot sense. And, most daringly, in the final phase of this stage: '[T]hat we find these analogies is a kind of proof that mind and body, thinking and sense experience are "made for each other".' It is thinking that Arendt has characterised as 'out of order'. Since thinking and speech both deal with what cannot be sensed, thoughtful reflective speech may also be 'out of order'.

Arendt's writing stages the process of thinking itself as a conversation, not only with the reader but also with herself. A writer's imaginary reader is their other voice and ear that checks what they say. Thinking comes into phase with writing to maintain its communicative, social, voice. In forming that writing (before anyone else reads it) the 'reader' calls thinking back to that underworld one visits only in thought. Unlike speech and writing, thinking needs 'analogy, metaphor and emblems' not only to convey *what* is said, but so as to say *what we are doing* in thinking.

Arendt's claim that the metaphors for thinking are 'irreversible' can unsettle us. We found her examples to be *reversible*. A rock is metaphor for fortitude and fortitude may be attributed to a rock. This will not wash out of her text as a 'slip' to be corrected by the learned commentator. She writes a double text – thinking is conformable with speech – they are 'made for each other'. But, thinking is on a plane that does not translate to speech or writing. The text heaves and tosses in the same way about the 'irreversibility' of metaphors for the 'invisible'. Her examples show metaphors for the invisible as reversible. It is in a different sense that they are not.

These tensions arise not from some erroneous observation but as within her *thinking*. We are not to be satisfied by what she writes in its aftermath. *Thinking* requires the reader's creative response, beyond the formal remedy of a re-definition to handle a contradiction. A 'flat' contradiction is stationary, the stultification of thought. In contrast, to be *contradicted* within thinking's conversation is a critically friendly re-animation of the conversation.

Ineffable absence

In preparation for dealing with *metaphor*'s way with the *ineffable* (LM, 110), Arendt enunciates some 'reminders' (Wittgenstein) to keep us on track that might be condensed thus:

> Language enables us to think because it brings in metaphor and image.
> Language permits sense-experiences to be carried over, de-sensed, into the language of thought.
> Appearances insert themselves into thought, superseding bodily and social needs.
> Thinking brings us up to what is far away, and places us far from the close at hand.
> The delusion of the two-world theory is not arbitrary or accidental.
> There are not two worlds, because metaphor unites them.

To explain how we can describe thinking Arendt revives the idea of what is *ineffable*. She takes risks in doing this. Thinking may seem ineffable because we cannot *sense* it. Imagination leaps from the standard site of a word (or phrase) to a place where it makes no literal sense. The sense of a new metaphor is wonderment that the user's private invention becomes a public carrier – readers can take the same flight. But Arendt has to breach Aristotle's security regulations for this traffic. If thinking is to fly with metaphor, observation cannot promise us security at both the departure and the arrival gates.

Of someone thinking we say they are 'somewhere else'. We anchor the metaphor in sensation – our exasperation at speaking into an empty room – and harness that to thinking's cart – '*It's as if you'd walked off without a word!*' '*Hello —!*' you cry, as if to call me back. But metaphors for thinking, anchored on one side, project over an abyss. The far side, the other's thought, is out of sight, even to the one who *is* thinking. They are preoccupied – lost in thought. No more than the one who calls out do they *observe* their thinking.

These last paragraphs are a kind of explanation of Arendt's 'ineffable' as used to characterise thinking and how it lives in need of metaphor. The word, though, echoes the myth that she rejects, of conscious activity as in the mind's secret box – that inner place dear to dualism that only the possessor knows and at which others can only guess. Arendt's intended direction in using 'ineffable' is that mental activities are 'driven' to language. In contrast with feeling and sensation, language is their only means of expression, to oneself no less than to another. That inward dialogue 'stands in need of outward expression' (to modify Wittgenstein), if it is to be 'activated' (LM, 121).

Coping with thought

Arendt maintains that the senses are adequate in *coping* with perceptible things, whereas language is not adequate in *expressing* thought (LM, 112). For all that, she continues, language and thought are 'made for each other'. Now, the senses do not *express* the perceptible world, well or badly. They *cope* with it, making some mistakes but not so as to impair their *coping*. On the other side, language *expresses* thought but does not *cope* with it, well or badly. Arendt's question is whether language *copes* as well with *expressing* thought as the senses do in *coping* with their sensory objects. What can we make of such a question?

How do we understand this metaphorical image of language as *expressing* thought? In being 'expressed', is thought 'pressed out'? The expression 'expression' does suggest how one makes an effort to speak one's thought. Though one easily says what one thinks it is not so easy to think what one says. Merely to say what one thinks is to fail to *express* thought. In the absence of the work of expression this 'what one thinks' is thoughtless talk. What of this image of *expression*? Expressing coffee from the espresso machine? If the infant does not make the effort to suckle, breast milk is *expressed* for them. This 'expression' is more deliberate. It manipulates … what shall we say … 'the milk of thought' … 'the thought of milk'?

As a physical metaphor, 'expression' expresses how circumstances may elicit my thoughtful speech without the usual effort.[14] This facilitated speech is still *thoughtful* in its need for *expression*. If sometimes it is easy to express what I think, this is because, when prompted, I have a familiar repertoire of 'expressions' – words, styles and registers of language.

Arendt began by saying that the senses *coped* well with their world. Presumably, thinking copes with its objects, subject (like the senses) to the usual run of mistakes. But how well does *speech* cope with *thought*? This question raises Arendt's sense of an 'ineffability' in thinking and the need for metaphor in expressing thinking and in saying what it is.[15] How well does language convey and evoke ('cope with') the annoying, baffling, evanescent character of thinking? We think of the language that we need as we thoughtfully utter it. Thought, for its part, has to 'cope with' questions of language – has to question the terms and the syntax that language hands it, *prêt-à-porter*. To be thinking in saying what we think is not just constative.[16] As a speech act, thought as conversation with oneself has illocutionary force[17] and scarcely predictable perlocutionary force[18]. (By thinking in certain ways we wind ourselves up.)

Perhaps we desire to reside in the world of thought to escape the world's pollution. As 'conversing with oneself', however, thinking involves the complications of illocution and perlocution inherent in speech and writing. If thinking is a conversation then *what am I doing* in speaking with myself? What am I doing in speaking to myself about *this* in particular? What *perlocutionary* force does my thinking possess? In my auto-conversation can I enthuse, frighten or panic myself? So we need limiting rules upon freedom of thought? Do not shout "Fire!" in a crowded theatre? The mind's theatre is so close to the playhouse?

---

14 In Arendt's view, only by metaphor can we say what thinking is. So 'expression' itself must be a metaphor.

15 We say, for instance, 'this way of putting the thought is better than that'.

16 The statement of something as a fact, abstracted from what one is doing in issuing the statement.

17 What we are *doing* in stating something: expressing our prejudices or warning someone of danger.

18 What is achieved in making a statement: annoying someone or preventing someone taking a poisoned drink.

Coming to know

By means of the senses we gain information about their proper world. Arendt states, in contrast, that only illusion arises from trying to gain knowledge by thought. One might challenge Arendt on this, arguing that she reduces her own writings to a paradox – if they express her *thought* they are not true (or false). But this would be to read her '*thinking is not the pursuit of truth*' as '*what we think cannot be true*'. As an inference from what she wrote, the objection involves a fallacy.[19] I think about the US invasion of Iraq. What I think about is the case, but it is not by thought that I *know* of the invasion. What of the idea that as pursuing truth her writing cannot be the expression of her thinking? I would suggest that to express thought in writing is closer to the pursuit of knowledge than is thinking. As visible it is designed to elicit information from others.

For Arendt, thought has a subtle and indirect relation to writing, as it does to action. Thought is Socrates' 'wind', disturbing our habits and deconstructing our familiar terms to release them from cliché. Thinking does not arrive at *knowledge* – it has left the 'world of appearance'. Truth is to be known by empirical means – directly or in testing theories. Arendt's writings *express* her thought but they are not her *thinking*. The thoughtful writing inspired by thinking displaces it. Visible action returns us from our withdrawal from publicity. As Eurydice vanishes when Orpheus turns to look at her in the underworld, thought vanishes when one goes to place it on the page. One must be content to leave thought waiting to be taken up the next time 'language takes a holiday'.

'*I think that …*' claims the truth of what follows. Not a claim to *know*, still, it can claim something that needs to be known. Certainly, knowledge may not be possible concerning some matters about which we think. (Moral, aesthetic and political issues according to Arendt.) There, thoughtful judgment must take the place of knowledge. But issues that can be known can still be thought about – that shows the point of thinking even though it does not *discover* truth.

Utterance and the ineffable

To be *thinking* blocks the declaration of it somewhat as *dreaming* occludes declaring 'I am dreaming'. Furthermore, '*I think*', a declarative, tends towards a conclusion. In contrast, to be thinking is not yet to be headed that way. After time spent in thinking I may then *think* (declaratively) that it would be best not to go the movies this afternoon. That is what I *happen* to conclude. I was thinking, but not *in order* to conclude that – or to conclude anything else. Only by accident could the conclusion fit the form of a deduction from its preceding thinking. One might object that 'whether to go to the movies' is not the kind of thing that can be known. Consider then a detective, thinking about which of various suspects might have committed a certain crime. (The factual 'Who did it?' rather than the judgmental 'Is the one who

19 This is a common misapprehension. See, for instance, Agnes Heller (Kaplan and Kessler 1989, 151–2). Beiner cites similar objections to her denial of a 'cognitive' status to judgment (Beiner 1992, 114–16, 136–7).

did it criminally responsible?'.) Coming to think that a certain one of the suspects committed the deed is not arguing (whether logically or not) that they are the one. We cannot, by thinking, know who is responsible. That emerges when concrete evidence backs up the thoughtful hunch. As Arendt would insist, the detective's *thinking* about the case, while a vital element, cannot compete (as if at some higher level) with the empirical enquiry that identifies the perpetrator. What the detective thinks when mulling over the evidence *can* turn out to be the truth and can be vital in giving direction to an empirical inquiry. Thinking, we may say in following Arendt's lead, can upset prejudices, expectations, and dull habits of inference. Thinking enables us to 'take a fresh look' at the facts and at the usual inferences we tend when proceeding beyond them. Of course it is according to the great cliché of detective fiction that the brilliant mind (berating itself for have been thick-headed), is struck by the blinding realisation of the perpetrator's identity. The pieces of the jigsaw fall into place, according to another cliché. This moment is not, however, the process of thinking (and here Ryle would join in agreement with Arendt). It is a *termination* – the moment of an achieved 'deduction'.[20]

Thinking cannot cross the gulf between thinking about who did something and knowing (with reasonable certainty) the identity of the perpetrator. So, Arendt says that thinking does not have 'cognition' as its aim. There is a close analogy here to a thought central to Sartre and Beauvoir's philosophy of deliberation and choice. To deliberate is a certain kind of thinking about what I will do. It may come to an end with the thought that I will take a certain line of action. However, no such deliberation amounts to the real choice of setting out upon that line of action. To take the initial step is the only real choice, in any effective sense. Taking that step cannot 'follow' from deliberative thought.

These reflections open up the question about the purpose and effect of thinking (including deliberation) upon what one finally does, or knows. Arendt's idea is that thinking has as its task the enrichment of life rather than the gaining of new knowledge. This quality gives meaning and significance to what finally we do know and the actions to which we commit ourselves.

Arendt says that there is an 'ineffability' about thinking itself, indicated in the fact that the process can be described only by the use of less than fully secured metaphors. In examining the meaning of this, we come upon her own 'take' on that distinction between speaking and writing that surfaces from time to time in what Plato gives Socrates to say, and is capitalised by Derrida, famously, in *Plato's Pharmacy*. What we find in the words she quotes from Plato is an interactive metaphoric system in which, first, thinking is described by metaphor as itself a kind of writing – a writing in our souls. Then, in counterpoint, thinking is described favourably in comparison with writing. Because of that comparison (unfavourable to writing), to call thinking a kind of writing would be to derogate it as a 'dead letter', a 'fatherless progeny', a 'profligate traveller' who cares nothing for the company it keeps.

---

20 A detective's deduction is the realisation of the most probable, or the only probable conclusion about the identity of the perpetrator. Given the contingencies of actions, it can never be, strictly, logical deduction.

We can now take up again Arendt's use of the myth of Orpheus and Eurydice to track the traffic between inaudible thinking and the sensible actions of speaking and writing. The allegory contains within itself a model for the gulf between them. When set against thinking, *speaking* and *writing* go together like shoes and socks. When speaking is set against writing, however, a gap appears between them that is strictly analogous to the one between thinking and *any* public expression of it. Just as thinking does not translate directly into what is spoken or written, what is spoken does not translate directly into what is written. Different codes apply; there are different rates of production and reception; there are different problems in determining reference from the base line of the linguistic act.

Just as *speaking or writing* must depart from *thinking*, *writing* must depart from *speaking*. Since speech and writing are each equally at home in the sensible world we can observe and analyse why speech cannot *become* writing. Thinking itself becomes less of a mystery, then. And, just as there is (despite these philosophical conundrums) the *practice* of rendering into writing what has been spoken, so too there is the *practice* of telling someone in speech or writing what one has been thinking. It is with the movement of speech into writing as it is with the traffic from thinking into speech or writing. In the translated result there is, but there is only, the spectral memory of what has been translated.

Chapter 5

Conversing

Solitude and conversation

We ready what we have sensed for our thinking about it:

> No mental act is content with its object as it is given to it. It always transcends the sheer givenness of whatever may have aroused its attention and transforms it into … an experiment of the self with itself (LM, 73).

Our thinking, invisible and inaudible, is on the verge of speech and writing. For Arendt's Romans, being amongst others comes under the sign of life; to withdraw into thought is as if to die. But perhaps, rather, thought means a temporary rehearsal for some oncoming phase of life. To think is to maintain and prepare oneself when alone. In forsaking the connections with others intrinsic to being involved in the world, still we carry with us that 'plurality [that] is one of the basic existential conditions of human life'. In thinking, I am conscious. I am 'knowing-with' myself. In thinking I *keep myself company*. By thinking I can exist in solitude:

> [It is] only in loneliness that I feel *deprived* of human company, and it is only in the awareness of such deprivation that men ever exist really in the singular (LM, 74).

Conversing with oneself is not bizarre like talking aloud to oneself. It is a way of being with oneself, by oneself. Arendt's emphasis on the plurality of the thinking ego destabilises the convention that the 'healthy' mind approaches a unified state called 'integrity'. Arendt is reassuring us about the lack of 'one-ness' we find when alone. Plurality of mind is the condition of reason – a measure of our distance from obsession, compulsiveness or fanaticism. When I exist in solitude, perhaps aware only that I exist, the inner theatre of conversation can seem to stage a dualism of mind and body. Cartesian dualism makes each 'I' necessarily isolated, however. Consciousness is a plurality, modelled on social conversation. Arendt points out that Kant's 'I think', which accompanies 'all other representations', 'guarantees merely 'the identical continuity of a self through [our] manifold representations, experiences and memories.' Arendt describes it, revealingly, as an 'altogether silent I-am-I' (LM, 74–5). Not merely silent as is all thinking. In being no more than consciously *the same one being* through my various experiences, I am 'silent' before myself in not having achieved the 'reflexivity' of thought. Plurality involves reflexivity; plurality is 'one of the basic existential conditions of human life on earth' (LM, 74). A conscious being is one of many interacting others of the same kind. The life of the mind in withdrawal from sociality must still map that plurality:

> [T]he mind can be said to have a life of its own only to the extent to which … existentially speaking, (this social) plurality is reduced to the duality … implied in … the word 'consciousness' … to know with myself (LM, 74).

The thinking in which I thus 'keep myself company' is 'inaudible', but this 'life of the mind' is 'never silent'. In reflexivity it is full of one's veritable chatter. One's pondering, recalling or hoping is always a *pondering-to-oneself*, a *recalling-to-oneself*, a *hoping-to-oneself*. This reflexivity is the 'inwardness' of mind, exploited in classical dualism of mind and body as 'immateriality'. Transactions between this 'immaterial' being and the body would be impossible to imagine. The site of the 'mind', however, simply is our power to withdraw from the world of affairs – to '*stop and think*'. One's 'thinking mind' is a transient state:

> I am aware of the faculties of mind only as long as the activity lasts … [T]he thinking ego of which I am perfectly conscious so long as the thinking activity lasts, will disappear as though it were a mere mirage when the real world asserts itself again (LM, 75).

The spectator

We can think only because we can bring objects of sense within a world of thought. Furthermore, we can *judge* and *will* because we can thus deal with things as objects of thought. Because we can distance ourselves from labour, work and action, we become (partial) *spectators*. Things become 'objects' for our thought. Stones, trees, human bodies, storms, conversations and meetings, growth, the constructing and the decay of systems, capacities, tendencies and proclivities – all become 'objects' within the structure of thinking. I am *thinking about* my car even if it has been crushed and melted down since I last saw it. I am thinking about the state of my car, even though there is no 'state of my car'. (These matters occupy specialist philosophies of mind and of language.)

The 'objects' of judging and willing are 'particulars with an established home in the appearing world, from which the willing or judging mind removes itself only temporarily and with the intention of a later return' (LM, 92). Arendt's 'objects of thought' do not displace the friends, car, holiday or income that one thinks about. The objects we think about are the things and processes of the world. In the mind's 'removal' from immediate involvement with these things we form objects of thought so that we *can* think about the world itself. *Thinking* makes its withdrawal only with the intention of later return. The structures of thought of scientists and philosophers defer this return on a longer-term basis. If a sense of reality is not to be lost, such specialists have to return regularly from their excursions into the 'world of thought'. Thought serves what we *will*, and casts before us the need to judge. In *willing* we deal with the 'particulars of the world' (at a remove). We are *going* to do something only in making contact with things and people as we deal with them.

Although it is in the very process of *going to do* something that we construct what we can think about, actual contact is possible only by because we have recreated what we deal with as objects of thought in a partial withdrawal. It is by thought that we continue to deal with what is yet an unachieved goal. What we summon up as objects of thought do not displace actuality since they were already vital to our initial perception of it. The perceptual judgment of individual things and events can be understood only on the basis of those objects of thought that we have as a (social) person within that structure of thoughts and feelings we call the 'life of the mind'.[1] Arendt maintains, nevertheless, that we take up a temporary role as spectator when we go to *will* and *judge*. Her idea is that judging requires a use of the spectator's point of view, not that judging is locked into it. Critics fail to recognise that her 'spectator' is only partially and temporarily separated from the playing field.[2]

Thinking as a 'negative action'

Arendt's production of *The Life of the Mind*, cut short by her death, is precisely contemporaneous with Ryle's production of eight essays on thinking during the early 1970s in the last years of *his* life (Ryle 1979). In those essays, Ryle has suggested *negative action* as a way of thinking about thinking. *Negativity* permits us to describe thinking in a mode that neither reduces it to behaviour nor elevates it above the body. What Arendt has in common with Ryle is her ability to evoke the phenomena of thinking while refusing dualism's positing of thinking as a process over and above physical activities (Small, 53–67).

The point of some actions is to *not do* something. When I swim, my conscious actions are witnessable. Warned of a rip I stand on the shore, holding off going swimming. You might guess at my conflict, but cannot discern what I am doing. Or, I *postpone* writing a letter. It is not merely that I do not write it. In contrast, I am not learning to speak Russian but I am not postponing or refusing to learn. It is nowhere on my agenda. That I am not doing something is no event. Negative *acts*, though, do occur even if it might appear that they lie beyond overt scrutiny. What I feel and want is part of the negativity of my act. So, if I am postponing the writing of a letter then I have to deal with my feeling that I had better write it, even as I find stratagems for putting it off: 'Surely procrastinating ... is the not-doing-it-yet of something' (Ryle 1979, 82).

But then Ryle rebels at his own intuition, '[Negative acts] have a factual, circumstantial and behavioural hollowness', and laughs at negative acts as *fully* acts: 'I should not be resting if I were thereby exerting myself' (Ryle 1979, 114). This witticism elides the difference between the infinity of acts that I am not doing, and my relatively few acts of *not-doing*. Procrastinating is 'far from the doing of something' claims Ryle. Yes, if I am procrastinating about the letter, I am not writing it. But procrastinating is its own doing. I take steps to evade thoughts of what might happen if I do not act promptly. This takes energy. Ryle's joke mis-fires. To rest involves control – slight exertion to forestall a greater one. Toddlers get hysterical with tiredness; they don't know that they must stop before they lose that reserve of energy needed for taking a rest.

---

1 Sartre's treatment of things as we think of them makes an interesting comparison with Arendt's 'life of thought'. Ryle also develops this theme (Ryle 1949, Chapters 1 and 7).

2 There will be a more detailed consideration of Arendt's account of this development in Chapters 6, 10 and 12.

Ryle alternates between the discovery of negative actions and minimising its impact. To *pause* is (briefly) to *not work* at what I have been doing. To pause is its own action and may involve a real effort. I may need the 'Coca Cola' pause – to enjoy the tautological equilibrium they advertise – REAL IS REAL: COKE IS COKE. It is *in* resting from what I *was* doing that I now stare into space, drink a glass of water and lean against a post. Ryle returns to this 'holding off' as a real action. We engage in it in response to advice; we may stop and start our negative actions. Being engaged in them occupies a period. But what fills that time?

I drive a car by starting the motor and pressing the accelerator, but waiting for a bus seems less than fully an action. There are no such ways and means of doing it: 'The mother lulls her baby to sleep partly by singing, the window cleaner polishes the glass partly by rubbing (whereas) there is nothing in particular by doing which I await the train.' (Ryle 1979, 107) He is minimising the sense of a negative action as an activity – not a discernible one and hence an inaudible process in realm beyond observation. Negative acts, however, resist being thus minimised. Singing a song lulls the baby to sleep; reading old magazines in the railway hall helps me continue to wait – to *not think* what is on my mind: 'a person who is holding something back, must be doing this consciously or wittingly. His doing it must incorporate … the 'thought' of the very retort which he is holding back' (Ryle 1979, 111). Ryle next thinks of a 'statesman' taking a vacation – this involves his *not thinking* about his duties. In resisting an allusion to conscious life Ryle makes a mystery out of this, however. He says, rightly:

> [The statesman] would lose … the benefits of his vacation if he did not … [put] aside all thoughts of what had been occupying him … But of course the statesman is well aware, in some other way … of what his fishing is a … respite from, yet without its being on his mind (Ryle 1979, 111).

But then Ryle adds, 'It need not pluck at even the fringes of his attention'. This cannot be right. If he had 'put aside all thoughts of his work' then work would not 'pluck at' his attention. He would no longer be putting away thoughts of it. Absorbed in his loch-side life, his fishing would be just fishing. As illustrating a negative *action*, in the event, he will have to make an effort to deal with thoughts of his work as they break in upon him. Just then, the problems of office do indeed 'pluck at his attention'. Negative actions help us to understand thinking because they give us another angle on our life of the mind.

Ryle finds his thread again. A boy jumps over a stream. Then he jumps across *to see how far he can jump*. As Ryle says, success in seeing how far he can jump is not the same as success in jumping the stream: 'A helping shove lengthens the jump, but ruins the experiment' (Ryle 1979, 112). He uses the difference as analogy for negative action. Success in a negative action involves thought, he now insists:

> [Negative actions] incorporate the thought of the negative action … as the boy's experimental jump incorporates the thought of how far he can jump … Our negative 'actions'… constitute … higher order 'operations upon' lower order positive actions (Ryle 1979, 113).

Ryle's sense of an unreality in negative actions, in contrast, is that the 'lower order' positive action is not performed. When someone keeps a secret, 'the ... actions of ... divulging [it] are ... un-executed'. Then, of someone who eats fruit as his policy of *not eating meat*, he writes:

> [O]ur behaviourist witness could [not] discriminate the fruit-eating of the vegetarian from that of his non-vegetarian neighbour ... [This can] help us trace to its source the puzzling unconcreteness, the ... behavioural hollowness of our negative 'actions'. It is a special case of the factual hollowness of denials of existence, occurrence or performance in general (Ryle 1979, 113).

But if negative acts were merely a special case of all denials of existence or occurrence then 'the interesting class of intentional non-performance' would collapse into the 'infinitely many other things that I am not now doing – '[N]ot sneezing, mountain-climbing or telephoning in Russian' (Ryle 1979, 105). A negative action involves more; waiting involves a 'putting off' operation. I arrive on time for an appointment and begin to read. After a while this becomes just what I want to do for its own sake. I am lost in the book when she taps me on the shoulder, 'You waited' she says. I have to admit, 'I was no longer *waiting* exactly'.

In Ryle's last example he strides past the 'village Miss Bates'[3] to avoid a conversation:

> In our village context, 'Not-halting-for-a-chat is as determinate as 'walking-on' and 'not-walking-on' as specific as 'Halting-for-a-chat.' Either can be nominated as the negative of the other (Ryle 1979, 118).

Given the narrator's reluctance, Miss Bates has forced him into a negative action whatever he does. If walking becomes *walking on*, he must have reasons to stop and deal with her questions. Walking on is thus *not dealing* with them. If he does stop to 'chat' this amounts to the action of not running away from the embarrassing moment.

A negative action is an act because it requires our energy and concentration. It may involve thinking, or occur within a public action as when someone stammers in his desire both to stay and to escape. The negative deed may be done quite within the person's mind – '[P]erhaps I held back my wounding repartee for only the few seconds before the quarrel ended' (Ryle 1979, 117). Ryle's examples amplify what his account of them tends to diminish.

Waiting and thinking

If we consider thinking itself as a kind of negative action akin to *waiting* then we can amplify what Ryle minimised. We can thus loosen some of the knots in our thought about thinking. While waiting for someone one is liable to converse with oneself. In waiting for someone whom you wish to meet you are already disposed to converse. To converse with oneself is one of the more significant ways of filling the time. So

3 'Our village Miss Bates' – a reference to Jane Austen's novel *Emma*.

waiting can amount to a form of thinking. What I engage in as *not-doing* something 'incorporates the thought … of what I am not doing' (Ryle 1979, 113). When my *not leaving* the scene no longer 'incorporated the thought' of meeting the one I'd been waiting for, I am no longer *waiting* for them. To wait is a kind of *thoughtfulness*. It might appear, then, that thinking (or waiting) is simply the (state of) thoughtfulness within which I talk with myself. This is what ensures that I am *conversing* with myself rather than indulging in empty-headed chatter.

If to think is to converse with oneself, then 'conversing' must include the painter who thinks of which paint to put next, where, in what style (Ryle 1979, 62). They do this without private muttering of the pros and cons. No less than the writer who internally voices trial sentences, the painter who interrogates their work in trying out differing juxtapositions of colour is *thinking*. *Thoughtfulness* must frame any inner life that amounts to *conversing* with oneself. I must make my inner utterances *thoughtfully*. On the other hand, I am thinking without making utterances at all when my reflection on the use of materials of art amounts to a 'conversation'. Thinking cannot be tied too tightly to the production of inner verbiage.

Is thinking, then, simply the thoughtful frame of mind within which I converse with myself (or reflect on the materials of my art) rather than some elusive *activity*? My saying and doing things self-reflexively would amount to 'thinking' in virtue of my thoughtful frame of mind: a tempting simplification that does not succeed. The 'thinking' that I do in conversing with myself *is* an activity. But thinking is both more and less than the activity that amounts to conversing with oneself. There is a *contingent* connection and yet a direct identity between specific instances of conversing and thinking. Thus, on a specific occasion, to converse with oneself may *amount* to thinking – an activity that comprises thinking just so long as it occurs within a thoughtful frame of mind. A frame of mind is a *readiness* to think, not *thinking*.

So, internal dialogue is conversation only if done thoughtfully – *and* there are forms of thinking other than verbal dialogue. These observations compete for our attention. To solve the problem that Arendt short-circuits in her emphasis on thinking as conversation, one must hold these propositions in mind, together. There is also a gap between knowing the meaning of the words a person may use, and knowing what they are *saying*. In the same space I am free ask what I am saying to *myself*. Am I really thinking, or just babbling to myself? What goes on internally is framed as *thinking* – as *conversation* with oneself – only as framed by thoughtfulness and an overall understanding of what one is *saying*. It is this same logical gap between performance and *saying* that permits us to ask what a painter is *saying* in their work. It can be an open question not only what I am 'saying' in a gesture but also what I am saying in a well-formed sentence. To answer it is to observe the circumstances of the utterance along with its tone of voice, guided by what could reasonably be inferred as the limits of what I might feel permitted to say. There is no special problem in the idea of what a painting *says* – what statement it makes. So there is no problem in extending thinking as conversation with oneself to one's mute interrogation of what one paints, composes, and so on.

On being 'two-in-one'

Arendt explains how someone who thinks is plural without being divided against themself. She quotes Socrates in Plato's *Gorgias* – 'It would be better if my lyre were out of tune that that I, being one, should … contradict me.' (LM, 181) Shocking as it appears, it is better that I suffer than that I commit a wrong. It may not be better for me as a military or financial competitor but it is better for me as one who thinks. To think, I must converse with myself. I must come to terms with myself. I cannot converse with a self whose basic aims run counter to my own. If I do what I take to be wrong I can maintain my 'conversation' only if I restore my friendship with myself. Until then, self-justifying monologue or obscurantism will replace conversation with myself. In words reminiscent of Lacan's,[4] Arendt observes how, as seen by another, I am a unified being. In contrast, as a 'thinking ego', my existence consists of fragments that (at best) maintain a conversation with each other.

Therefore, the integrity involved in honesty is a plural voice[5] – '[as] for myself … I clearly am not just one' (LM, 183). This integrity involves reciprocity between conflicting elements. Arendt describes this self-divided integrity at a more generally philosophical level: 'Everything that exists amongst a plurality is not simply what it is, but it is also different from others' (LM, 183). Writing against what Heidegger claims in his reading of Plato's *Sophist*, Arendt disputes his allegation that 'in itself a thing reveals no difference'. In the attempt to make a thing itself into an object of thought such an idea creates an 'eeriness'. (She cites Van Gogh's treatment of a pair of shoes – he imbues them with an aura that would transform them into a 'thought object'.) Difference exists within things themselves. Only a *thinking* being can (partially) unify its own differences. She observes, shrewdly, that it is only when the world intrudes upon thought that the self becomes (as if) one. Hence, the search for the pure unity of the *thinking ego* is a wild-goose chase.

Arendt writes of how Socrates accepts the need for plurality by a self in search of integrity. Plurality requires that the partners who inhabit the theatre of one's mind must be friends. As Socrates put it, you can't get away from your other. How can you be a murderer if you want to think? You can scarcely live on close, friendly and trusting terms with yourself in that case (LM, 188). Since I need friendship with myself, I need friends in the wider world. Socrates is again the guide here. That we *can* have intercourse with ourselves is vital, not to attain purity in integrity, but because the quality of thinking derives from our conversational intercourse with friends.[6]

---

4 Lacan's idea is of a 'mirror' stage, in which the one who seems to themselves as 'morcelated' sees in the mirror the ordered complete entity that they had imagined was the nature of the being of others (Lacan 1977, 4).

5 *Integrity and the Fragile Self* is an excellent defence of the reality of a plural integrity (Cox 2003).

6 Derrida has revived the cry 'Oh friends! There is no friend!'. The value of friends is that they will differ from you where they must. Yet in their difference they are still (as enemies are not) in accord with us. They mean us well in setting us to rights even though, in the crisis of our difference, we can feel that we are in mere disaccord.

Friendship with others and oneself depends upon each other. Our serious friendships with others require us to think hard for ourselves. At the same time, this thinking decays unless subjected to challenge by friends, from their position of inalienable difference (LM, 189). Arendt quotes Aristotle, 'the friend is another self', and counters this with the Socratic aphorism, 'the self is another friend'. In that case, friendship is the guiding experience here, not the glamorised image of a precious 'selfhood'. True, 'I talk with others before I talk with myself', but Arendt is saying more. Thinking is a kind of dialogue. That is possible only between friends, in the spirit of friendship.

Arendt shows that the plurality essential to thinking is more than bare 'consciousness' (LM, 187). As a term, 'consciousness' is quiet about the plurality required of thinking. The notion of consciousness is over-worked (and already was when she wrote in the 1970s). Talk of 'consciousness' clouds thought. Arendt is dismantling the metaphysics of difference and identity. Reality itself is an 'infinite plurality'. She connects this plurality with that of thought, in whose plurality that of reality itself is revealed. In the same gesture she re-instates her outlook about the essential role played by metaphor in making the life of the mind to appear in public as describable:

> As metaphor bridges the gap between appearances and mental activities, so the Socratic two-in-one heals the solitariness of thought … pointing to the infinite plurality which is the law of the earth (LM, 185).

Difference is the 'very condition of the human ego … which exists only in duality' (LM, 187). This ego must, as plural, exist as more than *two*, if the second were no more than the imaginary mirror-image called 'being conscious of oneself'. The 'thinking' of Arendt's that staves off solitariness requires more than a mirror. As conversation with my other, thinking returns to me something different from what I initiated. Solitude involves activity – it requires my art and initiative. Thwarting loneliness, solitude is a 'duality of question and answer'. Remembering goes beyond the having of images of one's past; thinking goes beyond having thoughts that pass through the mind.

In thinking, I ask what I *mean* when something is said, or happens. Arendt reminds us that in (Socratic) thinking, 'the criterion of the mental dialogue is no longer truth [but] … to be consistent with oneself'(LM, 185–6). To think is to be careful about the truth, but the discovery of truth is not thinking's long suit. Truth is to be discovered only by involvement with the world. Truth requires observation, calculation, and public corroboration. In logical deduction one may come to a new thought – the achievement of a conclusion from facts as given. To think, in comparison, is to examine the way in which the facts are presented, the terms in which they are portrayed, and what it means for the alleged facts to be as they are stated. This is why thinking brings us up (*via* our being willing to act) to the face of judgment – or even to face judgment.

Winds of thought

Our thinking, invisible and inaudible, is on the verge of speech and writing. Arendt always has in mind how thinking might free us within (or from) the established 'boundary conditions' – the mores and morality of our social life. The Athenians told Socrates that 'the wind of thought was a hurricane' that would destroy the city. Arendt's answer is that thinking is part of the process of life – to think and to withdraw from that withdrawal is to be fully alive. Thinking begins each day, just as life must always be lived-again. This 'living' to which I committed myself this morning cancels no existential debt to what this afternoon brings. Like thinking, life is 'written in water'.

Arendt had been using the figure of Socrates in his desire, above all, not to harm his friendly relations with the 'other fellow' he has to meet when he returns home from the market place. Arendt[7] cites Shakespeare's Richard III as someone who has avoided thinking by monomaniac ambition and ceaseless unreflective action (LM, 191). Before a crucial battle, the ghosts of those he has killed and whose reality he has kept at bay beset him:

> The lights turn blue. It is now dead midnight.
> Cold fearful drops stand on my trembling flesh.
> What do I fear? myself? there's none else by:
> Richard loves Richard; that is, I am I. (*Richard III*, Act V, Sc. 3, lines 182–5)

He makes successive attempts to shift on to others the idea of what is murderous in him, but he cannot avoid the danger to his own self. It is terrifying – unless it is absurd. Unpractised in thought, agitated, barely in control, he begins his conversation – a trial flight in turbulent air:

> Is there a murderer here? No; – yes, I am:
> Then fly. What, from myself? Great reason why:
> Lest I revenge. What, myself upon myself?
> Alack, I love myself. wherefor? for any good
> That I myself have done unto myself. (*Richard III*, Act V, Sc. 3, lines 186–90)

His mind reels under the contradictions of his warring elements. A self that attempts to define, appraise, protect, love and judge itself cannot escape them. Being divided against itself, the self cannot be whole-hearted or whole-minded in what it pronounces. 'Richard' could be made whole only by the words and observations of others, and in the loving regard of those who might have been his friends – under the judgment of those he had wronged. To accept that only others can see you as a whole (though partially) is to escape the impotence of self-division. It is to abandon the conceit that I can define myself as a subject – as a 'being for myself'. Richard would outwit his self-divisive voice. He strikes back upon conscience:

---

7 Michèle Le Dœuff makes the same reference for a similar philosophical purpose (Le Dœuff 1986, 22).

My conscience hath a thousand tongues,
And every tongue brings in a several tale. (*Richard III*, Act V, Sc. 3, lines 195–6)

The soliloquy ends in a kind of resolution, though a despairing one. Richard now proclaims neither 'I am I', nor 'What can I fear from myself?' nor 'Richard loves Richard'. He finds temporary stability by externalising his self-incriminating feelings, expressed as if by other voices: 'every tongue brings in a several tale/and every tale condemns me for a villain'. A division is required between the one who judges and the one who is judged. There he is – a villain. Over and against him are those who know him as that. When he engaged in condemning himself, his identity was unstable. Was he to identify with the voice in which he condemned himself or with the abject subject he condemned? In the process of (imaginary) resolution, he becomes less wild, forsaking his self-division. His body sweating in cold fear, he ceases to transcend his self-love. He makes an (unstable) resolution of his desire to protect himself, his self-love, and the voices that condemn him.

'*Alack, I love myself*' is the signal for that last detachment. It is 'alack' that he loves himself since it is self-love that still binds him to pursue the disastrous war that self-love brought upon him. And yet, distancing himself from his accusing voices he begins to resolve his ways of being. In this scene's drama of self-enactment he can finally say, steadily:

There is no creature loves me;
Nay, wherefore should they, – since that I myself
Find in myself no pity to myself. (*Richard III*, Act V, Sc. 3, lines 202–5)

Despite the intensity of the soliloquy this resolution is unstable. His admission of having done wrong vanishes as Ratcliffe enters, announcing the dawn. 'Thy friends are up, and buckle on their armour'. Richard recounts his nightmares, and as he gives his thoughts to another, his self-accusation turns to fear for his survival:

O Ratcliffe, I have dream'd a fearful dream! – –
…
Methought the souls of all that I had murder'd
Came to my tent; and every one did threat
to-morrow's vengeance on the head of Richard. (*Richard III*, Act V, Sc. 3, lines 210–15)

Though he does 'find in himself no pity to himself', Richard loves Richard. Realpolitik overtakes self-accusation; the voices of conscience become a rabble:

Let not our babbling dreams affright our souls;
Conscience is but a word that cowards use,
Devis'd at first to keep the strong in awe:
Our strong arms be our conscience, swords our law. (*Richard III*, Act V, Sc. 3, lines 309–12)

The challenging functions of amoral thought reveal it as a natural process rather than as a special prerogative of the privileged or those set apart by their intelligence.

Thinking is not a simple 'voice of conscience'. To think is to question even that inner voice that tells us what we should do. The voice that says what I ought to do might be that of the morality surrounding me, that I have been taught. (That was Eichmann's situation.) It has a character and consequences that I may not understand. In thinking I listen to this voice and converse critically with it, as with any other. Rather than the final judgment after thinking, the 'voice' of conscience is but one amongst the thoughts and feelings with which I engage when I think.

Arendt has drawn our attention to the disruption that the 'wind' of thought makes to the hardened surface of someone who has lived so fast that he feels no breezes. Thought also exposes (and is exposed by) circumstances when your culture becomes thoughtless but you go on thinking. The task of thinking – to question the very voice of conscience as well as to listen attentively to it – is then registered politically when you find yourself in a 'boundary situation' (LM, 192). Arendt lived at the boundary between thinking's withdrawal from events and judging for herself, as a German woman, the decisions made by the established leaders of her country. She lived at the boundary between thinking (withdrawal) and involvement. To live in thought one has to live with oneself. To live with oneself can require separation from the very culture that has fostered one's thinking. For Arendt this meant her acceptance of a 'stateless' life. She would never 'fit in', as she put it.

Jaspers, the philosopher who remained Arendt's intellectual companion after the break with Germany and with Heidegger, proposed that life as a whole is a boundary condition. That I must struggle, suffer and incur guilt frames the whole of life. Arendt observes that in political boundary situations, the very fact that one thinks becomes a point of radicalism. To think is to withdraw. Not to 'join in' brands you as an enemy of the State. One who thinks is thereby an enemy of any State that requires of its citizens absolute obedience and absolute disclosure.[8] To dismantle moral clichés requires thinking and makes judgment possible. This leads Arendt to consider the phenomenon of *judging*. As Kant says, 'judging deals with particulars without simply subsuming them under a general rule' (LM, 192). But we shall have to see how thinking's withdrawal relates to *willing* and *judging*, those other 'inner' acts that are on the verge of our return to the world.

---

8 Sartre writes about the effect on one's consciousness of that of another person who will not 'join in' (Sartre 1976, 287 and Deutscher 2003, 129–30, 158–9).

Chapter 6

Absence

'The only outward manifestation of the mind is absent-mindedness' (LM, 72).

Spectators and participants

Thinking, willing, and judging are 'three basic mental activities [that] cannot be derived from each other'(LM, 69).[1] Here, Arendt associates *thinking* with withdrawal from the 'world', *willing* with a withdrawal from the immediacy of desire and *judging* with a withdrawal from the arena of involvement to the ringside seat of the *spectator* of what people are doing. Before *The Life of the Mind*, Arendt had located judgment within social and political life.[2] Some commentators have, therefore, seen a problem in this shift to judgment as (like thinking) requiring a withdrawal from life's arena to its spectators' raised surrounds. What she says at this stage, however, is an elaboration of her earlier attention to judgment; this later emphasis on the need for a 'withdrawal' to the position of spectator is offered as an additional thought rather than as the correction of a previous error.

Judgment is required both in the midst of active life and when we take the 'ringside seat' of the spectator.[3] More intimately, the attitude of a possible spectator has to be imported into the active social and political world. In the setting for her ideas that Arendt first constructs in *The Life of the Mind*, thinking, willing, and judging[4] are activities in which we constantly engage in everyday life – within our involvement. Even thinking as a 'withdrawal' is defined as a bracketed paragraph within the text of active life. We are involved in '*willing*', which includes setting ourselves to do something, going to do it, resolving to do it, and maintaining ourselves in the course of what we are doing. Evidently too, in the everyday there is *judging* – deciding whether what someone did was right, whether some natural or created thing is beautiful, that some remark is witty or that some development in philosophy is promising.

It would have been excessive if even for one philosophical moment Arendt had moved judging entirely out of involvement's arena. Judging, including its spectatorial moment, involves me in an issue. When I judge that this is the moment

---

1 This line opens Part II of the first volume – *Thinking*.

2 See, for instance, her papers collected under 'Judgment' in *Responsibility and Judgment* (Arendt 2003).

3 This is what will be argued in the Part III of this work.

4 Along with others – pondering, mulling things over, imagining and speculating 'what would happen if …'.

to raise a difficult topic with someone, I do this as an involved participant, not as a spectator. Arendt is precise in her perception of the need to take up the role of spectator in being able to judge. Judging itself is a kind of action, and cannot but be involved and committed. And yet, this very commitment to justice and respect for relevant fact means that we must be prepared to make a partial or momentary withdrawal from the arena within which our judging must operate.

In court there is a 'judge' – a man or a woman who is supposed to play a role that fits Arendt's model of a 'spectator'. The judge is required not to be an interested party in the case that comes before them, and yet the one who plays that role is deeply involved in the making of the judgment.[5] Also, the one accused may well judge the judge, although within the proprieties of the court they do not have the power to put their judgment into effect. I judge that the judge is prejudiced against me on account of my race, the way I dress or speak, on account of my sex or sexual orientation. Briefly, in some spare corner of my mind, I become assessor of the process: I follow the case put against me. Thus I make myself partly 'spectator' of the judging process itself. Though within a situation that involves me crucially, I make a partial spectator of myself – by thought and judgment I am absent in mind from the formally defined judicial process. I refuse to sacrifice my autonomy to the judgment of others even when I must heed its force and take account of its consequences.

We judge that the First World War (in which most of us now alive were not involved) was a terrible but necessary thing – or we come to the conclusion that it has caused more destruction than the evil it was supposed to prevent. In so doing we involve ourselves in the questions of the legitimacy of current wars, events that we have the power to endorse or to oppose. Or we judge that some political candidate, despite their faults, would better represent us than some other. We are involved in this judgment. But as a true *judgment*, it implies judgments about the worthiness of candidates for other constituencies than our own – where our own interests are absent. To judge, then, requires a moment of detachment – the imagination of wider ramifications. There are judgments that seem too immediate to permit any absent-*mindedness* – any *mindedness* about what is absent, that is. Any moment of detachment and withdrawal might threaten the timing of the action that requires our judgment. I may have reflective time to judge that a book that I begin to read is one I shall be able to finish. It is not the same when, running at full speed, I judge that I can leap across a crevasse, or that I can continue to run at the pace I have set myself for the next 100 metres. However, without a partial withdrawal even *in medias res*, we act only impulsively, recklessly, compulsively or even, at the extreme, involuntarily. Withdrawal as inner reserve is possible without interruption to the flow of action.

Thinking, willing and judging. Each of these activities that are also withdrawals – absences from the world – is central to our 'life of the mind'. Arendt claims, too, that even though so closely interconnected, each is 'autonomous'. These activities are autonomous because each is 'subject to laws inherent in the activity itself' (LM, 70). Furthermore, each depends on our power to effect a 'certain stillness in the

5 This is evident in the Australian High Court where a bench of judges determines issues. However, in a jury system too, the judge's judgment is involved when they instruct the jury, oversee the proper examination of witnesses and so on.

soul's passions'.[6] This autonomy of each of these forms of activity, vital to them, means that each has inner limitations of scope and power. If what 'makes us think' is only 'reason's need' to ponder the puzzles thrown up by our life then we cannot expect that 'reason' itself will 'move the will'. We cannot expect that by thinking we shall come to the point of a *resolve* about what to do. Nor that by continuing to think shall we ever have made a *judgment*.[7] Arendt thinks no less of judgment for this. The limitation comes with autonomy's territory. She quotes Kant in favour of her view about the autonomy of judgment:

> To know how to apply the general to the particular is an additional 'natural gift' … the want of which … is ordinarily called stupidity, and for such a failing there is no remedy (LM, 69).

Arendt claims that this 'autonomy' of thinking, willing and judging implies that each activity is 'unconditioned'. 'Unconditioned', that is, not in the sense that nothing affects them or that they fail to effect anything, but in that 'none of the conditions of either life or the world corresponds to them directly' (LM, 70). Arendt's position here is unusual and, within the history of these problems, strikingly original. This 'unconditioned autonomy' has to be differentiated from the determinism that many think to be part and parcel of a scientific outlook on human action and thought. But her position is not a belief in the 'uncaused will' of traditional libertarianism. Indeed, at every point she is opposing 'dualism' – the notion that 'man'[8] is divided into two separate entities, mind and body. Though she writes in terms of 'mind' and 'soul', the error of dualism is revealed as the illusion in which we confound our real powers of inner mental reserve with a fantasy of some actual separation from the body. This need both to deny dualism and yet to use the terms of 'mind' and 'soul' can be understood in terms of its Aristotelian inspiration. The 'soul' of anything is the manifold ways of its 'matter' being composed and put together so that it *works*. To say this is to identify the 'soul' or 'mind' of a being with the manifold powers that that such a being can display.[9]

As an activity connected with thinking and willing, judgment is nevertheless autonomous and distinct from them. At the same time, in the attitude of a partial withdrawal required for judgment we are removed only in imagination from the hurly-burly:

> Men … are totally conditioned existentially – limited by the time-span between birth and death, subject to labour in order to live, motivated to work in order to make themselves at home in the world, and roused to action in order find their place in the society of their

---

6 Compare Socrates' discussion (*Charmides*) of 'temperance' ('tempered-ness' as we might translate it).

7 It is evident, after all, that thinking makes no demand for a conclusion. One may think, endlessly, about something one knows full well to be the case.

8 'Man' – that is, the 'human', that is, women and men considered in terms of their general humanity.

9 Ryle's explanation of the 'invisibility' of mind (Ryle 1949) was extended in the previous chapter to the question of describing 'thinking' in terms of negative actions, thus without lapsing into a 'mind/body' dualism.

> fellow-men. [They] can mentally transcend all these conditions, but … never in reality or in cognition or knowledge, by virtue of which they are able to explore the world's realness and their own (LM, 70–1).

We can *judge* what we find in the world even if we cannot change it. We can *will* that something be the case even if, in fact, it will never turn out. We can *think* of what is unknown and even unknowable, even though we shall never know it. Illusion arises only if we think we can thus *change* this reality which is for us 'totally conditioned existentially'.

Present *in absentia*

Arendt's 'The mind is never so present as in absent-mindedness' is a fine epigram. It is neither a definition nor an axiom – that is not Arendt's style. Rather, it reminds us of the various ways in which the mind can be 'absent', and how its various activities can be understood because we can comprehend the elusive phenomenon of absence. The 'absence' intrinsic to partial withdrawal, part of the life of the mind is not restricted to thinking. 'Withdrawal' equally characterises willing and judging. The difference concerns the activity from which we withdraw. For thinking it is 'the world' – those 'blindingly obvious'[10] objects of sense. For willing, it is desire from which we (partially and temporarily) withdraw. For judgment, it is our involvement in our interest in an outcome from which we must (temporarily and in imagination) detach ourselves.

These are all 'activities of mind'. As in Arendt's, in our time we still use 'mind' as a substantive; a term in search of its substance. As a thing the mind is always 'absent' – whatever is concrete and demonstrable is what it is not. Gilbert Ryle describes the Cartesian view of mind as that of a ghost in the body-machine. He mocks Descartes's certainty that the mind is a substance, albeit a 'non-material' one. Ryle suggests instead that we not take 'mind' as the name of any *thing*. We find mind not in matter or in spiritual 'anti-matter', but in the ways in which we are *mindful*. We discover it, without mystery, in imperatives. 'Mind out!' we cry, free of any metaphysical cringe. In a similar vein (adapting Hegel), Sartre and Beauvoir gave currency to the neologism '*néantir*' – to 'nihilate'. This is the ability to take in its negative aspect what is given. We can see that a friend is *not present* in the café we have entered. We can ensure that something *not occur*. We can think of the mind as a lack in the solidity of being – a lack that allows the emergence of creativity in thought and action.

Writing of perception and thought, Arendt ascribes to 'mind' the (negative) capacity of 'de-sensing' our perceptual experience as an object of thought and memory. Without this de-sensing, recall of the original experience would be 'witchcraft'. One would be struck as by a hallucinatory apparition of what one had experienced. In recall of a sensory experience there is an absence of its first impact. This is not a lack in memory, but the power of thought to deal with what is absent.

---

10 Just to revive those old days of Marx's perceptions for a moment.

It is the guilelessness (my term) of being absent-minded that permits the mind to emerge as an observable phenomenon. To see someone lost in thought is to see what it looks like to think. To have a mind is not only to act intelligently in relation to one's environment. The absent-mindedness that undoes the suave man or woman of the world is more than a loss of attention. The mind is absent only from those that expect its presence – the person who finds that his friend is no longer 'with' him. Arendt's epigram reminds us that absentmindedness is an absent-*mindedness*. Though not (presently) minded to be sociable, the friend is still minded to think.

The power to deal with what is absent (and to absent oneself) is not only the power to recall and to think more abstractly. It is also the power of imagination involved in perceiving something as real in itself. What we refer to *as* (and perceive *as*) a durable three-dimensional and mobile thing has to be mostly out of sight. A thing that could be taken in by a glance, leaving nothing more to be seen, would be a mere visual apparition. ('She's out of sight' expresses how much more there is *to be seen* in the person than what comes within present vision.) What I can *not* see of a three-dimensional moving object is brought into the picture of what I *can* see. These impositions of what is absent upon what is present show how thought is intimately involved in perception. By such superimposition I take someone as *to be seen* by someone on the other side of the room, or to be seen again later.

When we observe someone's face, gestures and bodily disposition we see them as perceiving or thinking. We can conceive of them as a physical thing and mechanism but we describe them, rightly, in wider terms – not as a thinking and perceiving immateriality that mysteriously inhabits that body but as the source of visible and tangible powers of 'nihilation'. The *invisibility* of mind and its operations becomes the visual metaphor of how things and people, vividly and strikingly 'present' to us, are present largely *in absentia*.[11] It should not surprise us that the mind is elusive. Consider what happens when we try to hunt it down. We may turn our attention from behaviour and expression to search out the mind in the cranium's fixed deposit box. But, whatever one can find there, whether grey matter or whether electrical activity within neuronal assemblies, provokes further uneasiness about the 'mind itself'. And although we cannot deny that the mind *is* the brain and that thinking *is* a brain process' (that thinking is *not* a brain process is the claim of Ryle's dualist), those identifications raise as many problems as they avoid.

Certainly, a physicalist identification of thinking and brain-processing reminds us of surprising new identities that emerge with new discoveries in scientific theory and experiment. Lightning *is* a discharge of electricity; the gene *is* a DNA molecule; the heat of a body *is* its average internal kinetic energy. The problem in *identifying* thinking with brain processing is whether it is *enough* of a thing to be a brain thing, whether thinking is *enough* of a process to be a brain process. You cannot identify a non-entity with an entity. A central uncertainty about 'thinking is a brain process' emerges. Does the identity reduce thought to a brain process or does it amplify brain processes to the status of thought? When we identify thinking with a brain process we must find new lodgings within electrochemical activity for negativity and absence.

11 These remarks are a sort of contemporary inheritance of Derrida's attack on the 'myth of presence'.

If thinking is a process (pattern of processes) in the brain when considered as part of a whole sensory and affective organism, then patterns of electrochemical activity must have the capacities to nihilate what is there to be perceived. Or, closer to the common sense of science, we may theorise that the human organism as a whole – the functioning body/brain complex – has these powers. Evidently brain processes support our mental powers but the identification yields no further information about thinking or about brain processes. The question of nihilation – perception and thought of absence – remains with us. Thinking is brain process (within an affective organism) but as a philosophical enterprise, it remains a conceptual and phenomenological business to describe what brain processes make us capable of.

We use the conceptual weight of thinking to lever upon the perennial problems of presence and of absence. It is in someone's having a 'mind' that things can be present. In that we can be present to (and for) each other, things can be present as amongst us as objects of shared concern. We are 'mindful' of them. It is because we need to be mindful of others that, in our *absent*-mindedness, we stand out amongst them. To 'have a mind' is to be capable of expressing, conveying and dissembling how it is with ourselves and the circumstances within which we are placed. To *have a mind* is *to mind.* In absent-mindedness this mind that still exists (we *can* mind) has gone missing (*we fail to mind*). Absent without leave.

For a time we will not *be* anything for them. What we call our 'will' and our 'judgment' require a presence of mind but also a sometime 'absence' of it. Continuing thoughtfulness with others (and with things) require us to think about circumstances and involvements. Perhaps we must determine a different will, or stand apart to make a judgment. A *presence of mind* (antithesis of the *absent* mind) requires of us a temporary detachment from the scene. *Minded-ness* – sensibility, acumen and judgment – depends upon this occasional absence. Arendt undercuts dualism by describing the phenomena of mind and thought that make the dualist fallacy stand out on theory's horizon, even while those descriptions resist reduction.

Many a mind

We keep more than one matter in mind at once. Bringing the potatoes to the boil we juggle the time of starting the steak (allowing for the few minutes for it to rest before serving), ready to flick the microwave to give the green beans a short burst when we take the steak off the grill. Everything to be ready at the same time. We answer the phone and bear in mind to turn the steak within the minute. Talking with a friend and handling children's pleas all the while.[12] In being ready to turn over the steak we are not 'absent-minded' about the potatoes or distracted from turning on the beans. To prepare the meal so that it can all be served freshly cooked on the instant is to take account of these stages in their overlapping phases of time.

Another time. You have put on the steak and already cannot recall where the second-hand was on your watch as you did so. You just remember to put on the beans, but ready to serve them with the steak as it has rested, find the potatoes boiled

12 (In your daydreams.)

out of their skins. Your reactions to your friend's confidences have been empty of sense and feeling. You had no imagination of the situation they tried to summon up. 'Hello! Anyone at home?' they say.

To be caught up in thought while trying to do things physically[13] is different from splitting your attention between various tasks. Any task that requires concentration (preparing a complex meal, driving a car, taking part in a public debate) runs an immediate risk of failure if you are caught up in thought. To be caught up in thought is not simply one more occupation to be fitted in with other matters to be dealt with at the same time. To have something on your mind refuses to sit as *one amongst* the various occupations that call for your attention. Absence of mind (for social use) impairs your capacity to pay attention to anything else you are doing. Thinking refuses to distribute attention to the various components and attendant matters of a task in hand within the one time frame.

To have something on your mind is to be *pre*occupied. The mind is taken up, taken over, before anything else can properly register. But what is a *pre*occupation as against an *occupation*? Why does thinking disable us from other activities in a way that is not matched by anything else that we do? Arendt's answer would be[14] that, as an activity, thinking is not (exactly) an action; it is not exactly something that we 'do'. This fits with our sense of something almost involuntary in being preoccupied. In contrast with what occupies us, what *pre*occupies us is an intrusion upon what we *should have been* doing.[15] For Arendt, the thinking activity is a quasi-action that displaces the mode of action rather than being yet another one. Or, thinking deliberately displaces action. Certainly, some other activities that fail to be *doings* also have little connection with thought – the almost reflex scratching of an itch while you go on doing something towards your main purpose, for instance. Such a half-conscious barely voluntary movement is scarcely a distraction. So why does being taken up in thought interfere so much with anything else that does require concentration? Being taken up in thought stands to mental and physical occupations quite differently from anything else to which we apply our mind.[16]

Ah! At that moment we come right up to the issue of mind and absent-mindedness. To think *occupies* one's mind – one might say that being taken up in thought *is* one's mind (so long as the preoccupation lasts). I am 'of a mind' to think, as I may be 'of a mind' to go for a swim, but thinking is not something to which I *apply* my mind. As Arendt reminds us, thinking is other than calculating, theorising, problem solving or the making of inferences. As being neither an action nor a simple passivity it lies outside the field of mental actions – calculating, theorising and so on. Considered as an activity, thinking is being use-less.

The expression 'I am in two minds whether to ...' clarifies this matter of being mindful as against having an 'absent' mind. There might be three differing and virtually exclusive things that I could consider doing. There might be half a dozen.

13 That includes conversing and making music – anything we do as distinct from our thinking about it.

14 She addresses related questions.

15 I acknowledge a suggestion along these lines by my colleague, Paul Crittenden.

16 Whatever exactly 'having a mind' is or involves.

But even as a bad joke you cannot speak of being in three minds (or six). If to be 'in two minds' were to be undecided between one thing and some other alternative, one could be in three or more minds. After all, there may be more than one alternative. But being in *two* minds is being in conflict whether to do something *or not* and that is why there is no room for 'three minds'.

I may be in two minds about whether to buy a certain parcel of shares in a company. The price may have bottomed or the present sharp descent may be only the first stage of a collapse. Being 'in two minds' makes it hard to think about other matters, or even to think clearly about the purchase itself. If four different parcels of shares were suggested by the broker I would move with a different kind of difficulty to decide on one (or none) of them. I would not be 'in four minds' about the merits of oil, minerals, heavy industry and income securities. It is the one mind that I bring to the problem of all of them. To be in two minds about oil shares, in comparison, is to be unable properly to bring my mind to bear on the issue. I may have begun to look at the issue, but as yet have no way of proceeding. This is what makes being in two minds analogous to being absent-minded. Being in two minds, I am in the state of thinking about the issue, looking to find a way of coming to *know* what to do.

Not minding

To mind is prior to *the mind.* This re-ordering makes more sense of negativity and absence as central issues of mind. As a thing, mind would be invested, rather, with positivity – a *substance*, as Descartes said in constructing his dualism of mind and body. This dualistic logic does not change when the mind is postulated as a material thing. The error is already made. To conceive the mind as the brain merely defers the commonplace affairs of mind that come under *negativity* and *absence*. It is *because we have a mind* that we can remember, but how a *thing* called 'mind' could explain this remains in the dark. In contrast, it is a basic observation that we can *bring to mind* what no longer occurs,[15] and imagine as *from within the mind* what we cannot sense. We deal with what is no longer, or what is not yet. We predict results for tomorrow, and form theories that we cannot (yet) verify. We make philosophical remarks upon *time*, or *matter*, on *thinking*, the *mind* or *being*. Timelessness has been attributed to *mind* because we deal with the 'timeless' objects of mathematics or metaphysics. As if the mind must have taken on that quality – like attributing a 'Russian soul' to one who can learn to converse in Russian? Or to find a child's mind in an adult because they write books enthralling children?

There is an indecipherable metaphor in the suggestion that the mind has something of negativity or absence within it so that it can deal with negativity or absence. As if there were a rent in the fabric of mind that would let in a world with its own pits and rents. The metaphor still pictures the mind as a kind of *thing* – a colander whose holes let in the fractured reality that surrounds it. Through these holes we gain a picture of reality as being absence as much as presence. Or the mind is a net we cast to 'capture' the realities about which we would theorise and upon which we would dwell in thought.

The mind as a thing – a colander or net-like thing – is a myth but it is no myth that we *mind.* We mind what we do and we mind what happens to us and to things.

To *mind* them logically involves our recognition of what they lack no less than what they possess. To bear the anxiety and risk involved in minding them is to accept what we lack in terms of knowledge of the conditions of their health and safety, and what we lack in terms of power to safeguard them. It is the mind's *absence* – the universal lack of a mind as a thing – that would permit us to *mind*. That mind itself is *absent* means that absence and negativity is homely. It is not the uncanny (*unheimlich*). With all its intrinsic gaps and lacks, thinking is ready-made to familiarise an alien world for us by close conversation – a *conversal*[17] of the world by thought.

17 Author's neologism.

PART III
Willing Myths

Chapter 7

Being Willing

'Not how you sing but how willingly you sing'[1]

Discovering the Will

There is an absence of the Will[2] as an experience or concept in early philosophies, Arendt observes. At the same time, the history of the 'operation of the concept' is not one of a progressive glorious revelation – as if an idea rough-hewn in one era became steadily more exact, comprehensive and entrenched through the centuries. Arendt will remark, acidly, 'if time marches on, the same cannot be said about what happens within it'.

'I do not do the good I want; the evil I do not want is what I do' cries Paul of Tarsus, displacing this world of temporal trial by the hope of an everlasting one. The Will and its struggles are obscured by these impassioned, stylish words. Words neither of passion nor of contemplative dispassion, they throw us into a tangle of thoughts and feelings. A predicament from which 'only a God could save us' (to parody our recent Heidegger). Paul designs his (proto) will to be impotent, constructing it to celebrate the inadequacy of our 'obedience to law' and the weakness of our obedience to better feelings. Only a miracle of 'grace' can save us from the ensuing paralysis of Will. Arendt extracts from Paul's self-flagellation a revealing model of the self-division intrinsic to 'Will' – the discovery of the 'inner man'.[3]

These days we have a lively scepticism about the very idea of Willing. The classical Greek paradigm did not recognise it either. Plato's characters discuss every theme but that of the Will. Following them, Aristotle uses '*thalein*' (to be ready or prepared) and '*boulesthai*' (to view one thing as more desirable than another) and coins '*proairesis*' (preference for some line of action). It might be thought obvious that Aristotle's *akrasia* does set out the problem of 'weakness of will', but Arendt argues that 'weakness of will' is a misnomer. It is Paul, much later, who will give currency to a Will that raises an intrinsic *counter-will*. In *akrasia* one fails to go ahead and do what one wants. This involves a failure of nerve or perhaps, ennui. In contrast with Aristotle, Paul expresses a new disturbance, not at his failure to carry through

---

1 *How Willingly You Sing* (film, Australia, 1975).

2 I use a capital letter for Arendt's problematic 'will'. As what I will *do*, the issue about Willing is glossed over.

3 Descartes establishes the scene for deconstructing that 'inner man'. Within his writing 'as if he could doubt everything', behind that 'mask', he places the 'inner man' under a spotlight, laying out the insoluble problem of the Will in relation to the 'laws' of nature. He establishes the era of suspicion about the 'I' and its 'Will'.

his plans, but with the character of his *life of the mind* – the dislocation between the 'good he wants' and the 'evil he does'. Contemporary scepticism virtually displaces Will as a faculty, and 'Willing' as some special activity that precedes action. This is a virtual return to the Greek heritage for which we 'will' simply in having a preference and acting coherently.

The lack of a concept of Will for the classical Greeks (perhaps they did *not* will, speculates Arendt) then goes with 'cyclical' Time measured by recurring sequences. The day proceeds from dawn to dusk and after night, recurs. From birth we proceed to death, and birth recurs. As one of Arendt's Greeks, I have reason to act so long as I can hope for fame and glory, which is secured so long as the *polis* is everlasting. *They* did not demand that an '*I*' (this precious ego as from the seventeenth century) should be 'born again'. In Arendt's words, freedom as 'I-can' (not 'I-will') is fundamental for them – the power to do as I please.

Arendt is prepared to date the issue of Will in terms of pre and post 'Christian' eras because the tortured Will appears along with the establishment of Christianity, with its cult of guilt and redemption. Moreover, that religion announces a radical break in the temporal cycles. There is no longer to be the same time for all time – as if time were no more than recurring cycles of day and night, winter and summer, birth and death, success and disaster. The first evangelists proclaim the death of Jesus as unique and unrepeatable – 'Christ born, crucified and resurrected'. The proclamation *requires* the break from a cyclical to a rectilinear sequence.

What marks 'modern times'[4] is first a suspicion and finally a downright rejection of the Will. There is no 'Will' that moves us unless that is simply 'the strongest desire'. Anything else that might be called 'Will' is 'what I choose that is within my power'. Arendt emphasises that the rectilinear vision of time required the annunciation of a unique event to establish it – as much for a scientific history as for theology. (Dating events 'B.C.' or 'A.D.' was convenient.) But the mathematical conception of a time continuum arises with that rectilinear vision. Then a *deterministic* picture also arises with the conception of an unbroken and successive order of causes that spray out an ever-widening set of irrecoverable effects. Within that vision, there is no plausibility in positing a 'Will' that might disrupt the series. To record an experience of initiating events is bad phenomenology – or else faithfully to represent an illusion.

Willing collaboration

Arendt borrows an idea from the philosophy of Augustine in the fifth century to clarify Paul's 'impotence' of Will and the 'omnipotence' of Will announced by Epictetus, the critical Stoic. The 'conflict' of will is between Will and counter-Will. Intrinsic to Will is a 'mental' act set up against it – 'Nilling' – the Will *not* to do what one's (other) Will says, or to perform its excluding contrary. This is far from the cliché of the (moral) will set against the (immoral or non-moral) desires and inclinations. For Paul, the only solution to the fact that the 'Law' is of no avail in bringing him

4 Arendt employs the usual frame of the rise of new philosophies and sciences in the seventeenth century.

to do what he feels he should is for him to await Grace. But this is horrifying, since 'Grace' is to be awarded on no discernible ground. He is paralysed by this divided subjection to the commands of one Law – of the Torah, of God – against the 'law' of the demands of his 'bodily members'. He can only wait upon this 'grace' of which he writes, and while waiting there is nothing for it but to 'mortify the flesh'. The sensationalism of this obscures Paul's emphasis on the problem of the thwarted Will as a conflict of *laws*. He appeals to the body's 'demands' (a loaded metaphor) as source of a *law* to whose quasi-legitimate *commands* (an extended metaphor) he is subject. What the body needs is conceptualised in terms of legitimacy and law. In consequence, the problem of not following what is good and right can no longer be represented simply as a struggle between forces in different domains – the 'spiritual' and the 'sensual'. In a struggle between two Laws, something more than *weakness* of will is involved when Paul enacts 'what he hates'. Like conflicting Law, Will cannot solve its own dilemma. It is the struggle of his *Will to Law(s)*, not a lack in his strength of will (when faced by desire) that makes his predicament insoluble.

Arendt places Epictetus very nicely in apposition to Paul's stalled struggle. Not Paul's 'impotence' but a new 'omnipotence' of Will. To be 'omnipotent' in my (newly constructed) Epictetan Will, I must Will only what does happen. I am to become like a child who gains the omnipotence of moving a railway carriage by the tactic of pushing on it only just at the moment when it is about to move off. Seeing my favoured team losing I do not despair. I will that the now winning team *should* win. This is the 'collaborationism' that Sartre exposes in a paper written in the aftermath of the Second World War.[5] Any one of us can feel the pull in our own daily politics towards that retention of Will's power by getting with the strength. The Howardian[6] right keeps up the pressure to define the 'centre' as always between its own goal posts. Each evening it shifts them that much further to the right in preparation for the next day of parliament by talkback radio. Being promised that we would be 'comfortable and relaxed' with how we were, it must seem churlish of us to object to this culture of the 'normal'. Their 'normality' feels no surprise at its own cruelty, and horror loses its grip on us.

Paul's 'impotence' approaches asymptotically the 'omnipotent' will of Epictetus, from the other side of the axis. Paul's Will would countermand the 'law' of his bodily nature, but attenuates to infinity in a 'sinful' ego while it awaits the unpredictable gift of 'grace'. The Will of Epictetus, in contrast, would be docile to all that happens, and to the body that maintains it. Will must be ready to attach itself to any trend. But that Will, no less than Paul's, attenuates to infinity in one who does not care what happens. On the other side of the fence from Paul's guilty impotence, Epictetus hoists his banner 'OMNIPOTENT WILL AT WORK HERE', standing in a barren inheritance. We spectators of history charge the Stoic with apathy.

Arendt sketches such an objection from Augustine to Epictetus. In a proto-Nietzschean gesture, however, she wishes Augustine had proposed a stronger argument against him: he needs a Will in order to 'nill' his Will to attempt projects

---

5 For a recent reference and context for this, see Bernard-Henri Lévy's *Sartre: Philosopher of the Century* (Lévy 2003, 264–5).

6 A reference to John Howard, ultra-conservative Prime Minister of Australia, 1996–.

with unpredictable outcomes. The Will to do what we may not achieve will dissipate of its own accord only if we no longer care what happens anyway. But our caring does *not* simply dissipate. As Epictetans we cannot risk Willing the abolition of our Will concerning what may happen unpredictably. How are we to ensure by Will that we *will* no longer care?

In reading these texts out of the first few centuries A.D. we are liable to be confused by our knowledge of Nietzsche's (nineteenth century) 'Yes' to the world, or Heidegger's (twentieth century) 'Will-not-to-Will'. There is a kind of love of the world in Nietzsche's thought experiment that we should be prepared to will an eternal recurrence of all that has been, with all our errors and all its disasters. That has a different mainspring from the gesture of Epictetus. If the Stoic strategy of omnipotence is to work its faked effect, we must be indifferent to eventuality. Yet the Epictetan proposal that we place a hand on the railway carriage of world events just as we perceive the train to be moving off is an attempt still to have the pleasure of exercising a power of will. So Epictetan stoicism asks more of us than to be spectators of the train's movement. (To exit the *vita activa* for the classical *vita contemplativa* is a different tale, a proposal under the sign of 'Thought' as nobler than 'Will and Action'.) Stoicism must Will not to will what is uncertain, in order to will only what does happen. This is my interpretation of Arendt's diagnosis of the Stoic's search for a calm Will in perfect collaboration with reality. Stoic Will seeks an environment of serenity, unable to accept Will's 'tense-ness', as Arendt puts it. But that serenity is thinking's reward, not given for *willing*. Calm is the compensatory payment to thinking for the loss it suffers in its privacy. Arendt reminds us how keenly the Romans felt that this privacy implies the thinker's privation. This is deprivation thought itself must suffer – involvement with the world.

My placing of an Epictetan hand on the carriage of the world's train may appear as a perfect charade to the unsympathetic critic of this kind of stoicism. Nevertheless, from the point of view of the phenomenology and the logic of the Will, in my detachment from caring about what will happen I do not, in this tale, merely *watch* the train set off. I do more than make a friendly wave from a distance, too. It is my *Will* that the train move off as it does. I am *willing* that it should do so. I thus retain active solidarity with events. But if I am to Will these events as they occur, my *caring* must be under *immediate* control of the Will. If I can detach from that *care* only in a struggle of will, I Will an outcome still unpredictable.

There is a trilemma for the Stoic strategy of ensuring an omnipotent Will. As a first alternative, I can leave Care in its own rightful place. But then I shall have to struggle against the tendency to Will to prevent what threatens what I care about. (I am to avoid a frustrated Will, and I may fail to avert the threat.) As a second alternative I can struggle against Care – it shall be my will not to care about any eventuality in any case. But I can have no guarantee of the success of that Will to indifference. To have that Will is an immediate threat to my stance of Stoicism. To take the final option, I must pay full attention to the distress of my caring concern with the world's eventualities. (I do this as an alternative to trying to extinguish that concern as threatening to provoke what will be an inevitably frustrated Will.)

We have conceded for argument's sake that the choice of that to which we pay attention *is* within the perfect province of the Will. This may be only a very rough approximation to empirical fact, but never mind. Although the Will may not be frustrated, the original intent of Stoicism has been subverted. Stoicism was designed so that by attuning my Will to the ways of the world I could avoid distress. But, since part of the world is my caring about what happens in it, I must either Will not to care (thus risking a frustrated Will) or I must fully engage my Will so as to accept my distress at what happens within the world. This chosen Will has to displace the Will to change the world. Paul's tortured Will has been replaced by that of struggling not to care, or else of somehow *accepting* the distress of care. And still we do not jeer at Epictetus from a citadel of logic. When the Stoic's conflicted desire for calm is spelled out thus, we recognise our own situation as we read the newspaper, daily.

Liberating the Will

Augustine, after the Stoics, also raises up the Will as essentially conflicted, a principal problem for thought. He locates the problem more explicitly, however, in the conflict of one person's two Wills, rather than between Will and some force outside its domain. One can compress Augustine's position into these key propositions:

	Willing something does not amount to being able to do it.
Nevertheless,	Willing something is necessary if one's power to act is to operate.
	Willing something draws upon one's power to do it.
	Unless one wills it, neither body nor mind is moved into action.
And finally,	In every 'I will' there is an 'I nill' – this is the essential conflict within Will.

When I contest some 'desire', it is conflict of Will rather than its weakness that is the problem.[7] Arendt reminds us of how Augustine's thinking occurs in two phases. In the first, the question is dominated by theology. How is there evil in the world if God is good? The discussion is inconclusive and postponed. In the second phase, though within a theological framework, the discussion is phenomenological and conceptual. Augustine rejects Paul's problem as being a conflict between two 'laws' to which he is subject – of the 'flesh' and of 'spirit'. The conflict is between Will and counter-will ('nilling') in relation to one Law – a Law that is addressed equally to Mind and to Will. It is by Will that we are free – neither reason nor the desires are free in themselves. So the problem is a battle, but not between 'reason' and 'desire'. Reason is *compelling* for Reason; desires are roused automatically by outside objects.[8] What we possess is a power to Will or to Nill – *Velle* and *Nolle* are 'actively transitive'. I can Will to do what I desire not to, since I Nill my Will to act out my desire.[9]

Augustine's *Confessions* reveal the Will as in an impossible position – a 'monstrosity'. According to Augustine's principles the body does not resist the Will since the body has no Will of its own. It is only when the 'mind commands itself'

7 Desire as threatening Will is closer to Plato's *Phaedrus*, but it is Reason, not Will that is threatened.

8 Duns Scotus will add that the Spirit, too, is free only through freedom of Will.

9 This 'nilling' seems very like Sartre's '*néantisation*'.

(the Will being one of mind's faculties) that 'it is resisted' (LMW, 93). Thus the 'monstrosity' of Will – why would the mind command unless it *did* Will? And, if so, how can it resist? This leads to the conclusion that what commands is the Will itself, not the mind. But the resistance does exist, and so the split occurs within the very Will itself. The mind is then its own Commander and Rebel. Commenting on Augustine's position, Arendt expresses this phenomenon in linguistic terms:

> [The split] is shown by the Will's use of imperatives … It is [thus] in the Will's nature to double itself [so that] there are always '*two wills neither of which is entire. [W]hat is present to one… is absent from the other … It is not that I was* '*in two minds, one good, the other evil*' but that the uproar of two wills in the one … mind '*rent me asunder*' (*Confessions*, Book 8, Chapters IX, X).

If it is in the nature of 'Will' to be divided against itself then the problem is how to make one's divided Will 'entire'. Will, as conflicted, must cease to *be* Will.[10] Paul had to wait for divine Grace. Augustine invokes a force outside Will, but within human resources to lend gravity to one's life – a kind of 'trinity' of memory, intellect and will – each 'comprehended by the other' and 'relating back to itself' (LMW, 99). Thought acts as an intellectual bond. (*Cogitare*, from *cogere*, to bind together.) Will binds thought and perception in their need for willed attention; memory collects the operations of thought and will and retains the past for every faculty. Yet memory itself stands in need of the directive and selective powers of Will.

This would be a cosy set-up were it not for Will's division with itself, which, unlike one's friendly auto-conversation when thinking, occupies a field of antagonists. Augustine suggests that in its essential daily services, Will is (in Arendt's words) 'so busy preparing action that it hardly has time to get caught in the controversy with its own counter-will' (LMW, 101). This is a sign of a more radical solution. A Will as a Command that exists only in relation to a resistant Will cannot be unified. That conflict of Will is resolved by action – a *coup d'état*, in Bergson's phrase. Arendt has prefaced this solution in her own distinction of thinking and will in terms of *tonality*. Motivated by hope of success and fear of failure, Will is marked by tense-ness. Neither thinking nor willing, but only action can resolve this tension.

Augustine also suggests love as what resolves the conflicted Will, offering hints about how this would work. (We must suspect some 'divine' love as the *load*stone.[11]) But for Arendt it is *freedom* that is the (philosophical) price of one's 'redemption' from conflicted Will. This freedom is *defined* not in terms of a traditional *freedom of will* but by a 'relative break' with normal causal succession. An 'uncaused cause', this would be merely the mystery of a divine being inscribed into our situation. The freedom that resolves a conflicted Will is our power to initiate a new series of events. As if Buridan's ass, in stasis between two bales of hay, were literally to apprehend lateral thinking by laterally Willing – to leap up and thus to fall to one side. Eager to broaden his mind with Apuleius, he'd leave his owner, shouting, far behind.

10 To be willing is to be resolved, and to have a 'divided will' is to fail to be resolved.

11 What you choose when push comes to shove is the only final criterion of what you most love – unless you render your choice useless by shilly-shallying after the choice is made.

The other part of Arendt's answer to paralysis of Will is that only action, not thought or willing, can resolve it. Arendt tells us that Kant invoked the idea of freedom as the initiation of a new series of events, only to be intellectually embarrassed by it. He had no need to be embarrassed by the possibility of initiating a new series of events in a world in which events must have causes, and these causes operate according to universal principles, she argues. 'All men are natals' would replace 'All men are mortals' as the initial premise:

> [T]he freedom of a *relatively* absolute spontaneity is no more embarrassing to human reason than the fact that men are born – newcomers again and again in a world that preceded them in time. The freedom of spontaneity is part and parcel of the human condition (LMW, 110).

I would add my word with Kant's: the trouble also comes from thinking of the imperative element in Will as the issuing of self-commands. If there is to be some *act*, 'to will', then telling myself what to do is the only candidate. Conceptually, the paralysis arises from thinking of Will as an act, and thus as a self-command that corresponds to thinking as *talking to myself*. Thinking is not doomed to paralysis or failure because it is as a friend with myself that I think. The problem about Will as Inner Command, however, is that I am inimical to myself in issuing orders against myself. I try to bring my subordinate into line, but only have to refuse in order that *I* become the Commander. Irresolvable conflict or a battle *I* cannot lose? Either way, nothing is resolved.

An embarrassment for modernity

Descartes maintains the power of the Will as within his dualism of mind and body. The body is a complete system of physical causes and effects. The will is not constrained by this fact, being a power of the mind that is not part of the physical order. And so are generated the problems of 'mind and body' that still form the staple of analytical philosophy to this day. How do the operations of this 'Willing Mind' fit with the operations of the human body as an already complete system of physical causes and effects? Interaction will flout the rules of the physical system. Mere parallel lines of mental and physical life make an illusion of our sense of making a difference to what happens by what we Will. Can we strictly identify mind and body in order to escape this impasse? And then, what kind of identity would this be, and how are we to account for the apparent qualitative difference between ourselves described in personal terms, as against the characterisation of the body and brain by physics?

Although Kant is 'already embarrassed by the idea of our having a power of spontaneously beginning a new series of events', he cannot escape the thought that this initiative is precisely what he takes, in the simplest act of getting up out of his chair. The real issue is between the old '*liberum arbitrium*' (a power of choice between set options) and the spontaneous initiation of a new line of events – an idea of freedom in will that is appealing and yet problematic. The idea 'appeals', not simply in that our experience appears to be as of such a capability. It is appealing to the whole modernist idea of progress that new, previously unpredictable lines of thought, enquiry, invention and action can be initiated. At the same time such 'modernism' is, for reasons sketched above, 'less than pleased', in Arendt's words, about the whole business of Willing.

We have see how the Will as created in Paul is conflicted as stalled between the demands of two conflicting Laws. Proceeding past Paul's situation of being stalled between the Law of God (or the Torah) and the 'Law' of the 'flesh', Augustine reads the Will as conflicted, not merely between itself and 'desire', but between Will and Counter-will. (It is in these terms that he begins to re-interpret Epictetus.) The Will cannot solve the conflict between itself and its own conflicting order. Even if God's grace, love, or one's own direct action rescued Will from this distressed stasis, a question stands over the concept of Will that predicates it as existing only in conflict with itself. For Arendt's Duns Scotus (only a generation younger than Aquinas), already bridging scholasticism and modernism, the solution to Will's conflict must be found within the human system. What is meant by the 'in-determination' of the Will simply is its power to Will or to Nill whatever reason or desire presents to it. Then it can strike us clearly enough that this freedom admits the existence of some kinds of causes of what we do willingly. In that Will 'wills' and 'nills' the same action, its defect is a power that it shares with the imagination's elusive freedom. (These reflections are not far from our own contemporary thoughts.)

Duns Scotus further underlines the real, though fine, line between the Will and our actually doing something, willingly. In falling to my death, having chosen to jump, my Will has no effect on anything I might do, and yet it can still remain my Will (or I may 'nill') that I fall. It is *contingency* that Duns Scotus underlines in advancing the cause of the Will and its freedom. Some matters are beyond our power to alter, but it is within our power at least to love or to hate what is presented to us. In this way, Duns Scotus takes one more step in linking love with the resolution of the Will – *amo: volo ut sis* – I love (whatever): I will that it should be. Love is a key to the possibility of freedom. Love itself is a contingency that freely chooses its object, being attracted to but not determined by it. Duns Scotus sketches an escape from *determinism* as following from *causality*. He does this in terms of the operation of multiple partial causes. Procreation is the paradigm of this – neither male nor female determine what the child will be like – each is a partial cause, dependent upon the contingencies of the other. This freedom to 'initiate a new series of events' is not the denial of causality, then, but the insistence on the primacy of contingency.

Duns Scotus admits, nonetheless, to not knowing how a Will can be a partial cause of what one does and how, precisely, it may have its causes without being determined by the considerations with which it must deal. The freedom of Will and the (apparent) necessity of a full set of all causes are attributed to 'different dimensions of mind' – a gesture that would seem to prefigure Kant's uneasy solution by appeal to a division of 'phenomenal' and 'noumenal' realities. Arendt thus sees Duns Scotus as leading us directly into the 'uncertain destinies of the willing faculty at the close of the [our] modern age' (LMW, 146). Arendt remarks how already (in 1611), John Donne has seen 'how drie a Cinder this world is' under the idea of physics alone.[12] Within the scientific Will to know and to change things for the better – the 'progressivism' of modernity – this very Will to science and progress is an intellectual embarrassment. It is not an idea *within* physics. Leaping forward into this 'modern age', Arendt points out how Nietzsche's sceptical undoing of Will identifies it with the inner voice of self-command. Nietzsche exposes the 'Will' as neither a divine gift of Grace nor a special part of the soul, set apart from body. Its voice is an inner theatrical trick in which *I* identify with it for the pleasure of being 'the one in command'. One expects an 'I can' when one wills, and by identifying with the one put in command, one can have the pleasure of success.

A new 'tonality' thus arrives on the scene. In freeing himself from the hopeless conflict of Will and Nill, Nietzsche repudiates both Paul's '*I-will-and-I-can not*' and, no less, the prudent utilitarian pleasure/pain calculus. He invokes, rather, a sense of joy in abundance – a thrill that can turn to Dionysian destruction. This 'Will' as a 'yes' to life makes his 'super man' strong enough to live in the thought of eternal recurrence simply as an acknowledgement of the full reality of the past as not to be hidden whatever it might have been. Resentful Will is that which is frustrated by one's inability to 'will backwards' – to undo the past. It is from its impotent rage that springs the thirst for vengeance and the desire to dominate. So we tend either to enforce insistence on Will or else repudiate it altogether. However, nothing short of the escape into action (as Arendt puts it) can resolve the Will's 'tense-ness'. The idea that the past simply 'causes' the present (and thus the future) is one more abdication of Will that abandons the future. Nietzsche's 'super' man neither encourages Will nor *Wills* to extinguish it. He transmutes it into a 'yes' to '*that the world is*'.

And so we come to Heidegger, in the next century after Nietzsche, almost catching up with our own trajectory. The business of Will is not an overt theme in the first major work, *Being and Time* (1927), but later Heidegger attacks the idea of Will as having been a disguised and malign influence within the work. Arendt finds him (in his first volume on Nietzsche) reading Nietzsche favourably, as endorsing the Will. Then, in his dramatic 'turning' (or 'reversal') that persisted from the later 1930s, Heidegger turns upon human Will as a force for evil. Instead of caring for '*Being*' (which involves the will to do so), we are to act and think at the behest of this *Being*. Thinking itself must 'let itself' be claimed by *Being*. Will's insistence on the future enforces an oblivion of the past – 'we would rather Will nothing than not Will', as Nietzsche says famously. Thus we can be led into utter destructiveness. As a response to *Being*, thinking is the opposite of willing. There *is* a history of understanding (*Seinsgeschichte*) but it is a history of *Being*, not of Hegel's *Spirit*. In its 'anxiety', the *Sorge* (Care) in *Being and Time* that Arendt proposes as his modern equivalent of Will, shared her characterisation of the tonality of Will as 'tense-ness'.

Arendt attempts a tentative critique of this 'reversal'. '*Being*' – the fact that things *are* – is personified as a Subject. In Heidegger's turning of thought, his earlier anxiously guilty Care is converted into a *taking-care* – of this personified *Being*. We must 'shepherd' it and 'house' it in our 'language'. Arendt rightly says that Heidegger

12 With our post-modern interest in biology, the scientific world *à la* TV becomes entertainingly colourful again.

takes up a 'radical understanding' of Nietzsche's Will that is 'destructive in its impotence to change what is past'. As paradoxical and conflicted as ever, Heidegger would have the Will become the '*will-not-to-will*'. Taking up Arendt's perception of the *personification* involved in all this, we may reflect, perhaps, that while 'Let it be!' may sound a gentle command, that injunction may be yet another enforced Will.[13] I have suggested that *being willing* is the resolution that can value thinking. In becoming willing, we can discover, and judge, what we are going to do.

'Going to'

We can find no activity called willing.[14] 'I will shop for dinner as soon as I have finished this paragraph' is not a prediction. The personal expression of the future tense becomes a declaration of *will*. (Marked in old, more precise, English as 'I shall'.) Or, as a declaration of 'will', I say 'I am going to shop for dinner', again, not as a prediction of what will happen. If I am mugged on the way, it remains true that 'I was going to shop'. In French, '*aller*' has the same double use. It is an active intransitive verb – '*j'allais aux cinéma frèquement quand j'étais en Paris*' ('I would go to the cinema a lot when I was in Paris'). It is also an auxiliary verb that expresses one's will: '*Je vais lire tous les livres de Jacques Derrida quand je resterai en hôpital l'année prochaine*' ('I am going to read all Derrida's books when I'm in hospital next year').

'Going to' as an auxiliary verb that marks (being) *willing* shares its syntax with the active verb 'to go'. The simple 'I am going' is not the present continuous of actions such as 'I am thinking' or 'I am walking'. 'I am going to Brisbane' as an answer to 'Will you need the transit lounge for Townsville?' while on the moving plane on its way there, simply announces my plan as already in operation. The same remark was apt in answer to 'Where are you off to?' when I was sitting in the airport lounge.[15] As an auxiliary, 'I will' expresses my 'will' as something beyond my desiring, thinking of or planning. If I 'will', that is what *I am going to do*. That what I set in train might become stalled does not cancel this original truth. These remarks, reminiscent of conceptual analysis, articulate our doubts about 'Will' as an act that figures in the life of one's mind. Free of the search for an activity, we can, with Arendt, take more seriously the issue of *willing*. Arendt is aware that the business of 'willing' is systematically elusive and she approaches it indirectly – by a detour behind the phenomena, a detour that is not a history of ideas, but a '*history of the operation of concepts*'.

Our moment of conceptual analysis exposes the artificiality of willing as an *act*. When a Victorian father utters to his daughter bent on her own career, 'It is my will

13 The next stage of this work will elaborate Arendt's reading and use of Heidegger on the Will.

14 When we force the issue we discover an everyday superstition. I find myself 'willing' a plane to land safely, as in the cited example of Isabel Karpin's.

15 'I go to Brisbane' does not inform you (in broken English) about my current movement. It is a fragment, completed by 'whenever there is a philosophy conference on there', for instance.

that you not proceed into that profession', he declares what he is 'set upon' and that he is 'going to do' something about it. So it is not surprising, when his child refuses to obey, that his language takes the form, 'Then you are struck out of my *will*.' But if he said 'Now I am engaged in *Willing* you to obey', his language would strain to cover an enforced intent. 'What *are* you willing to do about the situation?' we ask. He says, 'I'll worry about that later. I'm occupied in my *willing*.' We could retort, 'I wish you *were* willing to do something about it.'[16]

Forcing the Will

Arendt observes a 'clash between thinking and willing', marked by a distinction of 'tonality' in these 'mental activities (LMW, 34–9). The mental 'tone' of serenity that marks thinking does not co-exist with the 'tense-ness' integral to Will, in its oscillation between hope and fear. Only action resolves this tension. Only by action is hope fulfilled or fear validated. To *think* as a means to this release is to procrastinate, observes Arendt. We experience the difference of 'tonality'. The Will has projects, so the future takes pre-eminence over the past. Thought takes any objects; past, present and future are equally appropriate. It is as if thinking 'would conquer time', as Arendt puts it, creating an enduring present in its own 'land of thought'. Thinking is done for its own sake, but Will destroys all that.

Certainly this clash has had its theological underpinnings – the Will is strong – we refuse God's commands – or the Will is 'weak'. We fail to stand up to desire. But even outside such contexts Will appears only in the conflict between Will and Counter-will. I *Will* to do something only if I have a counter-*Will* to follow a contrary desire. It is Sartrean 'bad faith' to see my 'desire' as something foreign to me that *I* hate, and which prevents me from Willing what *I* love. My desire is part of what I am. Furthermore, even given contrary desires, if I have no will to follow one desire or another, I am not conflicted. Thirsty, but in enemy territory, it is my will to remain hidden. If I risk moving out for water this is a counter-will at work rather than some 'blind' thirst. Thus emerges an ancient problem, of willing 'unwillingly'. The 'unwilling' Will appears clearly once Will is revealed as essentially conflicted. Sartre will say that I am always 'free'. An action taken in consciousness and intention is always 'chosen'. He writes, hyperbolically, 'I have no excuse'. Austin writes a 'plea for excuses' – not all actions in which I have formed intentions are equally 'inexcusable' (Austin 1979, 175–204). For all that, the 'excuses' that I do plead are precisely in *mitigation* of how I am to be thought of or punished. To speak like Derrida, excuse is an 'impossible possible'. To *be* excused is to be 'without' (beyond) those blameless beings like stones and vegetation that are absolutely excused. Or the cunning penguin installs Gromit into trousers that walk wherever the penguin wills.[17] Here, no question of *excuse* for Gromit's transgressive movements can arise.

In contrast, when under 'duress', my will is 'forced' but still in play. Counter-desire co-exists with being willing. I have long desired to drive a getaway car in a

16 The power of intonation! Doing something tricky, my father would say 'It's how you hold your mouth'.

17 From *The Wrong Trousers* (film, 1993).

bank robbery, but have never been willing to. I have never been *going to do* that. I am seized by a gang (as one is) and someone I hold dear will be tortured until I agree (so crime-shows run) to drive the getaway vehicle. Yes, I decide to comply. I am willing to drive. Although later, I will plead that that I *had been* 'unwilling' to agree, to drive is now what I am *going to do*. The gang has secured *the compliance of my will*. I play my part with vigour, I don't lag in my driving nor shall I be distracted into fighting some agonising battle of wills. A failure of will might have been fatal. When I am forced to form the will to drive, this compliance does not amount to my doing it out of the desire I have long had. To act *willingly* in this fraught situation is a distinct new mentality. Though this mentality will collapse the moment that the conditions of duress disappear, it is into *being willing* to engage in a criminal act that I have been forced.

These last reflections may sound ill at ease in tone and style with those of Arendt's. They are on the same plane, however. Where my reflections have some affinity with the style of Ryle or Austin, the voice of Arendt takes more of a resonance from Nietzsche's and then Heidegger's. Perhaps, in the light of Nietzsche's exposure of the self-serving fantasies of the inner theatre of the Will, and, sensitive to the reasons behind Heidegger's later recoil from the Will, we must learn for a while to Will only *not-to-Will*. But this will not do, permanently or universally. *Thinking* of what to do will never amount to willing it. And, no less a difference exists between judging that something should be done and willing it. There is a stark difference between desiring some involvement and having the will for it. Certainly we need a disturbance of our complacency – either for or against the business of willing. Nevertheless there is something that used to go under the sign of Will – directedness, a *going-to-do* – and we can recover and mark this in our language. Thinking, judging, desiring and our involvements in the public world still demand *something* of us – some directed *going-to-do*. *Being willing* is the newly reformed 'something' that I have proposed. Deconstruction of the Will thus goes hand in hand with renovation of *being willing*. That is the lesson implicit in Arendt's heeding a detailed history of Will.

Within her own more historical and phenomenological approach, Arendt reads Gilbert Ryle's arguments against willing as an activity (Ryle 1949, 62–8).[18] She cites his attack on the Will and agrees that its status as a mental act is problematic (LMW, 25, 55). She takes an interest, herself, in the grammar of willing, and its elusiveness.[19] Insoluble conflict within the Will arises within the metaphor of 'command'. An inner voice speaks, only to spark revolt: 'My nill is as good as your will.' Such a 'will' brings us to a standstill. That the will takes the imperative rather than indicative voice is important nonetheless. Ryle's (and J.L. Austin's[20]) work supports Arendt's reconsideration of willing in terms of imperative speech acts. The will as a 'faculty' may have been a late discovery. For all that, we can now recognise it as a day-to-day reality.

---

18 She disagrees with his dismissal of the Will as a myth (LMW, 4–5) because she reconstructs the will.

19 The elusiveness of thinking had a somewhat different character. It is at least a quasi-activity.

20 See his famous 'Performative Utterances', for instance (Austin 1979, 233–52).

Chapter 8

Resolving Will

When I can live with what I do and am happy to recall it, there is no call for some (vain) Will. I am *more than willing.*[1] Such resolved living comes in hand with freedom – the fact that we initiate new 'lines of flight', as Deleuze would say. The question is how I can be willing (*more than willing*) without any need to suppress a contrary voice of inner command.

After the divided will

Nietzsche's phenomenology of will is important to Arendt's own reconstruction of (being) willing. This may be overshadowed by his famous attacks on the Commanding Will as an inner theatre of self-aggrandisement. One might well say that Nietzsche's writings are all about the Will – about the way in which the repression of one's powers produces bitter and conflicted inner voices. These resentful tones spill over into the public arena of revenge, punishment and the *will to nothingness* that leaps in to fill the void of not willing. For all that, to trawl through more than a thousand pages[2] is to gather in a bare page or two of references specific to the Will. In *Human, All-Too-Human*, we read that 'the nature of holiness and asceticism is *complicated*' (#136),[3] that it is a kind of 'lust over parts of [our] own nature' (#137), which results in a 'crav(ing) to let passions run their course' and a counter-craving 'to let [those passions] collapse like wild horses under the pressure of a proud soul' (#142).[4] Now victim of this cycle of *craving* and counter-*craving*[5] the 'all-too-human' human then falls victim to a stoic's desire for a 'cessation of feelings that disturb, torment and provoke' (#142).

About eight years later, in *Beyond Good and Evil* (1886), Nietzsche's formulation is more like our contemporary snapshot (*cliché*) of his language and views on the Will. The 'cardinal instinct of an organic being' is 'to *discharge* its strength, not to preserve itself' (#13). Nietzsche poses this operative urge to do what one has the power to (a natural organic 'will' as what one is set *towards*), against the Will as an

1 An expression put to me by Michelle Boulous Walker.

2 From *Human, All Too Human*, *Beyond Good and Evil*, *On the Genealogy of Morals* and that collection of all-sorts entitled (not by Nietzsche) *The Will to Power*.

3 The hatched (#) references are to the standardized paragraph numberings of Nietzsche's works, and can be found in almost all editions, as in those cited (Nietzsche 1967, 1984, 1996 and 1998).

4 An allusion to the theory of reason's control of the passions, attributed to Socrates in Plato's *Phaedrus*.

5 Nietzsche's terms satirise the noble Augustinian terms of *Willing* and *Nilling*.

inner command. So the Nietzsche whose blazon is *Will to Power* can be the same one who dismantles *Will* and *counter-Will*. The Will's conflict is a melodrama enacted in my inner theatre to distract its human director from his desires and propensities. He then directs his energies to destroy those others who are ready to live out their '*will-to-power*' – to do what lies within their power.

So, in *Beyond Good and Evil*, we find that Willing (in the Augustinian sense) is a 'complicated thing … a complex of sensation away and towards thinking and affect, particularly of command [in which] "I" am free and "he" must obey' (#19). One is 'at the same time the commanding and the obeying party'. In this internal theatre I take the role of one who must obey the commands of an 'other'; I 'know the sensations of constraint, impulsion, pressure, resistance and motion.'[6] It is this 'synthetic illusion … "I" [that makes me] believe sincerely that willing *suffices* for action.' 'Freedom of will' is then the 'delight' of identifying oneself as triumphant executor. This thought ends with a telling political analogy of how 'the governing class identifies itself with (that is, appropriates as if its own doing) all that the commonwealth achieves' (#19). In an image that presages the language of Sartre's *Being and Nothingness*, Nietzsche depicts, satirically, a '*causa sui* [that] would pull itself up into existence out of the swamps of nothingness' (#19).

It is here that Nietzsche switches from the illusory Will that he satirises, to the organic will that he would recognise: 'In real life there is not "free will" but strong and weak will'. In a dangerous use of the language, he thumbs his nose at religion's hopeless Will that is not strong enough to govern our desires and habits. Nietzsche's evocation of a 'strong' and a 'weak' will is of a resolved as against a relatively unresolved vector of the plural forces that compose an organism's life. ('*Willing is a complicated thing*.') He concludes with a shot against the image of causal determinism, too, that '*Nature's conformity to law*' might be read as a tyrannical claim to power – over words' (#22).

About a year later (1887) *On the Genealogy of Morals* is published and new characters – *promises* and then *debts* and *guilt* enter the Will's arena. Nietzsche mocks the division between 'man' and 'animal' (Aristotle's 'man is a rational animal'?) with the rhetorical question 'Can nature breed an animal *with the right to make promises*?'. When I promise, the idea of the Will arises from the need for 'a memory of the will so that what happens between I will and discharging the promise will not break the chain' (#II, 1). The elevation of the Will's ideal 'I' is also connected with this making of promises – 'in making a promise, having free will he is aware of superiority in being able to honour it' (#II, 2). Thus the connection of promise, Will and debt. If I have promised, I am obliged to honour my word. I owe that debt and if I fail to keep my promise then I owe a debt of recompense. My Will as 'free' is required for this obligation to arise – that I can owe a debt is a kind of honour: 'to impute freedom of the will is to hold the person as creditor of a debt' (#II, 4).

The phenomenon of guilt arises with the Will, coupled with promises that make me a debtor. I am guilty because I have not (yet) paid my debts. I have debts only because I have the honour of possessing (free) Will. So I have the honour of being (able to be) guilty. It is from this dubious honour that Nietzsche makes his

6 Here Nietzsche follows the phenomenology of Paul and Augustine.

double gesture (in Derridean terms) towards ascetic ideals. Insofar as the Will is the organism's urge to discharge its strength, the ascetic pursuit is part of this system. 'Instincts that do not discharge outwardly turn inward, leading to the internalisation of man.' (#II, 16) Hence, we are dissatisfied in not doing what we will, while in doing what we *Will* we feel guilt. This 'penance' is like the 'thinking' that Arendt spoke of as mere *procrastination*. It is undertaken as a distraction when only action could relieve the tense will. Penance is a pseudo-activity, compulsively repeated because it failed to release energy. It replaced the need to fulfil oneself, or tried to cancel obligations by injuring oneself. Harming oneself, distressing in itself, is frustrating. It must fail to achieve its object and easily flips over into an urge for destruction – 'We would rather will nothingness than not will' (#III, 1). (Nietzsche likes the line enough to repeat it in concluding the *Genealogy*.)

Nietzsche's words on 'asceticism' are a double gesture concerning the self that blocks the instinct to exercise its powers. Nietzsche as writer is implicated in the drive towards the *aesthetic* life – uncomfortably close to the ascetic impulse that he exposes as self-deluding and destructive. In terms of the 'Will' that he attacks, to succeed in an *aesthetic* way requires the 'will' to defer some 'minor' expressions of power in favour of a 'more lasting', 'greater' achievement. Nietzsche cannot stand off and attack this directly. Thus the double gesture. He cites Wagner as someone who succumbed to the risks in the aesthetic life – he 'wearied of his "inner" existence', 'fell victim to *velleity*' (#III, 4). He was prey to the delusion of a Will as inner command of a higher self that makes a lower one obey – as if that was the nature of his 'greatness'. Nietzsche's answer presages the 'death of the author': 'We must consider the work, not the artist, seriously' *(*#III, 4).

Implicated in his own criticism, Nietzsche asks, 'What does it mean when a genuine *philosopher* (Schopenhauer, *The World as Will and Representation*) respects the *ascetic*?' (#III, 5):

> The aesthetic counteracts *sexual* interestedness, finding the chance to repudiate one [delusory] hope of what aesthetic work can achieve. Is this 'calming' effect a regular one? Schopenhauer's 'interest' is that of 'a tortured man who wants to *gain release*' (#III, 6).

In rejecting a 'pure will-less painless knowing subject', he says that 'to eliminate the will, to suspend each affect, would mean … to castrate the intellect'. Arendt reads *The World as Will and Idea* as leaving no place for the will, and Nietzsche, to state his position against Schopenhauer, had to find a more credible idea of it. When Nietzsche warns that 'to eliminate the will is to castrate[7] the intellect' he wants to eliminate the Will as theatre of Commander and Rebel. To abandon *that* little chamber of horrors would *liberate* the intellect. *Affect* and *will* (*libido*, as Freud will call it) are more resolute than either habits of desire or the inner boss who orders about his rebellious servant desires.

We have our reservations about what Nietzsche is attempting. We note Nietzsche's tone and spirit but we must do our own work to understand this *will* that remains when self-domination is dismantled. In one of the epigrams collected within *The*

---

7 Such a choice (selective) sexual phantasmagoria! His anti-feminism saves Nietzsche the labour of widening it.

Will to Power, Nietzsche claims (as we have noted) that '*weakness of the will*' is a 'misleading' metaphor – 'there is no will, and consequently neither a strong nor a weak will' (#46).[8] This is in the same vein as his usual attack on the model of Will as self-domination, written with the same tone as 'for the religious, all changes are effects, all effects are effects of will' (#136). The 'Will' he rejects is the *mania* of Will – the (wilful) determination that all should occur in relation to my Command. This raises everything in relief as 'resisting, and to be brought in line'. This intensifies our sense of the reality of things – a mania that feels like tough *realism*. An encounter with realities, albeit distorted by egomania – like the *Napoleonic* view of Europe, perhaps.

Nietzsche's 'will to power' is one's being prepared to exercise power. The puritan of guilty conscience still *has* this 'will' but uses it as to control himself. Being confused at heart, this diversionary Will does not discharge his energy and he is disabled by the incoherence of his desire for control by Command. 'It takes courage to enjoy the feeling of power – to accept the "unfree will"', writes Nietzsche (#428). 'Unfree will' is an ironic flourish. It is *being willing* to do what one does, not riven by self-combat. Nietzsche's darling 'will to power' is not entirely free of division, however: 'The will to power [itself] appears only against resistances; it seeks what resists it' (#656). Nevertheless, its difference from Will as conflicted Command is clear. What resists the 'will to power' is reality itself. In doing what you will, you are brought up against the world's friction, but not against yourself. To act willingly in the world is not to Command the world, as if to repeat the way you used to (ineffectually) Command your lower self. The world appears in clarity to the one who would exercise their powers. No implacable foe, it is a reality within which you work and act.

Nietzsche writes of the Will he dismantles and the *will* that we can accept courageously in maintaining affect and libido. This 'will to power' relates to 'willing' as 'what I am going to do', for it goes beyond an 'act of commitment'. I am *willing* only in the process of what I am *going to do*. I 'commit myself' to give up smoking but I am only *willing to* (going to) give up smoking when next day I walk into a pharmacy to buy nicotine patches to help me through my craving. Nietzsche writes that 'willing' is distinguished from 'desiring', 'striving' and 'demanding' – this is true of his 'will to power' (#667–8). (It is interesting that, with all its negative associations, the word 'will' still appeals to Nietzsche.)

The structure of the self-divided disabling Will resembles that of the encounter with resistance, essential to the pleasure we take in the organic will to power. Nietzsche writes, 'There is a "yes" and "no" in the will to power – a force expends itself only on what resists it. But this displeasure strengthens the will to power' (#693–4). The difference, however, is that the division within the traditional Will entails its self-enmity whereas acting to express the will to achieve what we want, '*gives pleasure*'. Any '*displeasure*' that is experienced in the efforts to succeed, '*strengthens the will to power*'. Book Three of *The Will to Power* concludes with an

8 Presumably this (unreal) 'Will' is the inner Commander who overcomes his Rebel 'other'.

epigram of all these adventures of the *Will*: 'There is no will: there are treaty drafts of the will that are constantly increasing or losing their power' (#715).

Arendt – after Nietzsche and Heidegger

Arendt arrives at her formulation of the contemporary Will and its predicaments in reading Nietzsche, along with Heidegger's different receptions of his ideas. In looking for a way out of the cycle of resentment and destruction, Arendt finds in Nietzsche materials for renewing Kant's will as freedom – understood as the initiation of a new series of events – an origin of lines of feeling and conduct, freed from mores. As an exercise of the Will that internally orders obedience this search would defeat itself. Nietzsche's 'will to power', which requires us only not to suppress our energy to do what we can, falls smoothly into line with Arendt's project. Both want to have done with a Will frustrated by the duties (and guilt) from past wrongs that lie forever beyond its domain. The 'will to power' that is not *the* Will crosses the line between an imagination paralysed by an unchangeable past, and the free exercise of one's powers, oriented towards a possible future.

Arendt has led us out of the early history of the Will only to discover a predicament. Even as we dismantle traditional notions of the Will we need to 'overcome' being hypnotised by the past. We need a provisional version of 'willing' to get us through. A re-run of Epictetus and his overcoming of desires that make him will what he might not achieve? A new dominating Will to eradicate the old guilty one? Arendt's view of Nietzsche's solution is indicated in citing 'his final words on the issue'. The man who would go beyond resentment does not combat the promptings of the old guilty Will. Rather than bringing upon himself a new round of frustration in the effort 'to quell it to stillness', he *abstains* from combating the Will. 'All that is left is the wish to be a 'yes-sayer' – to bless what is for being' (LMW, 172).

Heidegger's change in his reception of Nietzsche marks his own rejection of the Will, with its new conundrum of a '*will not to will*'. Arendt remarks that neither the Will nor Willing appear in *Being and Time*. *Care* usurps the place of the Will. Care is free of the inimical divisions within the Will. Where Will existed as against counter-Will, care exists against indifference. Some nine years after *Being and Time* (1927), Heidegger completed the first volume of his *Nietzsche*, which Arendt sees as endorsing the ideas of Nietzsche that are signalled by the notion of the 'will to power'. Presumably he recognised that Nietzsche's writings corrode Will as internal command, but it seems reasonable of Arendt to associate this phase with his infamous 'Rector's Address' of 1933 that justified National Socialism in the name of the right of man to 'self-assertion'. It is in the second volume of the *Nietzsche*, completed in 1940, that there is the direct evidence of his *Kehre* – his turning or 'reversal' in thought.[9] In the second volume he turns against a 'subjectivism' that he alleges to infect the language and concerns of *Being and Time* in which he sees *man* as the being who must search for the 'meaning of Being'. Man is that being for whom his own being is in question.

---

9 Prior to this 'reversal' being announced in his *Letter on Humanism*, a major statement after the War, in 1949.

As Heidegger came to see it, this 'subjectivism' placed man at the origin of a 'quest' for a 'meaning of Being', a quest that has its sense in 'man' directing the question. This same 'subjectivism' distorted his reading of Nietzsche in that first phase where he welcomed the 'will to power', he decided. Almost seventy years later, in the aftermath of the horrors of the war that were perpetrated by Heidegger's Germany (then to descend upon it in firestorms), we can now look back over his textual actions and reactions. Heidegger read Nietzsche insensitively in the first place; he failed to observe that Nietzsche's 'will to power' was ill-named. We have seen how Nietzsche juxtaposed his favoured 'will to power' against his satire of the Will as self-glorification. His 'will to power' as the energy of the organism, its hope for pleasure in the use of its powers is not the desire for domination.

It makes one ache to think, now, of a Heidegger who might have developed *Being and Time* as a critical observation of the metaphysics of National Socialism as his Rector's speech. Heidegger had the conceptual resources to have exposed its mentality – exposed Nazi-ism by describing its mode of *being in the world.* The language of *Being and Time* understands a mentality in terms of the world in creates and inhabits, not in terms of its precious thoughts of itself. The process of understanding mentality in terms of a being's 'world' is precisely the move away from a Cartesian 'I'-centred discourse that Heidegger began to install (by 1927) into philosophical language.

In the second volume of Heidegger's *Nietzsche* (and henceforth[10]), it is *Being* rather than *Man* that is placed in the pivotal role. The consequence of the 'reversal' is, he thinks, that 'thinking is no longer subjective'. It is not on account of man's creative brilliance in *thinking* that *he* approaches Being. His thinking is 'of' Being, not simply in being *about* it, but as being possessed *by* it. As one might say that the moon is the planet *of* the earth. A moon possessed of the error that Heidegger exposed in his *Being and Time* would take itself to be *about* (of) the earth as if the earth were its object to be dealt with. After its Heideggerian reversal, it comes to realise, in due humility, that it is *of* the earth as belonging to it, and as being kept in its course by it.

The second consequence of the 'reversal' is that the entities that appear ('beings') only distract man from this *Being* of which his thinking is a dependency. When one's *will* is engaged one is involved in concrete or specific entities and issues. Hence, in terms of this 'reversal' in his thought, to deal with the world in terms of Will *is* to be distracted from *Being* itself. In the second volume of the *Nietzsche*, Heidegger has already proposed eliminating the 'willing ego' in favour of the 'thinking ego' on the ground that the Will's attention to the future forces man into an oblivion of the past. The past is the primary land of thinking, as the place of thinking's remembrance.

In his *Letter on Humanism*, Heidegger goes beyond suppressing *willing* in favour of *thinking*. He 'de-subjectifies' thinking, 'rob[bing] it of its Subject' – that 'I' who thinks and wills. Thinking becomes a function of Being itself, 'in which all efficacy rests' (LMW, 175). It is, Arendt decides, a certain interpretation of his 'reversal' that 'determines the entire development of his later philosophy' after the War. She

10 In his *Letter on Humanism*, in *The Question Concerning Technology* and in the lyrical *Building, Dwelling, Thinking* (Krell 1977).

explains, as personification, Heidegger's language of *Being*, which is addressed as an agency that controls thinking to the point of thinking for us. We must listen. *Being* as the 'being-ness' (*seiendheit*) of things[11] is simply '*that* there is whatever that is'. We can imagine 'letting *Being* speak'. We pay attention to what there is (whatever it is) and wait for thought to arise. Also we 'let Being speak' in not insisting on having something to say. This goes with the injunction to 'will not to will'. Obedient to what perception gives us we wait for words to come; we utter or write them without forcing them upon (the fact) that there is whatever there is, *being itself.*

Arendt now establishes her own point of view, taking up her observation in the preceding section that in using 'Being' as agency that can 'speak', he personifies it. Her description of his use of '*Being*' as personifying an abstraction awakens the reader from the sonorous gravity of the text. We regain autonomy as readers. 'Yes! This is like Keats's hailing one of the seasons in his *Ode to Autumn*.' We can then read Heidegger when he claims, 'history of Being can come to pass' when there is at last an audience who will listen. We can read his 'descent into the past [that] coincides with the arrival of the future'. The dead cannot reply and yet we cry out to them in mourning, and in mourning 'that which has happened' we recognise the 'historicity' of *that* there is what there is. Heidegger's *seiendheit* of *Sein*.

The 'will to power' itself becomes the '*seiendheit*', the *that*-there-is of what is. Nietzsche's 'will to power', as we recall, works at the level of organic life that strives with and against what surrounds it. So the abstraction about this 'will to power' is at the same ontological level as the personification of *Being*. Heidegger seizes on what Nietzsche accomplishes in his thought-experiment of the Eternal Recurrence. From there, he works out the consequences of his turning away from our Care with *Being*, to *Being*'s hold upon us. Heidegger inflects the *will-to-power* (in which we let go of resistance to our powers and use them) into his *will not to will*. We let go of assertion and *let Being speak*.

Heidegger thinks that the real contradiction in Nietzsche is between the rectilinear concept of time that is involved in the will to power's trans-valuation of values, and his will to power as a willing 'saying yes' to an eternal recurrence of life. This is a life one can imagine, as if from outside it, of something that has been lived through without perspective upon it, a life in which one moves towards a future and leaves behind a past. In the quasi-transcendental attitude of Nietzsche's eternal recurrence, one makes sense of life as something that has already happened and is to be repeated endlessly. Though thus regarded as if beyond one's control, still one is prepared to *will* that life *be* as it was, is, and shall be. As if to declare, 'I shall "will" what, as a whole, must remain a non-accomplishment.' So expressed, there is no contradiction between this 'willing' one's life while exposing the vain Will to undo the past.

Arendt criticises Heidegger for reading Nietzsche as a philosopher of the Will in the first place. Nietzsche uses 'will to power', but not to characterise something called the Will. As an alternative to passive acceptance of our inclinations it usurps the old Commanding Will. Arendt names her section on Nietzsche (preceding what she writes on Heidegger), 'Nietzsche's Repudiation of the Will'. She remarks that

11 The 'ontological difference' between beings and Being, is now between Being and the Being of Being.

the destructiveness of the Will is Heidegger's last word in the second volume of his *Nietzsche*. It is reasonable to conjecture that his desire to *correct* Nietzsche's past influence on him provoked Heidegger into his abdication of will. To escape the vengeful destructiveness of the Will, we learn the 'will-not-to-will'. Arendt proceeds in her usual fashion, understanding what is going on, allowing judgements to emerge quietly. She is dissatisfied with Heidegger's attempted resolution of the tensions in the Will. This is evident in her own 'last word' on Heidegger and the 'present' (1970s) state of thought about willing. She can make only a 'tentative' interpretation of Heidegger, but declares that 'Heidegger's denunciation of … self-preservation … as a wilful rebellion against the "order" of Creation as such is [extraordinarily] rare in the history of ideas' (LMW, 194).

Arendt calls Heidegger's denunciation of self-preservation 'extraordinarily' rare. This may be to speak of an extraordinary foolishness rather than wisdom. Looking for its sense, Arendt finds that it resonates with some lines of Goethe's:

> The Eternal works and stirs in all;
> For all must into Nothing fall,
> If it will persist in Being.

There is deep ambiguity in what Goethe writes. Is it a warning to us who *persist* in Being? An *injunction*, then, to let ourselves 'fall into Nothing'? Or is it a mortal vision of the 'Eternal' – that, persisting in Being as it does, still it will fall into 'Nothing'? For her part, Arendt connects Heidegger's ideas about the will to his change from man's quest for *Being* to *Being's* speaking to us. This change is roughly contemporaneous with his withdrawal of overt support for Hitler's National Socialism, after which he desires to stand outside the process as its spectator.[12] In his 'reverse turn'[13] he swerved from seeking Being to waiting to listen to it; he shifted from anxious care about man's existence to *taking* care of *Being*. Reversing his espousal of Nietzsche's *will-to-power* (mis-read by him in terms of the model of command and obedience) he turned to propose the 'will not to will'.

Arendt's understanding of Being

The sense of Heidegger's 'will not to will' relies upon his speaking meaningfully when he uses '*Being*'. In reading it as personification, Arendt makes easy weather of the metaphysical side of his language. She leads us readers through his forest – but then she leaves us on the far side of it with only a sketch of the way back. We have to make our own return. Recall, again, that Arendt accepts some antagonism between thinking and willing. While both 'make present to the mind what is actually absent', and both deal with what will be, only thinking deals with what has been. In relation to the past, the Will can only thrash about. But we can think about the past because we think for the sake of thinking, as we live for the sake of living. In contrast, we

12 That he refused to judge it, even in retrospect, has left his name tarnished.

13 This seems a fair combination, given the oscillation between reading '*Kehre*' as 'turning' or as 'reversal'.

Will for the sake of something we lack, dread or esteem. The will can do nothing about the past, but, as Nietzsche observes, it acts out of impotent discontent with what has been. The Will destroys the enduring present cultivated by the thinking ego; it routs the coalition of past, present, and future that thought gathered under its god-like eye.

In drawing from whatever phase of the history of thinking about the will that falls to hand, Arendt has formulated these ideas in her own way, making it easier for us to make our own inferences. Because of this rigorous preparation, she is confident in reading Heidegger's language of 'being' and the 'will'. *Being* is not reified ('*Being is not a being*'), and Arendt's 'personification' makes sense of *Sein* as a grammatical subject that 'calls', 'commands', 'summons' or looks for an 'abode'. As figurative speech it disarms us. The personification of *Sein* slips in under our radar to produce uncontrolled affect and effect – impressions of awesome depth or of an obscurity that smacks of charlatanism.[14]

In Heidegger's second stage of thought,[15] he writes, 'Man transforms Being's silent claim to speech', and, 'Man offers Being an abode'. This holding of *being* in his 'abode' amounts, not to man's creativity of thought, but to his response to '*Being*'s *command*'. *Being* is now granted the syntax of a commanding agent; it needs the compliance of the lesser beings (us) within whose house the muteness to which it is condemned while alone may emerge, articulated. Whether read as metaphysical speculation or as literary personification, such sentences follow the standard logic of relationships of command and obedience. The commander is figured as wielding power; at the same time he is nothing without the willing compliance (not to mention the intelligence, skills and social networks) of those whose business it is to carry out the orders. As with all personifications, to question the model remorselessly, renders it senseless. A mind that was truly of steel would require a mind to dispose its unthinking substance intelligently.

Outside the abode of language *being* would remain forever in 'oblivion' – mute, unspoken. Now, Being *is*, but not as a (most general) category of things.[16] To say that that something 'has being', that 'it is', does not describe it. A 'quest for the (meaning of) *being*' is not the search for a description. As such, there is nothing within *being* to be expressed. Since to speak of being is not to characterise[17] it, *being* can have no *way* of speaking. It is impossible, from the point of view of *being*, to say *how* it can have any right or power of command.

When Heidegger says to let go of *Will* and listen to *Being*, his language, as metaphysical, resembles the metaphorical.[18] More precisely, metaphysics is a

---

14 See, for instance, *Heidegger's Confusions* (Edwards 2004).

15 Arendt marks this 'later stage' in his second volume of *Nietzsche* and then in the *Letter on Humanism*.

16 Heidegger's states this plainly in the opening pages of the Introduction to *Being and Time* (Heidegger 1962, 22–4).

17 To write that *being* bears no characteristic would be clumsy – too much like Locke's mockery of substance as a 'bare characterless somewhat', which at the same time '*possesses*' all the characteristics of a thing.

18 A working definition of 'metaphysics' is that language which takes the most general notions such as *being*, *time*, *universality*, *individuality*, *thing* and *event* as its themes.

reverse metonymy. The paradigm of metonymy is the part or instance as standing in for the whole or the universal. The crown stands in for the whole system of royalty. Metaphysics reverses this process, taking the whole (or things considered universally) as standing in for a range of issues which, unspecified, are nevertheless particular. What does this *being* speak of, that speechlessly commands us to go quietly in *gelassenheit* and to listen to it and to speak on its behalf? What does it stand in for, metonymically? Sartre reminds us that in looking to uncover that immediacy in the (partial) openness of another conscious being he is not looking for some arcane or mystically rare experience. The presence of another conscious being as such is an everyday 'mystery in broad daylight'. It is what this involves and implies that requires our phenomenological work. It is in the same way that Heidegger reassures us that *being* is not some mysterious thing infinitely far off or impossibly difficult to describe – or even bafflingly hidden. If we are to redress the 'oblivion' of being, we are required to pay a particular kind of accepting attention to it.

Being stands outside the type (stereotype) of *a* being, exorbitantly grand, or a super-characteristic. The loss of oblivion of being, this *event* of 'letting *being* speak', is found in experience as we regain a feel for the world as something *that is*:

> In understanding Arendt understanding Heidegger about *being*, I've been pushing to 'keep the project going', to 'keep control of my picture of things and of myself', to 'keep myself from being flooded by what these others write'. I interfere with what someone is getting absorbed in. I see a cheaper option for her. She is angry. 'I'm sorry' but I still feel bad. I am bored, frightened. I'd been pushing myself in the fear of not getting going again if I lost my 'weigh'.
>
> I sit by the window recalling the last time I could feel at ease, when ideas and feelings came to mind and limbs. Still, I'm seeing the petals of some Impatience, the patch of industrial harbour a few hundred metres off, the running wooden slats of the balcony outside the window. These details, yes. But not *them*. I've seen them so many times. *That* they are – that these *specific* things are.
>
> I call this experience 'letting *being* speak in the everyday'. A shift in readiness lets things come to me and me to myself. In its collecting this thinking is almost remembering. This *being willing* is not an effort of Will, not the not-caring of the Stoics, not the 'Willing of whatever happens' of the collaborationists. There is no regress, I did not Will to become thus willing. *Letting being speak*, you let whatever is around or coming back or coming up at you make its impression. *Being* is that these things *are*. Some are possessed of beauty. You need only allow them to engage and you feel again the reality of the world. 'For the love of the world'.[19]

'Thinking lets itself be claimed by *Being*, to give utterance to its truth', says Heidegger. Can *being*, approached as personified, 'possess an unspoken truth' – or any *truth*? To ask this is simply to forget that though grammar requires '*being*' to go into the subject place if that is the theme of our discussion, we do not therefore reify it. That would be to mistake personification for reification. By personification we handle the

19 Author's reflection on 'being receptive to being'. 'For Love of the World' is a reference to the title of Young-Bruehl's book (Young-Bruehl 1982).

endemic tendency of thought towards reification by making an overt fiction of it. We gain the expressive and imagistic power without the mystifying appearance of arcane theory of entities forever hidden, working away in the (noumenal) background.

Antithesis of thinking

At the outset of *Willing*, Arendt described the antagonism between thinking and willing. Thinking exists in an atmosphere that can approach serenity, while the will lives, tensely. Thinking lives in its imaginary world of access to any time and place without restraint. Willing is baffled by the past. To *will*, one must let the past be and concentrate on what can be done. Thinking is not in every way to be celebrated over willing, however. In that direction lies self-deceit – and lies to others. To think as a way of handling the problems of willing is (she declares with earthy good sense) merely to procrastinate. Tacitly, then, she disagrees with Heidegger's swing against the business of willing, as if it traduced thinking and returned us to an 'oblivion' about *being*. Heidegger has overreacted to his first reading of Nietzsche.

With her properly explicit dealings in the history of thought about thinking and the will, Arendt has prepared us to come to terms with Heidegger's dilemma. Shall we continue to will and thus include times that exclude thinking as worthy segments of the life of one's mind? Or shall we 'try' to cease to will? If we do, how do we escape a dilemma? Either the *Will* (not-to-will) is reinstated, or we shall lapse into non-commitment. Arendt herself is not ready to bring these criticisms and the discomfort of the dilemma directly to Heidegger's door. By the time she is writing this *Willing*, she has travelled past the severe critique of him made in letters (and other writings) immediately subsequent to the War. In her famous (to some, infamous) contribution to the celebration, *Heidegger at Eighty*, she has reduced his active collaboration with Hitler and National Socialism to a 'serious error'. She describes it merely as the sort of mistake typical of the way intellectuals flounder when they leave the world of thinking and try to speak and to act in relation to practical affairs.

Arendt desired to bring Heidegger's most savage critics around, and to encourage them to see that his life and thinking does not reduce to that of some 'dyed-in-the-wool' Nazi. In particular, they were to judge his philosophical writing directly on its merits. To that extent we may agree with her. But, throughout these two volumes (*Thinking* and *Willing*) Arendt has pursued a strong line of criticism of both the scholarly and the religious ideal of the life of thought as a *vita contemplativa*. Thinking goes awry unless we converse closely with others, dispute with them, lay out our ideas for criticism, and learn what happens when we have to explain and defend them. Then, once we are in the public life of discussion, argument and defence, we are in the arena where words can lead to action and where ideas have their implications for what has to be done. It is not, then, that Heidegger erred simply in allowing himself to take up any social and political role during Hitler's ascendancy. Some of his mistakes are serious errors of judgment, such as supposing that he and other intellectuals could affect Hitler and the Nazi movement. Other acts, such as his writing letters exposing the lack of Nazi sympathies of some of his colleagues, and mentioning the Jewishness of some of them to his Nazi superiors are fearful deeds taken out of motives about which we can speculate.[20] But then to withdraw to spectatorship is only to abdicate from judgment.

So far as she has portrayed the state of thought about willing by the end of *Thinking* and *Willing*, Arendt is dissatisfied with it. This dissatisfaction seems fully warranted by the analysis that I have sketched about Heidegger's moral and political failure during the 1930s. Furthermore, since her own initial sharp criticism of Heidegger became muted during the years after the War, her own thinking is to that extent weakened. Clear judgments in her projected *Judging* would have exhibited the antipathy of her line of thought about thinking and willing in connection with Heidegger's actions (and failures to act) during the 1930s. Perhaps, even more intensely, the antipathy of her thought towards the evasive quality of his thinking and life after the War might have emerged.

Arendt was in a position to use a distinction between Willing (considered as a self-commandment with final executive power) and that state we call *being willing*. She has effectively criticised the former notion, exhibiting the irresolvable tension it produces between one's commanding and one's commanded self. The commanding voice is 'stronger', 'louder', or more 'authoritative' but has no intrinsic greater legitimacy. This phenomenon of drowning out one's inner complexity would have been rightly suspected by Heidegger of making its perpetrator deaf to the 'voice of being' – insensitive to how things are, whatever they are, and insensitive to the sheer fact *that* they are. Yes, thinking is a welcome relief after a bout on the inner parade ground listening to a bellowing sergeant major, or to a commissioned officer whose superior tones make one's other self to cringe. In contrast, when we think, the various voices to which we give rein can remain friends with each other. They may argue, dispute and chastise, but they do not order and obey. They must stop short of that alienated inimical relationship if they are to continue to be the voices of thinking.

But the relief of thinking and the thanks one gives to *being* as one thinks is no excuse or reason to downgrade the business of *being willing* to take one's life in some direction. To live thoughtfully is not only to 'stop and think'. We go forward in a *willing* life, listening to the considerations and needs of others, being prepared to put thinking aside when the occasion demands it. This is what Heidegger leaves out of consideration in his reaction against the Will. Certainly, he declares that his 'will not to will' is no mere passivity. Nevertheless, he cuts himself off from the conceptual resources that would distinguish, from some apathetic 'letting happen' of what one might have ameliorated, his favoured mood and tonality of '*letting-be*'. Not only this. In his language of 'listening to *being*' Heidegger re-instates the very model of command and obedience that he means to reject in rejecting the traditional

---

20 It is reported by Elzbieta Ettinger (Ettinger 1995, 96–8; 117–18) that at Arendt's first meeting with Heidegger after the war she was duped by him about the extent of his pro-Nazi actions in the period leading up to the war. He convinced her that the stories about him had malicious motives, and affirmed that he was free of anti-Semitic prejudice. Ettinger also documents evidence that even Jaspers, Arendt's most trusted friend and colleague, deliberately kept from her what he knew about Heidegger's collaboration. When he finally told her about it, twenty years after the war, she was not, by that stage, prepared to take it seriously.

demands of Willing. His 'turning' (from about 1936 to 1940) to a 'will-not-to-Will' is no more benign than his earlier 'will-dominated' (as he criticised it in retrospect) philosophy. While his philosophy is not a disguised theology, his solution to Willing shares difficulties inherent in the injunction of obedience to the 'voice of God'. Obedience to Being has the same defect as obedience to a divine voice. Without a critical challenge to any voice, one cannot judge between the malign and the benign. One may listen for the 'voice of being' – that what surrounds us *is*. But *being* is always the being of *some* being. One is paying unchallenging attention to the being of *something*. Is it to be the Holocaust, or Hitler's elevation of dictatorship as a virtue? The movement of a bird as it soars, then dives upon its prey – or when it flutters at flowers of grevillea?

In concluding the volume on *Willing*, Arendt declares that judgment frees us of the will's conflicts and dangers. In judgment we can understand willing in relation to thinking, and to action. The need to study judgment[21] frames the rest of our present study of *willing*. In her study of revolution Arendt connects metaphysical and political freedom within what we will. We shall make our dive into *judgment* – surf that breaks on our thinking and willing.

21 Part III of this work.

Chapter 9

Commandment

Obeying orders

Appropriating externality

The Will as an inner commanding voice tells me what to do. This confuses me both as commander and as commanded. Do I escape this divided Will when one of us exerts their will upon the other? When Moses has a conflict with his people, he ascends a mountain for an 'Other' source of Law. He brings down a rock inscribed with 'Ten Commandments'. An icon of externally imposed Will. The relation of Law to People is symbolised as an austere view upon the tribes of Israel enjoying food and drink, worshipping a golden effigy. The Law arrives as from an external source validated by a Being more powerful and knowing.

Reflection corrodes the sense of externality in this Command and reveals its troubled internalisation. Moses, a leader certainly, speaks still as a member of the tribe when he warrants 'commandments' as Law for them all. Had a power external to the Hebrews arrived bearing stone-inscribed commands, they would have lacked legitimacy. As subordinated to (Egyptian) alien rule, the Hebrews felt right in evading its commands.[1] Moses mediated the Commandments that have gained an external source as if not subject to the confusions within a human mind. In being brought 'down' by Moses, one of their own, the Commandments are converted (traduced) towards internality. The Laws are translated into the stonework of the people. Though brought back 'as from God', it is their own leader who hands them on. Initially the people refuse this new Will.[2] When the Hebrews decide to abide by them, the Commandments have their source in *their own* God. He belongs to the people, their Moses mediates the Law, and they need not enquire how he knows God is the source.

God is theirs but still the legitimacy of the Commandments derives from a Being other than themselves. This Being can 'belong' to the Hebrews because of the line of the prophets who are, each, *one of them*. Moses is of the same stuff as they who carouse and goggle at the golden calf. Moses rages at their 'corruption' as one who is dealing with his own need to let his hair down after the exodus and the ordeal in the desert. For their part, they are angry with him for banning their pleasures. Still,

---

1 If the rules coincided with their moral sense they might respect them, but not as *issued by an external agency*.

2 When the Hebrews refused the Law, Moses broke the tablets and had to go up again for a second edition.

he belongs to them and with them. Otherwise, they could not trust him as receiving the Commandments from their God.

The rage of Moses against their initial refusal to accept the Law is also a rage against himself. He breaks the stones that bear the Laws, lacking proper respect for them. He has chastised the people and must be chastised by the Law. The Law as issued externally has to be internalised by the one who mediates it. Interiorisation occurs within this icon of an externally delivered Commandment. Does this Will to obey an external Law divide against its countervailing Will? Authenticity and legitimacy bind, in a symbiosis of self-commandment, the mediator and those to whom the Law is mediated. The rage of Moses at the people is also his rage against himself as part of them. The Law they reject is what they fear must be true. It encodes what they have learned are the conditions of their strength as a people.

Extreme in self-division

There might be an earthly paradigm of external commandment, in which the will of the one who orders and that of those who obey are free from self-division. Though given as transcending human judgment, 'God's will' reflects their inner conflicts and the struggles between them as individuals. Appeal to 'God' enables them to discern the conflict between themselves and their 'leader' who embodies the Law as precisely what they fear to hear. When we look down at ourselves as from the mountain we can see our feelings, motives and opinions as a veritable tribe 'creating disorder in the realm of errancy', to borrow Heidegger's words.[3] His perception of 'the Will as a destroyer' appears within this picture of Willing as overseen by an external Force that gives impetus to a 'craving to persist' – to subjugate our forces of disorder. The status of the elevated view is imaginary, however, and our appeal to it has to understand this. Otherwise, in Freud's terms, the 'repressed' sneaks up to overtake the enforced order. Like the obdurate totalitarian state, our internal order can collapse in an instant. Writing of this 'craving to stall the forces of decay', Goethe wrote in warning: 'For all must into Nothing fall; / If it will persist in Being.' The Will as commander is destructive, we discover. So we must command the Waters to be still! Heidegger is mordant, or is he artless? Can he be ingenuous in his contradictory need to 'will not-to-will'? Well, the Commandments had to be engraved in stone, and this 'will not-to-will' may be something other than a plunge into Goethe's 'nothingness'. This 'willing not-to-will' may be prudent. We must not let the Will run loose to cause havoc by meddling with what it cannot control.[4] It might be as the determination of a group to impose control over behaviour that threatens its survival that we read this Will to raise up one unchanging Law. Yet, the same question that taxed the internally divided individual arises again between the members of the group. Its 'craving to persist' is another hazard. A new 'Israel' that is no longer 'Palestine' cannot deal with its internal division of 'Israeli' and 'Palestinian'.

---

3 Cited by Arendt in her discussion of Heidegger's essay on the Anaximander fragments (LMW, 191).

4 As the United Nations tried to Will the United States to not Will its career among the Un-united Middle East?

Metaphysics and metaphysical theology thus morphs into a familiar face – military politics. Arendt requires, theoretically, a politics of multiplicity to resolve the tension between willing and that thinking which, in its urgency, the will displaces. Perhaps, to accept the irreducible differences within any society and its ineluctable tendency towards strife can prevent it 'falling into nothingness' by an excess of will to 'persist in being'. That 'nothingness' is nothing abstruse. It is the result of the mania of willing that Nietzsche diagnosed: we will destruction rather than accept that we cannot will the situation as we would wish.

It is in judgment that we shall deal with the conflict of willing with thinking, and the need to mollify the over-determined Will.[5] If plurality is even partially to solve the conflict of thinking and willing that appears as obdurate conflict within a group, then it must be viable without some over-riding will. A source of coherent Will, that is, that requires no external dominant nation, no home-grown dictator, and no democracy that would enforce a unitary Will unchecked by justice and equity. Shall the nation as One 'into nothingness fall', out of its 'will to persist'? Or remain impregnable in implacable unity?

Formal compliance and autonomy

When a group that desires cohesion attempts 'self-regulation', the paradoxes of self-commandment leap up from individual to group in terms of economics, politics and social welfare. Marx's vision of a 'classless society' may be replaced by a vision of the 'end of history' – a world 'Reich' that will last for no mere thousand years. Every other system being 'irrational', there could be no room for opposition. An apocalypse of banality.

If obeyed willingly, a command is accepted within autonomy. In obeying automatically, behaviour remains barely legal. I may willingly tell myself to act, and willingly hear my self-admonition. In the same spirit, when I exercise my will to secure another's compliance, I may secure willing (thoughtful) co-operation. Nevertheless, I may 'obey' a law willingly despite the mutterings of a subordinated will. As there are those who will drive at whatever speed seems safe to them, out of pride and to enjoy a thrilling journey. An outright claim to speed as one pleased would appear irresponsible. I feel I may speed, but I cannot proclaim it as a right. I would fear to drive as I do if I knew that all drivers would follow the same principle of private judgment.

Within a mind that has internalised the Law and accepts its Reason, there exists a division of consciousness between its perception of the safety of speeding (in the circumstances) and its inhibiting sense of the law. Descending a valley I have a view of the whole road as it stretches and curves downwards. Shall I drive (so securely) at ten, at twenty, at fifty kilometres an hour over the limit? I know the reason for the Law. People misjudge the stability of their vehicles, and do not anticipate sudden changes in the road. A sudden dip in an old bridge can bring the car down hard, out of control. Inner dispute continues, though. 'These possibilities do not arise here. It

5 In Part IV of this work.

is superstition to drive here as if The Law were breathing down my neck', I think. For all that, I reduce speed if only for mental peace.

Obedience to the internalised voice of Law has the same form as obedience to self-command. 'Willing himself to countermand a conflicting will', the individual was described on analogy with a social group. His inner forces and private interests differ amongst themselves, constituting a warring group of individuals. We hear 'An over-arching Will is needed, to displace this anarchy.' This is a tautology! 'An-archy' means 'without an overarching ruler'. Perhaps an assembly *can* work productively and happily without any 'archy'. *Will* as what brings order out of chaos? What *is* 'disorder' – simply the lack of one over-riding Will? By what force do we obey a voice when we do recognise it as that of the *leader of our people*? When Moses brought down his engraved Commandments he risked making out-Laws of those who had followed him. The conflict between the mind's Will and those forces it commands shows us the possibility of *being willing* as the better spirit of operation, within one individual and between many. The enigmas of self-command pictured an individual as a composite group of different wills. Counter-will and non-compliance were built into the picture. Being willing is a resolved mind that, bearing the mark of thinking, goes beyond it.

Authority and outrage

The 'commanding will' as bringing order to quarrelling selves is no model for *being willing*. Rather, successful concurrence presupposes people who are *willing* to command and to obey. Will as Commandment has hidden another problem, a stark one for Arendt after the Nazi cult of obedience. What of the duty to rebel – the freedom to disobey commands? We have already noted Arendt's account of Heidegger's 'turning', his vision is of us listening to *being*, open to what it wants us to articulate. Within this benign language still lies the structure of command – the authority of an Other – the unimpeachable Other of *Being* itself.

Julia Kristeva criticises Arendt for dismissing the psychoanalytic dimension of fascism and its attraction for many (including intellectuals) during the 1930s (Kristeva 2001, 138, 179). Oscillation of feeling towards the Will has to be understood in its vexed relation to thinking, for thinking itself has its limitations, as Arendt insists. When exposing 'thought-less-ness', we must distinguish internalised self-expressive fantasy from the task of thinking.

> Thieves have broken into my car these last few years. I put a cover over it each evening in the imaginary hope that in these sporadic bouts of 'malicious damage' a covered vehicle might be passed over. Perhaps, it will be thought to have a car alarm, or that taking off the cover is time-consuming. One fine morning I am alerted that the cover has been sliced, the window broken, and glass shattered throughout the vehicle.[6]

Merely what happens all over the world every night? The police have no will to pursue such crimes. Mere 'nuisances', but even these minor crimes pose problems of thought and will for their victims. A crime is an outrage and occurs on a scale of

6 Author's anecdote.

magnitude – from misdemeanours like breaches of the peace, to grievous bodily harm, rape or murder. The victim of any crime has been subjected to outrage. Without compliance of the will they have been made part of the criminal world and the 'life of their mind' tends towards criminality. 'Good citizens' may be adept at self-repression and self-deception in keeping up appearances. In a situation for which their self-ideal has not prepared them they may act with ferocity out of all proportion to the harm done them. The 'decent law-abiding' householder shoots dead an intruder caught quietly removing their television set. And yet there are those who, not fleeing outrage into propriety or transcendent saintliness, avoid hatred and the desire for revenge. Nelson Mandela of course, and Martin Luther King. They are those with a will to resist being made passive victim or active criminal by the grievous harm done to them in the very name of the State and its Laws.[7] They escape the cycle of self-repression and violence by their manner of resisting their oppressors, not as saints who live as above grievances.

To be willing is to escape the frame of paralysing Will as commandment of oneself. One is willing to accept practical obedience simply for its economy in our dealings with others. When escaping the Will as a command of oneself, to detour into 'being willing' by 'obeying the commands of others' is to risk renewed outrage and interference. That raises emotions to a level where, in despair, you might be driven back to a world of repression where you 'command yourself to be reasonable', to be 'obedient'. Then, in resentment at those who will not put up with this you strike at them, if only by your support for a vicious use of the Law.

In being repressed into obedience rather than willing to be lawful, we 'grant licence' to our anger at a level of response inappropriate to the provocation. An insult 'requires' a blow; a blow 'requires' a gunshot wound; that wound 'requires' the obliteration of the perpetrator's family. Anything less is less than being 'true to oneself'. We will not pretend that the outrage means less.[8] Were we to become willing to feel what we do and willing to manifest our injury to the perpetrator and the wider world, we would go beyond telling ourselves 'to be reasonable' and managing to conform. To become willing to engage the law is to go far beyond the conventional demand to obey edicts because those *are* the laws and rules.

The word of another

The willing exercise of another's will requires my own complicity, but something is lost in dismantling another's will as 'external' to my own. In understanding another's will, I have a chance of escaping the divided mind that threatens when I depend upon my will alone. Something significant can be gained (or lost) in being subject to another's will. Yes, the Will to which I am subject has its own self-division. To deny this is to make a fetish of the other. I reify the other's will in a dutiful acceptance

---

7 They live this 'unthinkable' on a daily basis in their mind and body, through all the gritty events of injustice.

8 Such escalating response is typical of contemporary approaches to drug abuse and terrorist acts. Nothing less than endless *war* on *drugs (or terror) themselves* sends the 'right message'.

that marks my own authoritarian outlook. My *being willing* to respect another's will, however, is part of my autonomy. Yes, to allow myself to be subject to another can give rise to that old Will and Counter-will. For all that, my relationship to another's Will remains radically different from that towards my own.

Arendt's 'conflict' between willing and thinking recognises the support that each lends the other. Thinking as helping the thinker to live with themself rests upon conversing with someone as helpful to both. At the same time, thinking is no mere parasite upon conversation with others. Without *thinking* (conversing with *oneself*), conversing with others cannot manage its own business. Lost in social conversation unrelieved by thought, we lapse into conformity and lose our sense of judgment. And in the same way, we can lose direction and common sense if *lost in thought*. We cannot solve the problems intrinsic to thinking even by 'a good heart-to-heart' with others, just as we cannot escape the partial paralysis intrinsic to 'self-will' by remaining only within the social plane of subjecting and being subjected.

Thinking is not some mere ghost of social conversation, nor simply parasitic on it. The success of conversation depends upon our thinking. Thinking has its own dependency on outside interference, nevertheless. To be told to do something when you were 'just thinking about' doing it is like being overtaken by the surf when standing on the edge 'willing' yourself to go in. You are overtaken by surf in which you were *willing to find yourself*. Yet you could not enter it on your own. Your Willing to take to that rough element had found no purchase on your limbs. At the same time, if a child is *unwilling* to go into the surf then even a gentle and encouraging suggestion produces further resistance. The parents' will[9] works upon the child within its willingness or the adult will suffer the indignity of ineffectuality when faced with a mere child. Capitulation and sheer coercion become the only alternatives.

Being thoughtful makes *being willing* occupy the site that had been *Will as Self-command*. We may come to do *willingly* what we had been coerced to. Coercion or promise of reward cannot alone *produce* a willingness to co-operate, however. They produce rebellion (or sham co-operation)[10] rather than compliance unless they work upon my 'will' as my *being willing*. The point is, not that *being commanded or subject to the will of another* displaces my own will, but that another's will (along with their implied promises and so on) contributes to my actual *willingness*. Quite apart from accompanying threats and rewards, commands (as speech acts) can make a difference to my willingness. While I tell myself what I lose by not doing something and gain by doing it my 'will' may remain inert – I remain *unwilling* to proceed. 'Oh, come on, get on with it!' says some voice.[11] And so I do.

9 Even suggestions arising from a delicate sensibility require the other's willingness to listen.

10 Or jerky and ineffectual movements in the direction of what is desired by the one who coerces or bribes.

11 A familiar voice (or that of a stranger who sees my indecision) crystallises my effort at *becoming willing*.

Even as recall,[12] being revisited by another's voice can stir a process of resolution. A routine iteration of what my parents or teachers used to say, in contrast, occurs merely on the plane of self-commandment. In recall, however, a voice returns on a level outside what I will. Although 'within my mind', it is like being given encouragement to think rather than telling myself 'what they would say'. In being told something by another, their speech act normally carries some threat or promise, but the force of another's word differs from self-command in any case. That being addressed by another has a force of its own is an idea central in the phenomenology of Simone de Beauvoir and Jean-Paul Sartre. Being conscious of others shifts into being conscious of being for others – of being the object of another's regard.[13]

Willing difference

A 'commanding will' as the mind of one who is not yet *willing* is a faulty will – a function of a self or society divided in antagonism against itself rather than a multiplicity of partial members who encourage each other to contest what goes toward a sane and satisfactory life. Each is happy to be part of a multiplicity and pleased that this contestation be the order of things. For the commanding will, its divided parties are antagonists who assume that there must be *one* who shall rule, and rule *as one*. Though rescuing the Will in its history, Arendt mistrusts it, too. It becomes a cult. The Nazi machine made TRIUMPH OF THE WILL its heraldic blazon. This imagery was internalised by individuals. Officers in charge of the extermination camps who felt revulsion against what they did felt the 'voice of duty' speaking against their weakness of will. 'Would that they had lacking *will*!' Arendt might have said. Better to have been aimless 'degenerates'. (An epithet the Nazis liked for those without their Will.)

To get by and to live decently, we need more than thought and desire. *Being willing* as displacing the *will* goes beyond *deciding* what to do. 'Deciding', with its peremptory note of command, is a quite distant relation of *being willing*, whereas the process of *resolving* into (a) solution is its kissing cousin. To understand *being willing* is to escape the psychological as well as the conceptual confusions of *willing* as a *commanding will* and permits difference no less than harmony within the self and amongst us. Perhaps only to Kant, though, whose 'moral will' is what you would *will* as Universal Law, could a true account of *will* yield morally significant results.[14]

In *being willing*, moral evaluation and decision-making have their own autonomy. It is not some mighty 'effort of will'. To call upon Will to resolve thoughts and motives is to fear that unless *one* voice prevails over its antagonistic others, 'mere anarchy is loosed upon the world'. A post-modernity of multiple contestation sounds like weakness to conservatives. ('Neocons' and 'nostalgiacs' alike.) They

12 Recall is already in the Arendtian category of thinking.

13 May I cite my *Genre and Void: Looking Back at Sartre and Beauvoir*, Chapter 6 (Deutscher 2003).

14 The most economical version is in his *Groundwork of the Metaphysics of Morals* (Kant 2002).

mistake liberality (working within plurality) with the 'relativism' of their 'liberals'.[15] Individuals and societies that contest their plural perceptions and motives may still move to resolve their forces and act coherently. Certainly, this requires a steady 'will', but do not imagine that such a willingness guarantees any specifically *moral* purpose. Criminal intent requires a steady will, too.[16]

Political will and origins of legitimacy

Metaphysics of political freedom

It is disconcerting to many contemporary 'professional philosophers'[17] that Arendt creates her concepts during an historical detour. She approaches an individual's willing freedom ('free will' as against 'determinism') through the political history of freedom within the State. For Arendt, the significant distinction is that between what I *can do* (my material and political freedom) and what I *will* (my metaphysical freedom). However, political freedom and *my* freedom are divided by more than the simple difference between the rules and powers that exist in society, and the freedom I have in (being) willing. There is a conceptual space between the world of causes and the arena of the will. Likewise, there is a chasm between the laws and customs of the State and the origins of legitimacy of those laws. In thought, I am in horror at the gulf between the causes of what I do and my becoming freely willing in doing it. So too, as a society we fear the abyss in Law between its origin and its legitimacy. Arendt shows how the horror is not only of a theoretical *aporia* but also of thought's inadequacy. Thinking cannot take on the active responsibility we incur when we become willing, just as thinking about a State's legitimacy cannot become my endorsement (or rejection) of the State in which I live.

Arendt emphasises the dizzying gulf common to both fields of phenomena, but she does not blur the distinction between one's political freedoms and one's freedom in becoming willing to undertake specific action. We need a way around the impasse of 'free will' or 'determinism', as we need a way around the tension between thinking and willing – their competing claims upon us. We become transfixed by one picture of things and try to find a solution by ever-closer attention to that *idée fixe*. Arendt examines the history of the logic (along with the logic of the history) of the legend of origin a society narrates in constructing itself *anew*. A (Sartrean?) 'abyss of nothingness' opens up when, by revolution, we start a new series for which there is as yet no established pattern of cause and effect or of method and result. This is a challenge to nerve and wits no less than a puzzle in concepts, both for the one who forms a new will and for the society that constructs a new order.

---

15 Here I allude to a discourse common in the United States in which 'liberal' is a smear rather than a commendation.

16 We saw this earlier when thinking of how one might be *made* to become willing to act criminally.

17 Arendt uses this phrase to identify concerns defined purely within the academy.

Time in legitimacy

They cannot construct Rome anew, so the founders of the American Revolution construct a new Rome. They look to imperial legends as the ancient source for contemporary novelty. Religious morality comes to take its place in the interstices. Arendt evokes three ancient legends of State legitimacy for her purposes. First, she retells the Hebrews' story of seizing their freedom as a people in their flight from Egypt – an origin of a new legitimacy.[18] Then she writes of the Romans who construct a 'city-state' in a new 'time' while relying for legitimacy on a prior (imaginary) order. Finally, she considers the spirit of revolution in America – that all could be constructed anew, free of the strictures of 'Old Europe'. The conflict about legitimacy arises for the Americans as it did for the Romans. They relied on the British tradition even as they constructed their new State by a violent break from it.[19] They are 'good citizens' even while 'new citizens of a new order' in making the rupture.

Arendt deals with the 'necessity' we see in what happens once we can look back upon it,[20] in contrast with our sense of freedom in what we are presently willing to do. We freely initiate a new series of events. How are events as causes and effects, linked 'necessarily', to be understood as our initiating a new outcome? The situation of thought within which this impasse is insoluble includes one's mind as if already determined by the terms of the problem presented to it. We regain mobility of thought, Arendt suggests, from the fact that we are natal before we are mortal. Mortal in being natal, but defined first by natality.

Metaphysics of natal freedom

Once a child is born, one can reconstruct its development from conception to birth as a series of causally connected events, but there is no prior necessity in the child's birth. In trying to conceive we do no more than enhance the chances. Once conception occurs, to enhance the chances is all we can do about a successful pregnancy. There is no 'uncaused' quality to conception and pregnancy but because it involves living beings what happens to the woman and embryo remains unpredictable. She has to *be willing* to bring her duo to the first parting of its being – that threshold of a new bond that develops again with unpredictable character.

To insist that from a 'God's eye point of view' there is only a necessity of cause and effect in all that happens is *wilful* reversion to an old obsession. There is no 'God's eye point of view'. Metaphysics does not govern the sciences, whose language speculates how quantities are functionally related. Arendt defuses the problems of metaphysics. Political revolution is like creating something anew, as when we give

---

18 The Greeks' measure of time as from Olympiad to Olympiad is no myth of 'origin' for State legitimacy.

19 In the 'Great Southern Land' (an old title for Australia given new currency in popular music) the inhabitants, having made no such violent break, must specify national differences differently.

20 If we think of what we are living through as subject to later recollection we gain foresight of this 'necessity'.

birth to a new life, to a work of art, to a friendship – or to an infant. What arises from our new form of *being willing* becomes a gritty reality to be placed in apposition with the revolutionary dream of something freed of the burden of old failed arrangements. The frictions within what emerges from our initiative vindicate the hope for something new that is better *in* being new. What is initiated has liveliness beyond the control of its initiator. The birth of a child is both an example and a literary 'figure'. A 'birth' signifies something new that breaks with the past and enlivens it.

To charge birth with perfection is to reify it in a spirit redolent of fascism. To grow, the child becomes part of its society and is 'stunted' without it, and yet social pressure may make the child become a conformist rather than enlivened by social connections. The parents who were excited by their *new*born may come to see their offspring as vehicle for their religious and social practices, counting themselves successful in raising their children as reflecting the outlook of those for whom they have excessive respect. And yet, even if the newborn turns out to be an Eichmann who finds a life only in crushing others, still that child *did exist*. For each child and its parents there is the initial possibility of a novel life.

To desire a new human life is to desire the existence of, first, an embryo, before it has a being *for itself*. Its abortion may be considered. Those who fix upon the embryo as a *potential human* exploit its amorphous status. Where an embryo is already an object of loving concern it is no mere assemblage of cells to be used for medical purposes or terminated wilfully. Whether to terminate a pregnancy is a moral question, but not a matter of MURDER ACROSS THE NATION! It is a moral question because it *is* a serious choice whether to 'bring into the world' a new being. To represent only the choice of *termination* as the moral issue is to abdicate from the *choosing* of the new life as a human being amongst us. Critics have been 'troubled' by an apparently conservative dimension of Arendt's thought and language that co-exists with her radical critiques. Conservatives appropriated her critique of communism, for instance, not reading the intensity of her criticism of the repressions that develop within democratic capitalist societies. Liberal critics are dismayed by conservative 'lapses' in her thinking. In the same way, her vision of humans as 'those who have been born' could be co-opted by conservatives, mouthing off their 'family values' against a 'liberal permissive society'. What is the significance of our 'natality' – as individuals and as nations?

A new series of events

Eviction and liberation

Arendt avows that she was *made* stateless. She did not reject her nation and culture: It would have proceeded to kill her for being a member of it. In arriving in America she was forewarned[21] of the pitfalls for the immigrant who was never a willing emigrant – the conformism of the *parvenu*. She became a critical observer of American social

21 Forearmed by her studies of the history of problematic 'assimilation' of Jews into German society.

and political life. Not belonging to its conservatives, liberals or radicals was not her political *stance*, but her predicament. We have noted how Arendt examines the revolutionary spirit of America in its rupture with Britain. In a series of images, she takes the face of an individual's 'free will' that deploys causality and morphs it onto a people defining itself by rebellion within a structure of oppression.[22] Arendt understands the State and the life of an individual in its connection with it in terms of freedom, the will, and the constitution of 'we'. The Hebrews in fleeing Egypt, surviving in the desert, and becoming nationals in our contemporary life is the first of her foundation myths. 'The birth of a nation!' It is not to *idealise* being born that Arendt thinks of freedom's initiative as natality. She is the Socratic philosopher, not the political pundit; she dismantles ideas even as she uses them. At the end of 'Thinking' (Part One of *The Life of the Mind*), Arendt describes how the simplest of ordinary ideas becomes philosophical when subject to thinking about it. The simple integrity of an idea disappears, deconstructed by philosophy, and the idea springs into life. Freedom as initiating a new series of events is the same whether we think of metaphysical freedom of an individual or the political freedom of a nation, whether newly 'born' like America or newly constituted like post-revolutionary France. Only by appeal to origins is the novelty comprehensible, and legitimacy secured. And yet the novelty of what is established produces this abyss between past and present.

Establishing freedom

The Hebrews as a people hoping to become a nation arise out of *nothing*, as it were. In their flight from Egypt they had neither an identity nor the experience to form a nation. In its momentary freedom it was the adventure of the exodus that initiated the new series of events that began to create a recognised people. In the frictional details of their unpredictable life, their survival in the desert made their idea material. But then the Commandments! A bondage with no escape? The lines in stone never depart from their memory; they carry the Law with them in their new 'ark' – a portable permanency, constantly rebuilt.

Freedom as a break from the past into a future that cannot yet be described suffers a change of phase. Only liberation need be thought – until liberation is achieved. Until liberation ruptures the hold of the past the future cannot be conceptualised. That is the 'abyss' of freedom. In his telling his story of revolution in advance, Marx has to lay out how it shall work out – as if revolution were a science rather than an act of liberation. In contrast, the Hebrews' struggle in accepting the Law is their coping with the unpredictable events of a new existence. They are willing to be bound within a form they can come to *will* as their own.

In the foundation story of Rome Arendt finds again the haunting problem of a new beginning. As absolutely new it seems only arbitrary; as legitimated it is bound to the past. Arendt points out that liberation[23] does not bring about freedom. We know

22 This analysis concludes the second Part of all that came to be written of *The Life of the Mind*.

23 This is true of oneself escaping a constricting past as it is of a people who fall victim to an oppressive power.

that it may produce only further oppression. Liberation is an act of freedom, not a State with institutionalised liberties. So, after an act of liberation, it is constitutional rather than revolutionary work that secures freedom. A social, economic, legal and parliamentary system has to establish what citizens *can do*. It is within that constitution that each 'I' exercises its free initiative.

Still, political revolution is an act *for* freedom even if what happens is the 'Terror'. When a child is born a creativity emerges, though it may come to murder freedom: like Kant, though ready to deplore terror we spectators cheer the revolutionaries. Even as we pop the champagne after a birth we begin to watch over what the child becomes, for to celebrate the creativity of an initiative is not predict its outcome. An enthusiastic spectator of the French Revolution (as Arendt notes), Kant condemns all specific revolutionary acts as illegitimate, nevertheless. It is the freedom of people who initiate a new series of events that he applauds – their rupture with oppression. Like individual acts of initiative, the political acts that found a new political order present their perpetrator with an abyss. Faced with this 'nothingness' in the post-revolutionary phase, they proceed without any proper guide from precedents, laws and customs. And yet they must bear these precedents in mind, to retain sanity.

Time and times

How can a future, cut off from its past, still be comprehended? Arendt remarks upon the Hebrew solution to this aporia. The instigator of change creates time itself[24] along with everything else. If there was no time before the 'week' of creating Eve and Adam in their world then there was no prior order of causality to be understood. This origination is re-enacted in a visible and political form when the Hebrews escape and endure in the desert. The time of their bondage is incommensurable with that of their liberty. The formation of Rome is both similar and different. Arendt reads Virgil's *Aeneid* against his *Georgics*. In the Fourth Eclogue's celebration of husbandry of soil and land, Rome, now an imperial power, is legitimised as making possible the re-instalment of the (imaginary) age of sylvan bliss.

The wanderings of Aeneas (after the destruction of Troy) culminate in the glory of a new city – a civic order as if for all nations. His wanderings parallel that of the Hebrews, but the outcome involves a different tension. After the exodus, the Hebrews relinquish freedom in vagrancy and submit to Law, surviving their escape. In contrast, the security of the imperial order of Virgil's civic State makes possible the recreation of an ancient idyll. (Perhaps as new technology permits us new-Australian people to survive in the barely inhabited bush. We live within the capsule of a motor home like space-time travellers.)

Arendt argues that even in counting time from the foundation of Rome, the Romans evoke continuity in their restoring a prior glory. Hence, she suggests, the American revolutionaries who appealed to Roman models of civic life could not *legitimate* their State as emulating a Roman legend. They appealed to no prior idyll. (Subsequently, Longfellow's *Hiawatha*[25] projected nostalgia for a perfection of life

24 Time itself in a political, social or cultural sense.

25 My own choice of example.

before colonisation, but did not legitimate the new occupation and social system as if it re-established a revered past. The legend that grips America's culture[26] is the violent displacement of people who could then be forgotten.)

It is under the Law that the Hebrews find themselves, not as re-creating Eden,[27] but as becoming an autonomous nation. The Romans found a sophisticated city-state, but dream of a return to a 'distant origin in sylvan, rural, ab-original simplicity', as Arendt puts it. Their adherence to a system of laws is motivated, not by the Hebrews' reverence for the Law, but rather by pragmatic recognition that their laws promote a stable and prosperous life. The 'perfect' life lies, not in the Law as Justice, but in 'Saturn's Italic rule … where *no laws fettered men to justice*'. (Like the tension between the American ideals of hard entrepreneurial work and the symbols of success as lassitude in Las Vegas, the Caribbean, Miami Beach.)

Arendt argued that the American revolutionary thinkers plunder ancient history for models of freedom and the legitimacy of a new order. They are 'well acquainted with Roman as well as Biblical antiquity' (LMW, 206), and look to the Hebraic tradition of an exodus and nomadic explorations, and the adventures of Aeneas after the fall of Troy that culminate in the new Roman order. But, argues Arendt, the American revolutionaries do not examine the 'hiatus in both legends between liberation from oppression and 'actual freedom'. They think as if they would be 'free' because liberated from the British bondage –'they themselves had not settled there (in America) as exiles but as colonists.'[28] Their revolutionary spirit presents them with the 'bewildering spontaneity of a free act.'[29] Separation from Britain requires not a new system but only a 'great effort to reform and restore the body politic to its initial integrity'. (As if to found 'Rome anew'.) In the violence of the break from Britain, 'a very different task of constituting something entirely new' emerges in the 'abyss':

> [T]hose who had started as men of action … changed Virgil's great line '*Magnus ab integro saeclorum nascitur ordo*' ('the great order of the ages is reborn as it was in the beginning') to the *Novus Ordo Seclorum* ('the new order [of the ages]') which we still find on [US] dollar bills … [T]he great effort to … restore the body politic to its initial integrity (to found 'Rome anew') had led to … constituting something entirely new – founding a 'new Rome' (LMW, 207).

Thus, Arendt sees 'men of action' who, because of their violent break with their past, need radical thought about what freedom involves. With liberation achieved, they have to think what *freedom* involves in their new order. Willing action has resulted in the need for thought, and yet, even in the midst of her rich history of the Will Arendt cannot resolve the conflict between thinking and willing. She has only

26 Legitimation of their government lay, rather, in its continuation of British law and administration.

27 Or is this the meaning of Canaan as the land 'of milk and honey'?

28 The invasion/settlement of Australia as a convict 'settlement' placed the first arrivals as enforced exiles.

29 Imperialism emerges after 'independence'. Their ideals as from the French revolution soon lapsed.

begun to deal with the conflict when she writes of freedom as initiative within a causal order. In this frustration, she has turned, as she says, to the 'men of action, … hop[ing] to find … a notion of freedom purged of the reflexivity of mental activity'. And yet, those who, intent on establishing a new temporal order find themselves obsessed with antiquity. In their 'break with the past' they fear the abyss they have created. Lacking established ways of administering a new State and having only hazy concepts of what to bring about, in their fall they clutch at a ledge and cling to it come what may.

Abyss of spontaneity

When it comes to the *political* action of creating a new state or a state anew, 'the abyss of spontaneity, bridged by the hiatus between liberation and freedom, is covered up by regarding the new as an improved statement of the old'. This is a 'frustrating conclusion', she says, because we have not escaped the puzzles endemic to each person's freedom with respect to their inheritance and circumstances. There is something sardonic in this verbal flourish of Arendt's. Milton finds those who seek liberty in a world of causation 'in endless mazes lost'. Did she expect a clarity in political action to guide us out of the labyrinth?

Arendt reminds us of the metaphysical bearing of Marx's 'scientific' dream of a political freedom.[30] Instead of a myth of origins by which the new order is made legitimate, Marx appeals to a coming 'realm of freedom' that will amount to 'an end of all things' – a 'sempiternal peace' (LMW, 216). Arendt judges this 'peace' of the classless stateless state of a people to be an imminent death. A life of the mind can exist only in the perpetual challenge of one voice by another's. Arendt can hope that this challenge will be friendly when intimate, and at least civil when public. But any 'withering away of the state' is the loss of a public space for vocal interaction. Amongst other fearful consequences this means a 'withering' of individual thought as a reasonable and fruitful process, too. In her final two paragraphs Arendt reverses her series of images back from the public face of politics to the private sphere of a pure initiating freedom that displays over its doorway the blazon of *natality*. She remarks, wryly:

> If, as Hegel believed, the philosopher's task is to catch the most elusive of all manifestations, the spirit of an age, in the net of reason's concepts, then Augustine, the Christian philosopher of the fifth century AD, was the only philosopher the Romans ever had (LMW, 216).

Tongue in cheek, Arendt suggests that in his *City of God*, Augustine provides (centuries too late!) an 'ontological underpinning for a truly Roman or Virgilian philosophy of politics'. She explains this untimely achievement as Augustine's idea of God's creation of man as a creation of time. *Natality* saves us from a mere repetition of the species. It is because infants replace adults that human novelty and freedom are given a fresh start with each birth:

30 Is this freedom, too, a nostalgia for some past state of pre-political innocence?

> [T]he entry [into established adult society] of a novel creature who as something entirely new appears in the midst of the time continuum of the world. The purpose of the creation of man was to make possible a *beginning* (LMW, 217).

Arendt makes a daring parallel between Augustine's meaning for God's creation of humans and the Roman conception of the reason of the foundation of their city-state. A serious idea, because the Romans also took the creation of their civilising *civitas* as the very beginning of time. To date a calendar from the foundation of Rome is to declare that human life as more than animal existence consists in its occurrence within such civilisation. The creation of human time is the creation of the civic and civilised life. It takes nerve to make a parallel between Roman secular pride and Augustine's solution of the old puzzle about why a perfect God would create such an imperfect human being. In doing so, she casts her idea of natality into the civic sphere and leavens with elemental human sentiment the concepts that uphold even Roman's imperial power. (Arendt does not mention the part of the tale that does centre on infancy. Romulus and Remus survive because suckled by a wolf. Not the Christian picture of lowing cattle present with the humans at the birth of Jesus, but a figure of vulnerability and care behind the scenes of imperial Roman glory, nonetheless.)

Arendt accepts that the use she makes of Augustine's (and the Roman) concept of *natality* is less than adequate. Her language resembles that of her contemporaries, Beauvoir and Sartre:

> [T]he argument even in the Augustinian version is somehow opaque, … seem[ing] to tell us no more than that we are *doomed* to be free by virtue of being born … This impasse, if such it is, cannot be opened or solved except by an appeal to … the faculty of Judgment (LMW, 217).

Certainly we have no choice but to be born. We are born before we have a capacity for choice. Furthermore, it is only by birth that a human comes into existence. A fluency in dealing with Sartre's conundrum of freedom is helpful here.[31] *To be conscious* works for Sartre as does *to be born* for Arendt. To be conscious involves the creativity of 'nihilation' – to make nothing of sheer facticity – to establish that 'thin film of nothingness' by which we can slip from our past, our 'given natures' and very 'conditions of birth'. We can refuse our freedom only in the very exercise of it. The refusal is an act, in *bad faith*, of a conscious being. For Sartre, this (evanescent) consciousness that pretends not to be conscious can become an entrenched habit of bad faith. As such, it does some of the work achieved by Arendt's 'banality of evil'. We are 'doomed to be born' as we are 'doomed to be free'. So, like *freedom*, *natality* does its lively work precisely when we are in the process of deconstructing it. We can always trust its enemies to engage in the reification.

31 I have constructed a contemporary development of this 'freedom to which we are doomed' (GV, 41–87).

PART IV
Judgment

Chapter 10

Process and Judgment

From thinking to judgment

A 'new order of the ages'

Arendt has two paradigms of judgment. She may link judgment to the spectator who, observing life's arena, makes valid judgments. Within the other paradigm it is the involved participant who must judge, for to remain in retreat on the spectators' bench is to evade the world's demands – to refuse the very *being* of the world. We are in the world and make judgments, on the run if need be. As a thinker and spectator we are overtaken by events. (Arendt has remarked that events, not thinking, change one's mind.) In the concluding section of *Willing* (*Novus ordo Seclorum*) Arendt juxtaposes *thinking* (whose freedom must accommodate action) with *revolution* (whose liberating acts demand legitimacy). Thought gives way to action. Only by action can I release the 'tense-ness' of the will, and yet thoughtless or unwilling action only multiplies my problems.

To think, in this context, of my *becoming willing* suggests the hope of a resolution of a divided Will, or a chaos of desires and thoughts. I *give myself* to a line of (thoughtful) action. Wishes and thoughts then take a new shape within what I am going to do. Sartre writes of those moments when 'the prior project collapses … in the light of a new project [and] we let go I order to grasp and grasp in order to let go' (Sartre 1976, 476). Arendt finds in Augustine and Duns Scotus the idea that we escape the dilemma of a divided will in pursuing what we love. In acting out of love we are, as we discussed earlier, 'more than willing'.

Revolution, legitimacy, thinking and freedom in action – all of these involve us in judging. This concept eluded Arendt and when she died, she left an epigram for *Judging*, a book that was to have made a trilogy with *Thinking* and *Willing*. In 'What Makes us Think?' (LM, 129–93), Arendt coupled the Greek idea of 'spectatorship' with Kant's 'discovery' of judgment (more than twenty centuries later) 'as a separate faculty'. She went back to 'Plato's answer' – it is *wonder* that makes us think. Thinking out what we wonder at enriches an otherwise too detached 'spectatorship'.[1] Arendt delights in Pascal's 'impertinence' at the great Greeks, for all that:

> We can only think of Plato and Aristotle in grand academic robes. They were honest men, and like others laughing with their friends, and when they wanted to divert themselves, they wrote the *Laws* or the *Politics* to amuse themselves. That part of their life was the least philosophic and the least serious … If they wrote on politics, it was as if laying down

1 Like Heidegger, in *What is Called Thinking*, Sartre in *Nausea* and Irigaray in *An Ethics of Sexual Difference*.

rules for a lunatic asylum; if they presented the appearance of speaking of a great matter, it was because they knew that the madmen, to whom they spoke, thought they were kings and emperors. They entered into their principles in order to make their madness as little harmful as possible (LM, 152–3).

This impertinence leads us towards the Roman idea of the philosopher as a little mad, in a virtual death in opting out of politics and war:

> [P]hilosophy arises when the unifying power has disappeared from the life of men … Thinking does not arise out of reason's need, but has an existential root in unhappiness (Hegel, cited LM, 153).

In sketching her version of Socrates' reply to 'What makes us think?' Arendt begins to connect thinking and judging. Socrates' questioning of the meaning of happiness, courage and friendship (and so on) is constructed to be inconclusive, always generating the next day's questions and hypotheses. This is Arendt's paradigm of thinking. But what of judgment? We inherit a stylised legacy from Socratic thinking by centring upon Plato when he places eternal 'Forms' at the centre of philosophy's project. These would be the basis of absolute judgments rather than the stimulus for perennial thinking. This bias reflects the subsequent Aristotelian project of a scientific philosophy that needed a stable object of thought upon which to pass his judgments. The Socrates of open thinking does not attract him, since it is designed to destabilise our confidence in our most familiar ideas so as to set thinking in motion:

> [B]ecause Socrates, asking questions to which he does not know the answers, sets them in motion, once the statements have come full circle, it is usually Socrates who cheerfully proposes to start all over again and inquires what justice or piety or knowledge or happiness are. For the topics of these early dialogues deal with very simple, everyday concepts, such as arise whenever people open their mouths and begin to talk (LM, 170).

These concepts are those of our everyday words. There is an interesting consequence:

> When we try to define them they get slippery; when we talk about their meaning, nothing stays put any more, everything begins to move (LM, 171).

'What is a house?' Arendt asks of a familiar thing that resists the idealised *Forms* generated by 'truth', 'justice' or 'courage'. In this philosophy of the domestic we still want more than examples of houses. What we discover in thinking is not a tangible construction of wood or stone. In Arendt's adoption of Socrates we move from 'house' to 'housing'. 'To house', Arendt suggests, is 'the unseen measure' that 'holds the limits of all things' – all things of a certain sort. To 'house' humans is to give them a *dwelling*. Now thought takes off and discovers something about the noun, too:

> The word 'house' is something like a frozen thought that thinking must unfreeze whenever it wants to find out the original meaning (LM, 171).

Thinking 'unfreezes' meaning – it is not its business to arrive at a settled result. This is Arendt's step towards the value of thinking and the need for judgment:

> In unfreezing concepts, 'thinking inevitably has a destructive, undermining effect on all established criteria, values, measurements of good and evil' (LM, 175).

The Socratic philosopher as 'torpedo fish' stuns us. Thus we *stop* and think. Thinking lurches ahead *to unfreeze* our concepts. (Socrates as 'gad-fly'.) Thinking is dangerous and its results unpredictable, but not thinking poses a greater threat. Arendt conjectures that the alleged evils of thought (corroding morality) arise in a collapse of the philosophical project. People settle down with a their first new ideas, less considered, perhaps, than those they upset. Nihilism and cynicism are such petrified thought, new orthodoxies in radical cloth.[2] We can here condense to four epigrams the themes we developed from Arendt's *Thinking*:

> To think is to exist as a '*two-in-one*' – to engage in a conversation with oneself.
> To think is not to improve oneself; it has no aim beyond itself.
> To think is to wonder; to wonder is to discern what is good or beautiful.
> To think is to ponder what is not ugly or evil; the ugly and evil do not excite wonder.

Working from this basis we are on the way to a *judgment* upon nihilism and cynicism. Thinking cannot settle down into *positions* called 'nihilism' or 'cynicism', but how do we move from thinking to judgment? Just to *think* is not to judge what is evil or ugly, good or fine. Does thought raise some barrier against evil and ugliness in being unable to ponder it? Now, Socrates maintains (infamously) that *it is better to be wronged than to do wrong*.[3] This involves a judgment. Better for whom? If to think is to converse with myself then I must bear my own company. I can face myself in having been wronged, but not in doing wrong. (When it is wrong to accept wrong being done to myself as much as to another, I must then resist wrong being done.)

To explain why it is worse (for the 'thinking ego') to suffer wrong rather than to do it, is to connect thinking with judgment. Callicles maintains that it is worse to suffer *being* wronged. Socrates says it is worse to *commit* wrong. Arendt says that they speak of a different 'I'. The 'I' of Callicles' will never converse as if between two. The fanatic has no desire to think – to 'return home to himself'. The one who thinks, *stops*. The fanatic who *carries on* will not see the harm he does himself in doing wrong. The thoughtful ('philosophical') person may commit evil nonetheless, but cannot be pleased by it. Understanding what it means to do wrong may deter us, Arendt suggests. Reflection is the beginning of judgment. Resolving not to do wrong in the understanding of how wrong-doing puts thinking out of joint, goes beyond thinking itself. This is what judgment must do.

---

2 Egoism, the sensation-ism of the Italian futurists', and perhaps 'economic rationalism' are further examples.

3 'It is better that my lyre be out of tune than that I (being one) be out of harmony with myself.'

To think and to judge

In thinking, one is in solitude. As not calculating or theorising, thinking 'has the criterion … no longer [of] truth … [but] to be consistent with oneself' (LM, 185–6). If one's premises (the 'facts of the matter') become the prime issue, one breaks out of thought into empirical tests, mathematical calculations and gathering evidence.[4] Arendt is contrasting the adversarial relation I may have to another, with the *differing* of myself from myself that is essential to my thinking. If I become my own adversary I contradict myself and get nowhere. As a metaphor for thought, *conversation* means more than empty talk. Conversation involves differing from another, but if differing turns to contradicting, conversation is at an end. Once quarrelling breaks out, thinking flies through the window and declarations usurp judgment.

Attempting to approach judging, Arendt differs thinking from mere consciousness:

> What thinking actualises … is difference … as a raw fact in consciousness; only in this humanised form does consciousness then become the outstanding characteristic of somebody who is a man and neither a god nor an animal. As metaphor bridges the gap between the world of appearances and the mental activities going on within it, so the Socratic two-in-one heals the solitariness of thought; it … points to the infinite plurality which is the law of the earth (LM, 187).

The *differing*, typical of thought, is challenging, even embarrassing. Arendt reminds us how Socrates refers to 'a very obnoxious fellow' who always awaits him 'at home [to] cross-examine him'. 'He is a close relative and lives in the same house' says Socrates, drolly, to the thickheaded Hippias (LM, 188). Base people, caught in contradictions like Richard III in attempting to converse with himself, 'avoid their own company'.[5]

When consciousness becomes the plural conversation of thinking it does the work of conscience.[6] That 'God-given' voice becomes as natural to us as breathing, being musical or humorous. Thinking, and the love of it, is not confined to the highly intelligent. As Arendt points out, scientists, scholars and 'professional' philosophers may foreclose on thinking:

> Everybody may come to shun that intercourse with oneself … [Though] thinking accompanies life and is itself the de-materialised quintessence of being alive … a life without thinking is quite possible … [yet] it is not merely meaningless; it is not fully alive. Unthinking men are like sleepwalkers (LM, 191).

If we are to think, then our 'two-in-one' must 'be friends and live in harmony' even while they *differ*. Arendt stresses that 'this moral side-effect is a marginal affair'. It is not in order to be in harmony that we think. Nevertheless, like any art, thinking does some good in the margins. There are also times of emergency

---

4 Arendt does not prize thinking above all else. The 'thirst for knowledge' is of more use to society.

5 See this work, Chapter 5, 63–67.

6 The discussion runs closely parallel to Gilbert Ryle's (Ryle 1947, 159, 315).

when thinking as living within oneself is a political act. Arendt uses Jaspers's idea of 'boundary conditions':

> When everybody is swept away unthinkingly by what everybody else does and believes in, those who think are drawn out of hiding because their refusal to join in is conspicuous and thereby becomes a kind of action (LM, 192).

For Jaspers, 'boundary conditions' extend to the whole business of being alive – 'I cannot live without struggling and suffering; I cannot avoid guilt; I must die':

> Existence itself forces me to take account of a past when I was not yet and a future when I shall be no more. [Thus] … when I begin to reflect on this past, judging it, and this future, forming projects of the will, thinking ceases to be a politically marginal activity (LM, 192).

The deconstruction of ideas by thought 'has a liberating effect on … the faculty of judgement, which one may call … the most political of man's mental abilities' (LM, 192). For Kant, judgment deals with 'particulars without subsuming them under general rules which can be taught … and grow into habits'.[7] This is the gist of it:

> [Thinking] actualises the difference within our identity as given in consciousness and thereby results in conscience as its by-product [whereas judging], the by-product of the liberating effect of thinking … in realising thinking … makes it manifest in the world of appearances where I am never alone and always too busy to think … [Judgment is] a manifestation of the wind of thought [and as such] is not knowledge (LM, 192–3).

This 'judgment', this 'manifestation of the wind of thought', is not knowledge. It is 'the ability to tell right from wrong, beautiful from ugly'. By differing judging and knowing Arendt secures the political significance of thinking and judgment. I can discern[8] good and evil because to think is to have heard various sides of the case within myself. In being (temporarily) a spectator, I have been with both protagonist and antagonist. Thinking makes it possible to judge – that is all. Thinking results in no infallible or absolute truth, and judgment must surpass the thinking that engenders it, as thinking surpasses the sensory knowledge that engenders it. So, if to judge does not guarantee good judgment, and good judgment is no species of knowledge, we cannot know that we have rejected evil. Judgment is carried forward by the 'wind of thought'. Thinking means only that when we 'descend' to the world of affairs, what we declare will not be thoughtlessly conformist. We shall have taken into account what we should know. Knowledge *lies behind judgment* in prompting the *thinking* that judgment needs.

Eichmann does not judge (or misjudge) because he does not think. Arendt typifies his actions as 'thought-less'. Mary McCarthy complained that the word suggested Eichmann was merely careless. ('If only he'd stopped to think!' might be uttered

---

7 Elsewhere she points out that we also judge that a particular comes under a certain given principle, but without deducing it. Judgment co-ordinates sensory perception and intellectual grasp.

8 To discern is to judge, not to know as one knows a fact by research and observation.

as a cliché.) 'Thought-less' has grave connotations. Being *thought-less* is like my mind being *weight-less*. I need gravity – *substance* – to judge what life throws at me. Being pursued across the rooftops (you know the scene) I leap across a gap. I had to judge the distance along with the risk of being caught. (If I would certainly be killed if captured and judge that I can probably make the leap, it would be a misjudgment to pull up at the edge.) So I may fail in judgment of the distance or of the consequences of capture. However if, being desperate, I just leap anyway and fall, there no misjudgment since there was no judgment.[9] (A prejudiced judge may *issue* ('*declare*') a judgment without having *made* one. On appeal it may be found contrary to law or to have ignored principles of evidence. Though decorum requires the language of 'misjudgment' there may have been no *judgment*.)

Kant installed judgment as applying principles to instances, and discerning new principles in instances. Judgment about any specific instance goes beyond knowing the principles that apply. We have to judge principles, too, in relation to what they deal with. Not only in ethics, aesthetics or politics but in science too, we have to judge principles. It is not enough to sum the evidence and to make a deduction from it. There is judgment in the choice and use of principles of research and in the weight placed upon evidence. Good scientists are more than good technicians – and good technicians need their own judgment, too. Arendt has (limited) hopes that *judging* might resolve the conflict between thinking and willing:

> [N]o less mysterious than the faculty of beginning [is] the faculty of Judgment, an analysis of which at least may tell us what is involved in our pleasures and displeasures (LMW, 217).

Judging, like thinking and *beginning* a 'new series of events' is a mystery 'in broad daylight'. The extraordinary that lies within everyday life and language.

Judgment in recession

Process in judgment

> I walk up and down, thinking of the submissions for a literary award. I am judging while walking but not in the sense that I am thinking while walking. So long as the judgment has to be made, I read the submitted books and write notes. What I am doing amounts, eventually, to my *having judged*. Judging is not (as are thinking and writing notes) in the present continuous. I read the entries, think about them and compare their merits. Then, all is said and done and my judgment is *made*. '*I am judging*' is a truncated expression; I cannot *not* haul judging into conscious presence.[10]

These questions of concept and syntax are at the heart of Arendt's success (and difficulty) in accounting for judgment. Ronald Beiner writes:

---

9 We say 'just' just when there is no justice. Just doing, like judgment, transcends specific reasons.

10 Author's anecdote.

> [W]e arrive at the end of … *Willing* in …[in] a theoretical impasse. Willing … implies an 'abyss of pure spontaneity' [which, as Arendt put it] 'cannot be … solved except by appeal to another mental faculty, no less mysterious than [that] of beginning, the faculty of Judgment' (Beiner 1992, 90).

Arendt continually defers the question of what judging is, as did Kant. Arendt does not procrastinate. The problem lies within the phenomenon. Like thinking, we need to write about judgment, and yet it eludes each probe. Arendt explored the elusiveness of thinking which, like Eurydice, returns to the shadows if the writer turns to face it full on. Arendt has studied the troubled history of the Will as an inner Command, always already debilitated, and born in strife awaiting a higher power. We can call off the chase for the process of 'willing'. We can take seriously the Will that goes beyond what we most desire or are habituated to do and still abandon *Willing* as the putting down of a rebellion by a commander. We should not expect the same diagnosis of the *deference* to judgment (a solemn business) and the *deferral* of our description of it. Judging is not in the present continuous like speaking or writing,[11] conversing or arguing.

Process and culmination

Thinking is a process, but I cannot, while engaged in it, announce the fact. In asking 'What are you doing?' you interrupt my train of thought. I might answer, 'Well I'm replying to your query, now.' Another elusive process is *dreaming*. The impasse in bringing present thought to public expression reminds us of how one cannot recount a present dream. In telling you what I dreaming, I am awoken from my dreaming. (I might dream I have been questioned, but that is no interrogation. To dream that a lion is eating me is not to have been gnawed.) But what blocks me in telling you of my present continuous *judging* process is different from these occlusions of the process by the stating of its ongoing occurrence. Judgment is a culmination rather than a process. I cannot report my present *judging* because there is nothing to speak of until it is over. To adapt from Ryle, the runner can answer (if they have the breath) how they are running, but not how they are *winning*. Winning must be announced in the past tense, for, like judgment, it sums up what *has happened* (what has been accomplished).

Consider, once more, the ways in which thinking, though elusive, still comes within the category of process and activity. Mulling things over with a friend approximates voicing current thinking without cancelling it. I am not attempting to tell you what I am thinking even as I go on doing that. I am not first thinking thoughts and then converting them into speech or writing. In voicing what I think to someone I trust I approximate to thinking while speaking with another. Still, in speaking to another I am not 'purely' thinking. I am speaking aloud, overcoming physical inertia. I am speaking *to* another, securing reference for my expressions. 'Just which holiday were you thinking of?' Thinking can well up into almost speech. In just 'thinking

11 Yes, the judge writes their judgment, and that underlines how judging differs from any process.

aloud', I take it that no one else is present. Someone happens to be there and asks 'What did you say?' I reply 'Nothing!' I was not trying to *say* anything.

That interiority of thinking may be physical, like one's mysterious control of the bladder's sphincter. To think of thinking as a physical inhibition makes more apparent its intensity as inner life – and how we may exaggerate its importance. We may develop a false pride in being silent about what we think, as we cultivate pride in sphincter control – as if its very *privacy* amounted to a special depth of purpose. But thinking's elusiveness does not impugn it as a process. 'What were you doing as I came in?' 'I was thinking about the war in Iraq.' And I shall be going on thinking about it when you leave. In writing these very paragraphs, I spend time now *thinking about it*, then over the next few days. I shall write some pages of a next chapter, put down some lines as they come to me, then go back to thinking.

From thinking to willing

There is no process of 'willing', either, analogous with that of thinking.[12] I am 'prepared to do what is required', though 'I don't much fancy doing it – it goes against the grain'. I declare that 'my will is now quite settled.' And yet, even as we fail to find *Willing's* present occurrence, the phenomena of 'Will' emerge more distinctly. As I go to grasp that rainbow of willing's process I find a pot of gold. I find a 'mode of being', this 'I am willing', encouraged in its being by the very performance of uttering it without inhibition or constraint. As what I *am*, *willing* emerges as real in itself.

Being willing (*that I am willing*) has grammatical stability. 'I shall be willing when I've rested', or 'I was willing to do that for him, until I learned about what he'd been up to.' These tenses carry this *mode of being*, with no insinuation that willing is something we do, though there are the processes and actions involved in 'resolving issues', 'gearing oneself up' and so on. Some are acts we undertake, and some are processes that we allow to occur to aid and abet the 'formation of the will'. Acts of self-command (sometimes to disguise what we are *going to do*) persist within our inner theatre in which a commanding officer raises up a rebellious Other whom he will take pleasure in proving to be his inferior.

We shall not, however, mistake these fictionalised deeds for our *being willing* to do what, within the theatre, we agonise about with delicious agitation. This theatre, along with the plays we perform upon its stage, has its place as we rehearse enacting the choices we make. These enactments then become part of our *thinking* – a more dramatised and emotionally charged version of the conversations with oneself that are thinking's paradigm. So, if thinking is a process, while willing is a mode of being, what of that achievement we call judgment? Thinking defers it and willing has been all too willing to forget it. Perhaps because we apprehend the need for judgment we contrive this deferral of thought about it.

12 Textually speaking, with Arendt, we write over the erasures in past texts that bore the name of 'willing'.

Turning to judgment

When philosophers discuss the Will they set out from *thinking*, remarks Arendt. Constitutionally, it is by reference to thinking that a thinker would give an account of willing. A similar trouble besets the thinker's account of judging. How can a thinker avoid taking thinking as the paradigm from which judging is to be represented? For is the thinker to think about judging, or to judge it? To make anything of judgment, we must extend initial credit to the phenomena of judging, just as we had to be willing to taking willing seriously. With all its difficulties, judging may be no less apparent to us than thinking itself. We have had to leave thinking only partly described, and only partially removed from its cloud of mystery. So too, even as recognised in the mode of *being willing*, we have had to be content with partial success in representing it. Arendt confesses that she lacks a concept to mediate the conflict between thinking and willing, despite the progress she made in understanding them. Do they differ so radically in mood? To enter one of those phases of life – is that, *ipso facto*, to depart from the other? Are these changes of phase between thinking and willing quite arbitrary, then? Is the change from willing to thinking (and *vice versa*) unthought and unwilled?

The change may occur without mediation, as when we are caught up by a breaking wave, and, shortly, dumped on dry land. Or, we may move from thinking to willing as when we wade through the shallow water back into the sea in graduated stages. These planned and thoughtful changes of phase involve judgment whether, as it were, the surf is too strong and there may be a rip, and how long to stay out there. The fact that we can judge makes sense of the fact that one may have thought long enough. To be willing to act is irresponsible if it is thought that is required but to go on thinking when we need willing resolution to end the tension is to procrastinate (as Arendt puts it). Further thinking cannot move us out of thinking into resolution. Nor do we move from thought to will by an act of 'pure will'. It is a matter of *judgment* when to make these changes of mood and direction.

Thinking would seem mysterious if we took willing as the paradigm of the mind's life, and approached thinking only from there. Looking only at the will, what is this 'thinking' that we fall into when willing leads us into a mess? Willing seems a mysterious 'other' to thinking if we set out only from thinking. It strikes like lightning[13] and brings us to a point of change that no stretch of thinking could account for. In the same way, *judging* seems mysterious when we come to it last, having attended only to thinking and willing. We can connect the concepts and phenomena of *thinking*, *willing* and *judging*. Our separated periods of attention allow time for familiarity with them and we make a geography of these concepts (as Ryle puts it). They become part of the lie of the land; their areas of application lie ready to hand. Periods of one's life may be marked as predominantly one of them. For a while one *thinks*, and then it is a time of the *will*. One resolves and acts. One writes one's immediate 'memoirs' in a spirit of judgment. In stating these ordinary facts it is apparent that to separate them as if separate lives is an artifice.

13 Like that 'amazing' grace that Paul of Tarsus waited upon?

We have observed that 'I am judging' tells you not what I am doing but what I am *to do* – what I *shall have done* when the work judgment requires is complete. Judgment is located first in the ambiguous zone between thinking and willing. As if it thrived in a rock pool where, bordered by land plants and insects, a specialised sea life develops. Thinking that thrives on the border of willing has its specialised forms, and the willing that borders on thinking has its varieties particular to that border. Resolution and action flourish, more thoughtful than action's inland can support. The tidal border may be devoid of thought in a violent rock fall. Within this ecology, is judgment a sea or a land creature? If judgment flourishes in the pools that form the border life between thinking and willing then we shall find judgment there neither as a fully formed land animal nor as an adapted marine dweller. We shall find judgments, taken on the move, that are judgments nonetheless, or judgments so long considered that they have become lame ideas. Thinking, bordering on willing, is found in the thick of resolute action, just as thinking wells up within active life to take us unawares.

Thought carries a high iconic value, but to think is a risky business, as Arendt points out. You know how it goes – you don't stop to think and you make a fearful error. Next time, like Epaminondas in the story, you think hard and long, form your will, make your judgment and take action. Wrong again, and worse recrimination. 'You knew what you were doing. Premeditated stupidity!' In other ways, too, it is risky to think, for you see possible initiatives and aspects that others wish not to have acknowledged. You come to see that something is required that otherwise you might have ignored So you approach the telephone, legs heavy, each movement of a finger to the touch-dial at the limit of your power. A moment's lapse in concentration and you walk away in a flurry. 'Oh! I'm taking all this much too seriously!' A panic reaction – an abdication from a well-judged action in which we clutch the words of mature wisdom.

Arendt devoted whole sections on 'what makes us think', and on 'where we are when we think', evoking what we deal with thinking and with willing, giving the different moods they require their due. Judgment has thus entered the scene. It is tempting to stare at it, hoping to discern the extraordinary qualities by which, as Superconcept, it leaps with one bound the obstacles that stultify mere thinking and willing. We had better admit judging from the start on the same level of familiarity as thinking and willing. They can make their own contributions to judging that empower it to return them the favour.

Immediate and reflective judgment

Arendt changes her emphases on judgment. Sometimes it appears as part of the 'active life' and sometimes as practised as by a 'spectator'.[14] Judgments are involved as much in those activities that leave no time for reflection, as when we have the luxury of time. Having no time to pause and consider, still I must *judge* ('on the run') whether I can clear an obstacle in a leap. As spectator, I might calculate whether a runner will clear it. Their velocity and the height of the obstacle might be entered

14 Ronald Beiner's 'Interpretive Essay' (Beiner 1992, 135–44) raises this as a problem.

into a computer and a prediction issued almost as the runner clears the hurdle. Or the spectator might judge on the basis of the runner's past performance and present style. Runners themselves, however, must judge on the moment, in the event, that they can do it. The same goes for what we say 'on the run' in a conversation.

Such judgments lack the gravity of Arendt's concerns with judgment in times of moral and political crisis, and judgment as mediating between thought and action. Nevertheless, they demonstrate the need for good judgment made *in medias res* – a 'faculty' that cannot be replaced by thinking, inferring, calculating or knowing. Arendt will concentrate first on judgment from the point of view of the one involved in a situation[15] and then as a reflective practice. Our familiar examples indicate how judgment is equally the achievement of a reflective spectator and a 'doer'. Judgment then makes clear why it is the same achievement, despite the different circumstances. There may be no time to pause to deliberate but one exercises judgment in taking the leap. To just leap would be to abdicate from judgment.

Whether in action or when judging as if a spectator, to judge (even if instantaneously) is more than to be single-minded and unwavering. To see the need for judgment is to be always ready to stop and consider, to size up the situation and to consider less risky escape routes. Nevertheless, to judge without a moment's hesitation, may be still to act with acumen. One keeps in play a sense of one's resources, imagination and 'muscle-memory' of past 'leaps', together with an appreciation of the urgency that makes sense of the degree of risk.

In examining judgment on the run we see why Arendt's attention to thinking and willing generates a surge of thought about the need for judgment with all that that involves. If I had time to stop and think, I would not have to judge at this very moment. The involved participant need not therefore despise the 'spectator-like' character of thinking. We need to have taken time for thinking and coming to judgments, when we do have the luxury of time. It would be bad judgment to stop in the midst of a concert to rehearse a *bravura* passage even if that would improve one's playing. Forging ahead, hoping for the best may be the only thing to do, but emphasises the need to have already rehearsed, thoughtfully, technically difficult passages. Only after practice and rehearsal can one act with good judgment in launching into the passage under the spotlight of an audience's attention and expectation.

There is a parallel between thinking and acting, and rehearsal and performance. Rehearsal does not guarantee good performance, as thought and preparation do not guarantee good judgment. The quality of the judgment is only measured in terms of what you do in the event. Alternatively, things may go badly in rehearsal and well on the night. One can rehearse too much and be worn out with rehearsing and therefore perform badly. And yet, though the link is loose and not strictly reliable, rehearsal, careful, thoughtful and intelligent, is vital. To rehearse well is to avoid ingraining one's errors. It is to be determined to understand the causes of why some passage leaps out to bite you. In the same way, we think about what we shall have to say on an important issue when we know that a prepared speech will be out of the question.

15 'Actor' or 'agent': terms strangely common in philosophical discourse. Strange, because these are words that imply a secondary relation to one's deeds while attempting to express how one is peculiarly the author of them.

To think well is to avoid thinking too much – not to make the issue stale before we speak of it. To be thoughtful is to have the patience to think precisely, with detailed imagination of what one is going to do. Only such rehearsal makes it responsible to launch into the abyss of the irrecoverable event or the conversational interchange. In the event, what we say may be quite different from what we had prepared. All the same, we have improved our repertoire to handle the changes that immediate circumstances throw up. To retain this touch, this 'tact', is one form of the exercise of judgment.[16]

We can, therefore, judge while in the midst of an involvement that makes it impossible to 'stop and think'. Such urgent need for judgment accentuates thinking as a condition of one's judging rather than a persistence in rigid 'decisiveness'. And, in the grandstand from which the spectator is supposed to able to make their reflective judgments the trap we have to avoid is that of having 'all the time in the world'. In such an exaggerated sense of having gained 'perspective', we forget that we shall be required to judge. Thinking becomes a useless surrogate for will and judgment. Usually, a turn of events shakes us out of this reverie.[17] We easily lose our sense of the need to judge. This, as Arendt has explained, is to lose one's conscience. Within the reflective, more scholarly or spectator-like situation there is a slow urgency about that need to judge – no less intense for being taken with a measured step.[18]

Whether involved in action, or detached as spectators in thoughtful perception, it is equally possible to exercise judgment. The difference between action and observation is not a gulf, with judgment stranded on one side or the other. Detachment is its own kind of involvement. It is a relief to have 'time out' to think, but even Husserl's transcendental ego cannot bracket out *every* object of experience and thought. The drama critic is no more able to assess their own current critique than is the actor, while playing out their role, able to write it.

16 The will has been left in the background in this social phenomenology. To describe the connections of any two out of the trio of *thinking*, *willing*, *judging*, one of them is left tacit, framing the others.

17 In *The Phenomenology of Spirit* Hegel illustrates, with much irony, how after each stage of enlightenment comes the next pratfall. Matthew Karpin, in his tragic-comic *The Thesis* (Karpin 2004) explores these recursive pathways.

18 Think of Kant's habitual morning walk – and of how a certain lack of judgment made him break his routine.

Chapter 11

Working Magic

'The dream of philosophy is to be above the fray' (Michèle Le Dœuff).

Judgment – from Kant to Arendt

Taste

In Kant's *Critique of Judgment* (the third and last of his great 'critiques') aesthetic judgment – judgment in matters of taste – is the paradigm of judgment's possibilities. Surprisingly, it is judgment's very complicity in taste that, for Kant, is the reason it can help resolve the impasse between theoretical and practical knowledge, between nature and freedom. In fact, Kant gives currency to this term as from the first *Critique* (of 'pure reason'); it is at the heart of philosophy's nature and problems. To understand how he can imagine or hope that judgment as domesticated in aesthetics can assume the great role of bridging the phenomenon of experience and the noumenon of moral principle and freedom, we must read his terms as freshly minted in the 'Transcendental Aesthetic', within the (first) *Critique of Pure Reason*.

Let us begin with some contemporary reflections on what our various inflexions of the 'aesthetic' have come to mean for us. Our technology that so smoothly supplies *an-aesthetic* recalls for us the flavour of Kant's *aesthetic*.[1] To be aesthetic is to be alive to the world as immediately given in sense. It is this responsiveness that makes judgment possible. To take seriously this *being* aesthetic, then, setting out from an enlivened sensibility, is to cultivate judgment.[2] Aesthetic judgment, like sound judgment in general, is founded in keen sensibility.[3] The degree of detachment that we need sometimes is a far cry from any disconnection of feeling or of indifference. It is sensibility that makes us confident to judge – we can resist the tendency of judgment to fall into authoritarianism. The need for sensibility reminds us that we live with the constant hazard of lacking 'sense' even though our senses

1 'Un-aesthesia' – a lack of aesthesia. '*An-aesthesia*' – to drug oneself into a stupor. We may aim to regain aesthesia: ecstasy rather than grass; crack rather than opium. A loss of sensibility on all counts.

2 An 'aesthete' cultivates an outlook within which judgment seems like a loss of 'cool'. The *un-aesthete*, the *an-aesthete* and the addictive 'high' of the *hyper-aesthete* are alike to the aesthete, since none are in any condition to make a judgment. The lack of any will to judge appears within the group as a tactful loyalty.

3 Kant's *Critique of the Power ('craft') of Judgment* (1793) centred on taste. Then we were given *Sense and Sensibility* by Jane Austen (1811) and John Austin's *Sense and Sensibilia* in 1962.

are in working order. Furthermore, it is not only that judgment is born in sensibility. Making judgments within our world of immediate experience and sensation itself is one of the conditions that maintain our sensibility as lively responsiveness. The will to make judgments, and the resolution required in making them, and the nerve required in order to be answerable for making them, shakes us out of the passivity inherent in our reception of sensation.

Thus, in not being prepared to make judgments about what is happening and about the way we are receiving our impressions, we begin to fail to experience what is presented to our senses.[4] We judge what we experience (both the object of experience, whether things, events or people) and our experiencing of these 'objects'. This is a condition of taking seriously – as real – what we sense. And we maintain this sensibility, too, by the public and private expression of what we sense. That is, it requires us to think (privately) and to speak (thoughtfully). Thus we develop our experience and judgment from the corrections of experience and of judgment that we gain from the responses and challenges of others.

It is extraordinary – a brilliant stroke – that Kant should attempt to deploy judgment as in matters of taste so as to describe the possibility of a bridge between the (noumenal) world of freedom and the (phenomenal) world of nature and causality.[5] Building on Kant's beginning, Arendt has made such *common sense* crucial to a recovery of judgment. Though judgment is founded in the lightness of the aesthetic, Kant and Arendt press it into heavy theoretical work. It is the lightness of judgment's origins and associations, nevertheless, which prepare it for the task. If judgment were *pure* reason (the heavyweight of the *Critiques*), it would lack direct connection with what we do. Pure reason operates only in the realm of thought. And then, if Kant had tried to make willing (even the good will of the *Groundwork* and the second *Critique*) the source of judgment, it would have been answerable only to the transcendental principles of practical reason. As such, judgment could have operated only in the noumenal realm, uselessly free of reason's appeal to natural causality. Kant needs judgment to cross the barrier between the noumenal and the phenomenal realms. Judgment is at home in sensibility, and sound judgment, arising only from within that, goes beyond clear sensory reception. In judgment I express my pleasure in what I sense, but go beyond the fact of my taste, posing it as answerable to critique. I enter the circuit of reasons and reasoning.

Relieved of the burden of practical reason's moral responsibility, judgment is sent to work within taste and feeling. Each person as receiver and user of their own taste goes beyond reporting and expressing what they like, while still remaining within experience. Judgment, hovering between raw experience and things as they are in themselves, offers itself as mediator between morality's freedom and nature's causality. For Kant, judgment has no place with regard to moral law, which is recognised by pure reason. Pure in its application to principles that are practical

4 '*Are you experienced?*' enquires Jimi Hendrix, exploiting a fine ambiguity between one's being capable of properly taking on our experience, and our being open to the fact that we are being experienced by others. '*Being for others*' in 'being for oneself', as Beauvoir and Sartre would put it.

5 How Kant does this is detailed later in this chapter.

imperatives, reason determines the will as good and the will determines conduct as obedient to moral law outside any collision with cause and effect.

Judgment is required in moral life, nevertheless. We *judge* individual cases of character and action, deciding how they fall under the concepts and principles of moral law. Not pure reason, speculative or practical, but only judgment gains purchase on the particularity of sensibility. It is judgment we need to decide the motivation for an action, too. Though observable in the phenomenal realm, an action is based on noumenal principles. Kant needs a firewall between the noumenal and phenomenal, to protect a free good will. All the same, that will is exercised in the phenomenal realm. Otherwise (as he explains in his *Groundwork for the Metaphysics of Morals*), moral responsibility is a farce:

> The subjective impossibility of *explaining* the freedom of the will is the same as the impossibility of … making comprehensible an *interest* that the human being could take in moral laws … the foundation of which in us we call 'moral feeling' … the *subjective* effect that the law exercises on the will, for which reason alone provides the objective grounds (Kant 2002, 76).

Kant must separate his spheres of sensibility and of pure (practical) reason. A good will is determined by the validity of its maxims and yet *influences* conduct. Kant concedes, however, that it is 'entirely impossible for us to have an explanation of how the universality of the maxim as a law, hence morality, should interest us' (Kant 2002, 77):

> [Interest is] that through which reason becomes practical, i.e., becomes a cause determining the will. … [C]reatures without reason feel only sensible impulses [but] reason takes an immediate interest in an action only when the universal validity of its maxim is a sufficient determining ground of the will. Such an interest alone is pure (Kant 2002, 76).

So, judgment must succeed in linking pure reason's grasp of the moral law with the world of experience and motive. Arendt has her own way of reading this troubled division between an action as caused and as done out of regard for the moral law. For her, the division shows the need to find the place of freedom prior to that of moral reason.[6] For Kant, to act with a good will is to act within one's understanding of the moral law. For both of them, to act freely is to initiate a new series of events and break with habit and tradition.

Critiques of Reason and Judgment

In the first *Critique*, judgment was invoked to bridge the world we experience, with the noumenal domain of freedom. In the (final) *Critique of Judgment* the *imperatives* issued by practical reason (*Vernunft*) connect intellect's objects of pure understanding (*Verstand*) with the world of action. A critical position on Arendt's adaptation of Kant must proceed into contemporary issues of judgment. With Arendt's help we

6 For both Kant and Arendt, at the heart of freedom is the power to initiate a new line of events. They leave aside the old conundrum, 'Could I have done otherwise?'.

have to re-work the distinction between intellect and reason, to recast the problem of how what can be 'grasped' by reason' works within a 'noumenal' realm beyond reason's power to describe it.

So, how do we understand 'intellect' and 'reason' in our informed conversations? Kant attributes to (intellect's) understanding the power to supply concepts to synthesise the manifold of experience. We too consider one who can bring the right concepts to grasp an issue as a person of 'intellect'. Such a person succeeds because they have a wide repertoire of concepts and are trained in thought, educated ('led out'). They are not hidebound within one professional discourse but have fluent access to a variety. As to reason, there is a difference in the feel of Kant's German and our English, with its constellation of Latinate terms like 'ratiocination' and 'rationality' that surround 'reason'. These (and corresponding Greek words) are ideas of proportion – the ratio of one quantity to another. Yet, though Kant's *Vernunft* moves in a different etymological constellation, our contemporary 'reason', too, would distinguish understanding from the overall practice of reason. Reason appears most clearly, in relief, when someone has 'lost it'. (An evocative new idiom.) I can lose my reason and then recover it. Only in an accident or by surgery would I lose my intellect on some occasion. We lose our powers of intellect gradually in the normal progress of life, whereas we lose our powers of reason when overcome by emotion or exhaustion, when depressed or elated, and when terrorised or apprehensive. There are the quieter moments of a moral failure of reason, too. Unable to face a changed situation I go into denial. Refusing to 'face the facts'; I throw up a smokescreen by the usual practices of illogic. I attack the one who brings the news; I represent faint possibilities as high probabilities. I make unwarranted inferences while I balk at making my usual sound ones.

Kant's division of intellect and reason, however, is designed to go beyond such an everyday understanding. That Kant's *intellect* can operate in a 'different world' is part of the project of the *Critique of Pure Reason*. *Intellect* supplies concepts for experience by which we operate within a 'transcendental' logic. He uses reason in a critique of reason to determine reason's limits. Intellect enables us to use reason in this process of self-regulation, exhibiting the conditions of sensing the world: 'Although all our cognition commences with experience, yet it does not on that account all arise from experience' (Kant 1998, 136). Are there, Kant asks, 'any cognitions independent of all impressions of the senses?'. Only such cognitions could be called *a priori* and only the *intellect* can possesses them (Kant 1998, 136–7).

In the opening page of the last *Critique* Kant morphs the *theoretical* and (pure) *practical* reason of the first two *Critiques* into 'nature' and 'freedom'. The distinction of theoretical and (pure) practical reason, though 'sound', is made derivative from these dichotomous concepts of *nature* and of *freedom*. Now, what is *known* in philosophy is less than what is *thought*. We *know* freedom only as what is *not* determined by natural causes, and this is not to know what freedom is 'in itself'. Nevertheless we proceed to 'determine the will', and philosophy leads us to 'practical legislation for reason based upon the concept of freedom'.[7]

7 Kant's 'practical reason' has to do with the moral 'What shall I do?' not the practical 'How can I do this?'.

Kant cuts 'theoretical' from 'practical' reason, and divides the activity of the self in its phenomenal world, separate from the will of a noumenal self that knows nothing of the 'before and after' of causality. From that moment Kant's text 'pitches and tosses'.[8] No sooner has he maintained nature and freedom as 'antithetical' principles than he goes to bring them together again – only to react against this accommodation. A synthesis of nature and freedom would be achieved at the cost of freedom, since there can be no limit to the application of scientific principle in the world of nature. It is by the craftiness of judgment (*Urteilskraft*) that we attempt a salvage operation: 'the critique of judgment [is to be] a means of linking the two parts of philosophy into a whole' (Kant 1987, 15). It seems that to achieve what Kant needs, however, judgment must be a work of magic. Kant must separate the realms of nature and of freedom if his world is to be open to science and yet safe for freedom. At the same time, they must be connected if a pure moral will is to have any significance for our actions. This 'separation of powers'[9] by the *Critique of Pure Reason* assigns nature to the phenomenal realm and freedom to the noumenal. Freedom becomes ineffable, being consigned beyond what is phenomenal – that is, beyond what can be described. Yet even as we snort at the ineffable, Kant would whisper, 'If things *as they appear to us* comprise the phenomenal world, what of the world of things as they are *in themselves?*'. Things 'in themselves' as against what they are 'for us' descend to us (via Hegel) in Sartre and Beauvoir's version (1943).[10]

What, then, is expected of judgment if it is to connect the 'noumenal' pure will with the 'phenomenal' action we experience? Kant creates no problem about judgment in the *Critique of Pure Reason* (in 1781),[11] but uses the notion constantly. In differing 'analytic' from "'synthetic' propositions Kant calls them '*judgments*'". He needs the word. Of any proposition we must *judge* and not merely *state* that it is 'analytic' or 'synthetic'. The power of judgment is our 'faculty' of recognising how individuals are instances of principles, and of deriving principles from individual cases, an art invoked by the first *Critique* when identifying pure principles *a priori*. The last *Critique* (of judgment) exposes the gulf between the necessity of a proposition and our identification of it as such. The *judgment* of a proposition as 'necessary' is not itself established of necessity. Because of the universality implied in a judgment, the making of a judgment puts one in the dock of public criticism. This achieves objectivity, but not certainty. In exposing our judgment to the judgment of others we depart from self-certainty. Unlike 'pure reason', judgment feeds off the world of our likes and dislikes. Can such subjectivity then bridge causal nature to willing freedom?

---

8 An expression I have from Michèle Le Dœuff in her discussion of Beauvoir's thought (Le Dœuff 1991, 114).

9 There is a parallel here with liberal democracy's separation of powers between the legislative and the judicial.

10 They worked out the *in-itself*, the *for-itself* and the *for-others* in terms of what appears, so that Kant's 'transcendental aesthetic' becomes aesthetic. Their phenomenology makes Kant's 'transcendental' conditions of appearance and of freedom appear within sense and sensibility.

11 Seven years later (1788) he publishes the *Critique*, where judgment is a kind of art. An idea introduced cursorily in the first *Critique*.

Kant's constructions

With Arendt, we are reading Kant as dealing with the relation of thought and will, with judgment bringing the conflict between them to a head. In the *Crisis of European Sciences*, Husserl challenges Kant's intellectual constructions:

> Husserl believed that Kant's great attempt to achieve and understand the viewpoint of transcendental subjectivity failed. For Kant, 'so many *presuppositions* are "obviously" valid, presuppositions which in the Humean sense are included within this "world enigma" of how objectivity based on subjectivity is possible, that he "never penetrated to the enigma itself"' (Husserl 1970, 97). … Kant's attempt failed also in its results because he created mythical constructions – the noumenal object 'behind' sensible experiences and the noumenal self 'behind' conscious describable acts and experiences (Deutscher 2003, 3).

Husserl shrewdly diagnoses this flaw. It arises from Kant's accepting an empiricists' picture of perception as subjective experiences that, at best, represent some real world by mediation:

> Because he understands inner perception in this empiricist, psychological sense and because, warned by Hume's scepticism, he fears recourse to the psychological as an absurd perversion of the genuine problem of understanding, Kant gets involved in his mythical concept formation [of 'pure' transcendental forms of understanding] (Husserl 1970, 115).

When Kant instructs us to think away these 'sensuous' experiences when we search for the transcendental conditions of experience, he represents them as mere 'representations' that sully the 'purity' of the understanding. And yet he (rightly) warns us not to construct a new dogmatic metaphysics on the basis of transcendental principles. These principles make sense only in being applied to the empirical realm of phenomena. Kant divides from 'pure' understanding (whose concepts are given *a priori*) what presents to us as a phenomenon, and it is judgment that has to cross the divide. We must cross it. Moral intuition must bear upon the world of phenomena – the world in which we are responsible for what we do phenomenally. Arendt owes the structure of the problem to Kant. Then she reads Kant's text as something to be made credible and workable.

Now, Kant does warn his readers against an illusion. We are liable to take his demonstrated limits of reason as principles of a new systematic metaphysics. And yet, as Arendt observes, Kant himself sometimes treats his work as a sort of 'science'. As a science, it would be systematic knowledge of that very 'noumenal' domain of which no science is possible. But, for the most part, Kant steers clear of the illusion, recognizing that pure reason (*Vernunft*) simply *limits* the realm of possible truths. He points out that this is not knowledge of another realm of truth. Within its province *Vernunft* intuits what is *a priori* and yet *synthetic*, but to regard it as an infallible organ that produces a science of infallible truths in a new realm 'purer' than the phenomenal is a fantasy. The ideas of 'pure reason' have the reality of a *schema* of thought, Kant insists. Kant warns us that these pure ideas neither represent reality as delivered by the senses nor some otherworldly reality (LM, 64).

Though, as Arendt says, Kant can 'veil this fact' and turn meaning into an 'intention' or 'purpose' (as if to instate *Vernunft* as a higher version of common sense understanding) he does recant. He can declare that '*pure reason is in fact concerned with nothing but itself*' (Kant 1998, 610). This declaration is a defence of a 'critique of pure reason' as a possible project. The use of judgment in recognising the transcendental principles is crucial. Our judgments about the limits of sense do not amount to knowledge, but they are more than mere opinion. Those judgments do not fall into the abyss of scepticism. The appeal to judgment to lay hold of limiting principles of reason is indispensable. Only after a critique of judgment itself can the first *Critique* can be fully comprehended and clearly stated.

We have to clarify what we understand by 'intellect', 'understanding' (*Verstand)* and 'reason' (*Vernunft*) in Kant, and what Arendt makes of those distinctions. 'How are synthetical judgments *a priori* possible?' is the 'proper problem of pure reason', Kant writes in section VI of the Introduction to the *Critique of Pure Reason*. To make synthetic judgments *a priori* is a task of 'pure reason' rather than the proper problem of 'pure *intellect*', or of 'pure *understanding*.' As a 'critique', his philosophy only sets limits to what can be known, but this might raise a problem. These limits are stated and defended, as if ascertained to be true. Conspicuous arguments are constructed that the limits are as Kant states them. If Kant's arguments to set the limits of reason are conclusive, then it is by means of the Critique's transcendental enquiry that statements of these limits appear as if to be known. This question about Kant's position is given new force when we extend Arendt's study of judgment in relation to thinking and willing. Arendt associates Kant's *Critique* with *thought*, and argues that thinking cannot amount to knowledge.

Is Kant constructing a speculative line of *thought* in his first *Critique* or has he created a new *science* of the limits to knowledge? In concluding the 'Remarks on Transcendental Aesthetic', Kant writes that synthetic propositions *a priori* are possible because we possess 'pure a priori intuitions [of space and time, that enable us to] go beyond the given concept [to a fresh conception that] is discovered synthetically connected with it' (Kant 1998, 192). It is the 'understanding' (*Verstand*) that takes the lead as we approach the *Categories*. Where the 'synthesis' of representations requires 'mere imagination', it 'is a function of the understanding' to reduce this synthesis to concepts. Where understanding is our comprehension of laws or rules, judgment is our ability to *subsume* particular things or events as 'standing under' a given law or rule (Kant 1998, 268). To require a law to guide the application of a law to particular cases would be logically regressive. The power of judgment is 'specific to so-called mother-wit, the lack of which cannot be made good by any school' (Kant 1998, 268).

Truth exists within an isolated domain of experienced phenomena that are synthesised and made intelligible by the concepts of the understanding. Kant uses the trope of a 'northern island of truth'. We shall risk a voyage on the seas beyond this island, says Kant, but this dangerous journey is taken for the purposes of thought. Knowable truth is left behind within the shores of the island. This is the situation at the outset of the 'Transcendental Doctrine of the Faculty of Judgment'. Kant nominates the 'region of pure understanding' (within which we form concepts of what lies within our possible experience) as the island of truth, even as he moves to divide phenomenal from noumenal objects. He is to set out on the 'stormy ocean' that lies beyond the island of phenomena, risking shipwreck on the icebergs of illusion. All this in order to pursue a pure line of thought concerning what, though falling beyond possible experience, has to be countenanced in his philosophy.

This is not territory to be *known*. Even the principles of 'pure understanding', true *a priori*, are 'nothing but only the pure schema, as it were, for possible experience' (Kant 19098, 339). This 'pure' understanding can make only 'empirical use of its *a priori* principles, indeed of all its conceptions' (Kant 1998, 340). Kant pursues the consequences. Conditions that are 'transcendental' (as conditions of the possibility of experience) do not 'transcend' experience towards a thing 'in itself'. The pure categories (of space, time and causality) 'have merely transcendental significance, but are … not of any transcendental use, since this is impossible in itself, for they are lacking all conditions of any use in judgments [which would involve] the subsumption of any … object under these concepts' (Kant 1998, 346). They can be applied 'empirically', but cannot be applied to an object.[12]

Arendt's own way of thinking about thought, the will, and their relation to judgment moves almost hand in hand with Kant's. She poses afresh the question of how we can relate the world revealed as an object of thought with the world within which we must act.[13] In Arendt's terms, the thinking ego lacks the traction to haul what it thinks (and things as it has thought them) back into the arena where decisions must be made and commitments entered into. So she has retained the structure of the Kantian problem while re-interpreting its terms. So long as reason is confined within the limits of possible of experience, the world can be known. Practical (moral) reason requires that we act rationally within materiality and the constraints of cause and effect. Practical reason requires, with equal force, that we are free. This freedom has an ontological character. It is not the merely forensic concept as outlined classically by John Locke, say, according to which to be free means only that we are not under compulsion or constraint, and are therefore subject to social or legal sanctions in what we do. As Kant and Arendt envisage it, to be free is to be capable of initiating a new series of events. These take their place within the phenomenal world of visible responsibility and their causes lie within that world. The origin of our initiative, however, has another kind of explanation, in different terms.

Thus, Kant's 'solution' to the problem of freedom within the natural order of cause and effect is radically ambiguous. Like the composed vase that suddenly appears instead as two faces set towards each other, his 'solution' can switch without warning, to appear instead as the problem itself in a yet more dramatic guise. Suppose that freedom does exist. In that case, it exists only in the noumenal realm that lies beyond all possible experience and to which even the transcendental conditions of experience have no application. We cannot experience such a freedom, and we can in no way describe it in itself. It is simply an empty 'that which' makes possible the radical initiation of new series of events within the natural order. By the same token,

12 Kant must mean an object *in itself*, rather than an object as given empirically, as a phenomenon.

13 What happens is that we return from thinking into willing as Orpheus returns from Hades. We cannot look back from the world still to see our Eurydice of thought.

we can have no understanding of how, in its special way, it can operate within that of the natural order without being a force countervailing to natural sequences of cause and effect. We can say only that since freedom does exist in an radically different order of existence, there can be no formal contradiction between what is asserted to occur in the phenomenal (natural) order, and what is speculated to exist in the noumenal one.

Arendt knows her Kant well enough, along with the history of the struggles to do something within his framework. She knows, therefore, that it would be vain to attempt a solution while leaving his framework quite unchanged. As Husserl has put it, Kant has 'created mythical constructions' that in fact *prevent* him from 'penetrat[ing] to the enigma itself'. At the same time, it is a real problem that is presented to us in the form of Kantian myth. Arendt's analysis, a re-writing of Kant's problematic, thus runs parallel with that of Gilbert Ryle in his diagnosis of the simpler sort of dualism that marked the Descartes of the *Discourse on Method* and the *Meditations*. Though a myth, the tale of a 'ghost' in a 'machine' freed up philosophical thought that was still transfixed by Aristotelian models of internal committees and internal orders of command. Remarks about 'states of mind', experiences, thoughts and emotions as 'inner' or 'hidden' are in a different category from those about states of the body, and the various traumas and disturbances and movements of the body, considered as such. We surpass Descartes not by refuting him, but by deconstructing his myth and then building a new narrative on a site that we admit to be strongly marked by the ruins of the old one. So, we must review how Kant constructs a divide between the worlds of speculative intellect and of reason that contains our possibilities of knowledge.[14] We must ask again how judgment could bridge the divide. In this process, too, we shall have to re-evaluate and re-describe the nature of the division between the phenomenal and the noumenal. We might then stand just far enough off from Kant and Arendt to make our own judgments.

Bridging worlds

There are three *Critiques*. In a footnote to the third, Kant mocks his always finding *three* of everything, but takes the question seriously enough to explain that it is not some *idée fixe* of his own, but that it has its origin in the nature of the categories of thought:

> It has been thought somewhat suspicious that my divisions in pure philosophy should almost always come out threefold. But it is due to the nature of the case. If a division is to be *a priori* it must be either analytic, according to the law of contradiction, or else it is *synthetic*. If it is to be derived in the latter case from *a priori* concepts ... then to meet the requirements of synthetic unity in general – [a condition, a conditioned, and the concept arising from the union of the two], the classification must necessarily be threefold (Kant 1987, 38, fn 43).

Kant simply repeats his practice of establishing a triad upon a dualism of category. To say that it is 'in the nature of the case' is to say, on his own principles, that it is

14 That is, in Kant's first and third *Critiques*.

how things must be according to the concepts of his understanding that bring unity to a manifold of phenomena, whether empirical or logical. Kant's attempt is to resolve, within his triad of categories, the standoff between nature and freedom.

The things we do simply *are*, as *causes*, and as *being caused*. Judgment takes this into account, but considers these acts, though taken in the public phenomenal order, to be assessed by principles of reasoned morality. That an act is in accord with principles can then have a noumenal origin in a sense other than that of temporal causality. Kant has argued persuasively that there is no outright contradiction in the situation (Kant 1998, 537–46). To know this, however, is far from understanding the meaning of his philosophy on this issue. Early in the third *Critique*, Kant sets the place for judgment in the way that he describes what is achieved in the first two. He reminds us that the first *Critique* does issue in a doctrine, but constructs a way of thinking that sets limits to doctrines. Similarly, the second *Critique* (of practical reason) does not put forward moral doctrines, but attempts to arrive at the limiting forms of what constitutes a doctrine as moral. In the first the intellect discovers the world as governed by laws of causality ('What causes what I do?'), in the second, the will reveals a freedom that operates by a reason of practice ('What shall I do?'). The division between the two forms of reason emerges as the fact of this difference. The problem for reason is that there seems to be no way of relating the two forms. Thus arises Kant's hope:

> What cannot be included in the division of philosophy [into theoretical and practical] may yet be admitted as a principal part into the general critique of our faculty for pure knowledge if it contains principles [that is, of judgment] that are not in themselves adapted for either theoretical or practical use (Kant 1987, 15–16).

Thus arises the need for a critique of judgment. Not being theoretical knowledge or practical reason, judgment might bridge the gap between the phenomenal and the noumenal orders. Judgment, it is hoped, can survey, equally, events as governed by the laws of cause and effect, and willing activity as governed by a rational grasp of moral principles. Concepts of nature, the grounds for theoretical knowledge gained by the law-giving intellect can apply to the phenomenal order. Concepts of freedom, the grounds for all practical precepts *a priori*, gained by pure (practical) reason can apply to the noumenal order. The division seems intense, but the will itself already spans, tenuously, these separated fields. The will is serious only as operating phenomenally, and principled only if subject to noumenal principle. It is the *power of judgment* that secures the link. In willing, we are within either the phenomenal or noumenal realms. In judgment, the claims of the noumenal will are informed by facts, while the will is made thoughtful in being judged according to principle. This is what Kant describes as a non-temporal causality that governs us, even as phenomenal beings.

Kant promises only to demonstrate that it as *not impossible* that freedom should exist even while the phenomenal order is subject to cause and effect. Kant offers us the ground, too, on which judgment 'may be linked with another order of our imagination'. It is not only theoretical knowledge and practical reason that is subject to judgment:

> [Judgment also deals with] our capacity for pleasure and displeasure, and our power of desire. To be able to feel pleasure lies between the power of knowing and the capacity for desire, just as judgment lies between intellect and reason (Kant 1987, 16–17).

Thus, Kant suggests, we may 'provisionally assume that, [like the] power to know and to desire, judgment contains its own *a priori* principle' Kant 1987, 17).

The ideas in Kant's provocative argument operate as analogy. Since pleasure is necessarily connected with desire, judgment 'will effect a transition from the faculty of pure knowledge (from concepts of nature) to our faculty of freedom'.[15] It is 'in the same way' that judgment ('in its logical employment') effects the transition from intellect's knowledge of causes and effects to practical reason's principled determination of the will (Kant 1987, 17). His rich text raised Arendt's hopes for a rapprochement between thinking and willing, and yet her line of thought might stall, caught between Kant's promise and the sketchiness of his solution. Just how this double life is achieved by judgment remains in partial obscurity.

Looking back at Kant and Arendt, I would think about 'being determined' and 'being guided by principle' in terms that do not set up a chasm between causality in nature and morality in a separate world of principle. Your freedom in *being willing* rides on the back of causality. Your resolute action ends a cycle of oppression. You were *fully determined* to make the change. For justice, you could have done nothing less. Knowing this, someone still says, 'You chose to risk everything.' Yes, the choice was made and you are responsible for at least the consequences. But others only imagine that you could have quit the scene. You thought and experienced the situation and found yourself with an utterly determined will to act. This determination *is* your freedom – your capability of *being determined* by such considerations. To suggest that, as a 'free agent' you could have taken off for a holiday is a fantasy. To be free in one's willingness is to become determined. The question that remains is how we 'form a will' – *how* we become willing.

15 Is it the powers of knowledge, pleasure and freedom or the concepts of these activities that are connected?

Chapter 12

Willing Thought

Existential deconstruction

'Outside the square'

To take *judgment* as a principal concept, activity and theme is to loosen the grip of *causality* and *freedom* upon our imagination of what is possible. In the antinomies Kant has little trouble in showing how, starting from the exclusive point of view of each, the existence of the other appears as an illusion. Still, it is not an arbitrator who appears *ex machina* that we need. Nor can we expect a resolution to the conflict by the victory of one side, either. Since the solution is neither from some outside vantage point nor by the elimination of one point of view, it must come from dismantling the issue internally. So, if *judgment* is to help here (whether the act itself or the concept of it) it must assist as initiating or supporting this process of deconstruction. Just to begin, we can say in one sentence why *judgment* destabilises the stand-off between causality ('nature') and freedom. It is an existential point[1] involving the demands of existence that require us not only to understand the causes of events but, as participants in them, to take upon ourselves the responsibility that accrues to those who have a degree of freedom. The acting point ('*stand*point' is not apt!) required in being willing is that from which one takes on as one's own (or as part of one's group's), an initiative in producing a new line of events.

A line of thought may be just such a 'line of events'. Suppose that in philosophy, say, we set ourselves not just to rehearse and to play out the parts that have already been written for us by the 'determinists' and the 'libertarians'. In that case we are claiming this freedom to initiate a new line of events. We lay hold of this freedom no less than do those who 'act' to initiate new systems of building, of medical cures, or of political governance. Arendt may have overlooked (or downplayed) this fact when she described thinking as a *withdrawal* from action. It is, of course, a withdrawal from the action about which, instead, one thinks. However, thinking itself is a kind of action in which we either assume our responsibilities for a new initiative, or capitulate to established conventions and clichés. To recognise this is to risk absurd self-aggrandisement. Not to take that risk, however, is only faint-hearted. Let the task of thought be however modest when considered within the great scheme of things, still it is the effort, as Deleuze put it, to create concepts and to initiate 'lines of flight'.

---

1 It is existentialism's renewal of Kant's 'reasoned critique of reason' that leads on to the various 'post-modern' activities that include, particularly, the practice of deconstructing metaphysical conundrums.

Ronald Beiner (Beiner 1992, 89–155) has observed that Arendt sees the true home of judgment sometimes in its exercise in practical affairs by an involved party, while at other times, without announcing a change of mind, she appears to recognise judgment only in our moments as detached or disinterested spectators. It is not hard to explain this (apparently) puzzling shift. We must always move between those paradigms of judgment, simply because of what good judgment requires of us. The shift is not that of some aberration in a writer's approach. Judgment, which we need in addition to the power to calculate and to infer, is needed both within our most busy involvements and in our reflective moments of recollection and consideration. Involved, we may be prone to *hasty* judgments. That is in the nature of the case. A 'hasty' judgment is not inevitable, merely because of a lack of time to 'stop and think', however. As if by magic, judgment succeeds where calculation and inference are inappropriate or inapplicable. The possibility of successful judgment – that moment when we simply 'take the plunge' and declare that a much praised movie is an empty folly. We may, after wrestling with conflicting considerations, judge that the US ought not to have invaded Iraq even though it is good that Saddam Hussein was driven from power. People formally appointed as 'judges' may deliver their view that an indigenous system of land occupation and of territorial limits must take its place along with the British-based system of ownership.

The possibility of success in these judgments derives from our development of skills, familiarity and practice. Judging does not reduce to its related terms of thinking, inferring and evidence. One can proceed to detail the various kinds of things we do judge. One can describe how experience is incorporated into practice so that a person becomes confident enough to deliver, or to act upon, their own judgment. One can emphasise, too, how some sort of conceptual step is taken when we judge – a step not required when we calculate or infer. When we infer or calculate, all the concepts we use in the conclusion must already have been introduced in the basis for our calculation or the premises of our inference. That is the *sine qua non* of accurate calculation, of valid, and of probabilistic inference. Arendt develops the idea that Kant pointed out, that when we judge, we introduce a concept to a thing or situation, or we draw some new principle involving some new concept from some exemplary individual thing or situation. Arendt's incomplete trilogy leaves us to work out how the very fact that judgment exists and can be successful, bridges the gap between the 'natural' order of cause and effect, and that mode of life in which we are willing (or 'nilling') to do one thing rather than another. The principal hint we are given is that in being willing, we exercise our freedom to initiate a new line of events. We have already begun to examine how *natality* – the fact of birth – is a model for initiating a new series, though the process of conception, gestation and birth evidently is one of cause and effect. The question is how to go further than citing this metaphor of birth, prone as it is to degeneration into cliché.

Moods and modalities

In her study of *Willing* Arendt set out with the idea of thinking and willing as differing in mood. In thinking, one is in a different frame of mind from that in which one becomes willing to do what thinking might suggest.[2] Considered apart from extraneous upsets, thinking is marked by a mood of calm. Willing, in contrast, is marked by tension. In being ready to set out to undertake some line of action one is, intrinsically, beset by hope and by fear. There is something that needs to be done when the will is involved. There is some hope of achieving it, or one would never set out. At the same time, that one must 'bend one's will' to the task is because the result is no foregone conclusion. One has some apprehension of failure. This tension cannot be resolved by thinking. (Unless it happens that by thinking one comes to the conclusion that, for concrete and moral reasons, one should not have undertaken the venture in the first place.) When something needs to be done, to persist only in thinking is, as Arendt remarks acerbically, mere procrastination. We have here at least one source of the 'gulf' between the 'world of thought' and the 'world of the will'.[3]

Arendt makes another point, congruent with this. Accounts of the will are distorted in being, inevitably, constructed from the point of view of thought. In making of the will an object of thought, its work of surpassing thought into risky commitment – the business of willing – is neutralised. This is not so much a problem that can be overcome as a distortion of which one must be warned. The observation is borne out by the tendency of those whose prime business it is to think, to overlook the existence of the will, or to reduce it to some function of thinking, calculating and observation, or else to deny its existence as a total illusion. One does not find any parallel tradition of philosophers of the will in overlooking, reducing, or denying the very existence of thinking.[4]

All this seems so true and yet, when I hear that thinking distorts willing to suit its own interests, I overhear myself complaining to Arendt:

> So how am I to write about willing?' Am I to write without thinking? Even then I might turn out thoughtful writing. If thinking introduces its own bias when addressing willing, I must do more than to avoid thinking. I should write of willing, willingly. And, 'willingly' not only as the opposite of 'unwillingly', but as being in the mode of the will when I write – and more than that – in the mode of the will in writing. Don't I have to be in the mode of the will when writing, though? Yes, I might write listlessly, without any clear aim. Yet, even this almost collapse of the very project still requires the will to set down in print, rather than to let thoughts run through my head, sensations flow over me, or to leave the study and to converse with someone.[5]

Arendt admits that

2 Or 'nilling'.

3 In terms of 'nature' versus 'freedom' the world of 'thought' is the world as envisaged by the sciences, as an object thus of intellectual contemplation, and the world of the will goes on the 'freedom' side of the divide.

4 The reader of *The Life of the Mind* will be aware that Arendt attends to some – Duns Scotus, Nietzsche and Heidegger (in his first phase), who have attempted to give the will a primary place, with a priority over thinking.

5 Author's parenthetical thoughts.

> when we directed our attention to men of action, hoping to find in them a notion of freedom purged of the perplexities caused … by the reflexivity of mental activities [that is, thinking] … we hoped for more than we finally achieved. The abyss of pure spontaneity … was covered up by the device … of understanding the new as an improved re-statement of the old. In its original integrity, freedom survived in theory … conceived for the purposes of political action … only in utopian … promises of a final 'realm of freedom', … a sempiturnal peace in which all specifically human activities would wither away (LMW, 216).

In was in the first lines of this venture that Arendt warned us, as we observed above, of

> an inevitable flaw in … examinations of the willing faculty …that every philosophy of the Will is conceived … not by men of action but by philosophers … more inclined to 'interpret the world' than 'to change it' (LMW, 195).

It is not only the interest in change (and thus in willing) shown by men of action that gives Arendt a field of phenomena changed from that of thinking. It is that these 'men of action' look to actions taken by groups of people rather than by individuals. Certainly this was an advantage for Arendt. It gave us new figures, new images, narratives that differ from the ego-centred tales of Paul, Augustine, Aquinas and Kant. Nevertheless, as with the philosophers who preferred only to 'interpret the world', this change 'covered up' the need for men of action to take up a reflexive attitude in order to describe the past actualities or future hopes of political acts of freedom and liberation. Had they only acted, while saying and writing nothing, Arendt could have found no account of freedom to compare with that produced by the mere 'professional thinkers'. Certainly, there is something more outward looking in the narratives that interest the political theorists – at least in comparison with the soul-searching of Paul and of Augustine in particular. For all that, one might have foretold of the men of action who turned to writing about the nature of freedom that, simply in taking up the process of writing, they would fall into the 'bias' of the thinkers.

In the end, it is not the bias of thought in addressing will that is the problem. We can admit that a predisposition to thinking might encourage writers to downgrade willing in relation to it. This is not inevitable, however. Except for thought itself, everything that is thought about is other than thought. If the habit and preference for thought tends to downgrade willing because the will is a competitor with thinking, so too will the preference for thought tend to downgrade every reality that is other than thinking. One might remark, indeed, on the tendency to some form of idealism, which every systematic thought displays. Arendt herself shows how modern forms of materialism, in their universal conception of things, mime the structures of the idealistic systems of a century before them. So we can take ourselves to be given fair warning of our likely '*déformation professionelle*', but not therefore to have an excessive mistrust of theories of the will in particular. To put it shortly – a theory of will is not an instance of willing, no matter who produces it, whether 'professional thinker' or 'professional activist'.

Willing and thinking in judgment

It seems to be a time for incessant reminders. Indeed, Wittgenstein (typically in *Philosophical Investigations*), practised philosophy in the assembling of them. We recall that it is not as an extraordinary concept or activity that Arendt pinned her hopes on *judging* as leading her out of the difficulties associated with willing, in relation to thinking. Each of these activities is recognisably different, and their autonomy as activities is essential to what each has to offer. Nevertheless, only in terms of what each has to offer the other is their value assessable and their nature fully describable. Arendt was right that the bias of thought is to take a dim view of willing – to denigrate its competitor in its absence. From the point of view of willing, this seems a particularly unfair exclusion. It is thinking itself that sends willing off to the wings. Thinking takes the centre stage and in a blaze of glory makes condescending gestures towards the minor characters – willing and judging. Since thinking has defined its own theatre (of the absurd?) in order to showcase describing and explaining, willing is going to cut a poor figure if called in to make a major speech. Like calling on the stage hands, unrehearsed, their heads full of other urgent matters and making them appear stupid in not delivering a fine speech impromptu. So thinking has no option but to honour willing and judging in their absence. It must take care not to abuse its privilege, but it perpetrates a worse injustice by expecting to hold them to their own proper parts and yet to make a good representation of themselves. Thus by summoning up thinking, willing and judging as if they were autonomous agents we generate thought about how each is distinct and yet interdependent for its value and effect. At the same time we are dealing, if in personification, then in myth. Though there are risks in this strategy, the personification of the fabulous three as agents disputing their respective status is succinct and flags each brightly for our attention.

Arendt practices such a figuration too, even though when assessing Heidegger's evocation of the dangers of the Will she comments on the practice of personification as a risky one. We seem to introduce a kind of clarity of distinctness when we summon up these worthies as characters in music-hall melodrama. What we lose in the personification, curiously, is the vision of them as roles rather than as the actors who adopt them. Still we accept a temporary role for personification itself since without it, we lapse into iterated abstractions. 'Will', 'thought' and 'judgment' are words by which we set aspects of ourselves before 'the mind's watchful eye'[6] in a reified form that promises a simple essence for each. To that extent, personification is less risky since the presence of art in the argument is made explicit. Reification is more deceptive too in that it appears to achieve an (impossible) ideal of objectivity in relation to the roles that are intrinsic to the very existence by which we attempt to stand off and describe them, rather than simply proceeding with the play.

In relating judging to thinking and willing, then, we shall have to re-examine Arendt's original demarcation of thinking as a withdrawal from the world (of social and political engagement). In this sense 'world' names the site of our being willing

6 How natural personification seems in thought's arena – another virtual personification appears as inevitable.

– and, to stretch a phrase, of being nilling. (Nilling as *willing-not*.) Conceptually, we have left the site of the will in withdrawing to think.

A parallel emerges here with Husserl's 'transcendental' attitude of 'bracketing out' all natural objects of perception, thus disengaging from our involvements with the world.[7] As with Husserl, one must recall that in disengaging from commitment to the natural objects of perception one does not escape involvement as such. As with Arendt's retreat to thinking, to be in Husserl's 'transcendental' mode is to have gained a new involvement in the very process of losing the one that precedes it. Thus we realise a limitation on detachment as a condition of objectivity. If to be objective is to at least to enhance one's chances of drawing ideas and understanding from the 'object', then every detachment must coexist with an involvement with the 'object'. Faced with a situation bearing in on us we 'stop and think'; we resile from the mode of being willing. This abstention exists, however, only in relation to the situation that frames what we do as 'thinking about it' rather than 'acting in relation to it'. As an abstention from acting, thinking is an abstention only from that activity from which one disengages so as to think about it. 'Thinking is an abstention from acting', while true, obscures the fact that to think is its own action of a sort, and involves being willing to think. Thinking is itself an activity, which we practise willingly or unwillingly.

Yes, one may think idly, as if doing nothing, and for nothing. But so too with overt actions. I doodle; I lie in the sun; I go on listening to music that fails to interest me. The failure of will (that is, the failure to become willing or nilling) or the sheer absence of will (because nothing seems to be at issue) is a possibility that attends any activity over which I can have any degree of control. The fact that we challenge someone to become willing to think about a difficult issue shows this.[8] Furthermore, one might think idly, of and for nothing. This demonstrates such un-willing thought as only one mode and throws into relief what it is to become willing to think. Being willing is one of the modalities of thinking itself.

Certainly, one may be willing in one's thinking without having a plan or strategy. But let us observe that in the same fashion, one may be willing in anything that one does without having formulated a plan for success. It may be desirable to plan, but that does not arrive as within one's being willing. Rather, in being willing one tends to become ready to draft a plan and to formulate a strategy to achieve what one wills. We have observed earlier how a gulf was set up for Arendt between thinking's calm mood of contemplation and willing's tense mood of hope and fear – a mood that is relieved only by taking action. This correctly reflected the first dramatic achievement of stopping to think, of remaining open to an issue rather than closing it in action. There is no dichotomy between thinking and willing as such, however. As with overt action, to become willing to think may require considerable work.

So, thinking is like action in being done, sometimes willingly, sometimes unwillingly, and sometimes without any proper formation of a will. A sort of action,

---

7 There is an idiomatic account of this in my 'Husserl and Transcendental Subjectivity' (Small 2001, 3–24).

8 For example, where the possible outcome goes against the grain of their interests or prejudices.

thinking is in some ways other than an action nevertheless. It is at least typical of action that it invites the question 'What are you doing that for?" whereas, typically, thinking has no specific or immediate purpose. I may think *because of*, but not (except for special reasons) *in order to*. Results of thinking are relatively unpredictable and connected very loosely with one's process of thought. It is in order not to become lost in a mystery about how thinking can relate at all to willing and to judging that we reminded ourselves that the process is not in *all* ways outside the category of action. Both (being) willing and judging are intimately and almost immediately connected with what we are to do. At the same time we recall that thinking does lie awkwardly within the category of action since otherwise there would be a mystery about its lack of need for a purpose. Furthermore, the ways in which thinking is unlike action show what thinking owes to the will and to judgment. We need thought for well-judged action.

We have observed with Arendt how the mood of willing is in conflict with that of thinking.[9] At the same time, the value and good name of the will (particularly when one thinks, as did Arendt, of its contemporary abuses) depends upon one's capacity to retain the benefit of prior thought. Thought must have the force, though slight and uncertain, to leave a trace upon willing and doing. For its part, will must have a receptivity to thought's shadow even while in the fraught state of proceeding towards actions whose real nature and consequences must always far exceed anything one entertained in thought and imagination. To parody Kant on sense and intellect[10] – thought without will is idle; willing without thought, violent. So judgment appears on the scene, to solve the standoff between thinking and willing. Judgment has the required degree of autonomy from each to be able to achieve the task. To judge is not to think, since, for one thing, it is not a process like thinking. Nor is it simply the final point of thinking – the moment at which thinking comes to its end. A judgment is neither a calculation nor an inference. Useful as calculation and inference are, they do not bridge the gap between what is open to the intellect and what is required of the will.

What then is this 'judging'? Something remarkable and entirely familiar. We want to describe and to locate judgment as we practice it – not a process and scarcely an 'act'. Like conscience, we learn to ignore the call to judgment just as we learned the need to heed it. It is precisely because a judgment does not mince matters that we manage to ignore it, dismissing judgments as 'just your point of view', as 'dogmatic'. In moral affairs, it is precisely because there is a *judgment* that we seek to dismiss it as 'moralising'. We fail to make judgments because we lack the resolution we need if we are to be clear-cut. We inhibit ourselves from judging because we fail to distinguish making a thing of morality ('moralising') and seeing what is currently at stake in an issue.[11] Also, it is in being fearful that in making

9 We have yet to consider how it stands in relation to judging, in this respect.

10 'Thoughts without content are empty; intuitions without conceptions are blind' (Kant 1998, 193–4).

11 On being liberal (63–77), being open-minded (107–21) and being arrogant (169–80), see Deutscher 1983.

judgments we express nothing but our own subjectivity that we become heedless of the need to make them.

Though judging is not thinking, one fails to judge – even badly – unless thought was involved in the making of it. The 'judge' who misleadingly directs a jury because he or she has already decided on the guilt of the accused on extraneous grounds of prejudice has not made even his or her own private judgment about the guilt of the accused. He or she has failed to exercise judgment in the first place. Though there is no mysterious inner act called 'the act of judgment', the judge must *judge* if there is to be a judgment, whether good, bad, wise or reckless. If the judge has not brought him or herself to that 'moment'[12] at any stage of the court process then what he or she pronounces in the sentencing is a sham judgment rather than merely a bad one. There is a parallel here between judgment and the will. Though there is no inner deed called 'the act of will'[13] a person who takes a certain course of action may not have formed any resolution to do what they have begun even though they decided upon it at the outset. Faced with a tension, between their life before the new initiative and the consequences that arise for it, they have no basis for deciding what to do. They start to blame 'life' with its 'infinite perplexities', rather than their lack of resolution and judgment in living it.

We can collect some of these connections. To act, though being willing to, without having thought about the nature of the act or without a continuing thoughtfulness in doing what one wills is cruel. To persist requires the person involved to be no less than callous, perhaps outright destructive. However, someone may fail to exercise judgment even though they thought about the matter. They may fail to continue to be thoughtful when making their pronouncement. That is, their thinking may fail to continue to inform their will. It fails to be translated into it. To think is not yet to judge. To think and then to act is still not to have committed oneself intellectually and emotionally to the value (and the priority over other things one values) of what one is taking on. Similarly, to judge requires one to have thought about the issue and to be thoughtful in making the judgment.[14] Furthermore, if I thought properly this must have involved my being willing to think. This holds even though to think is not to will and even though, when thinking is willed, willing is no part of thinking. There is one more connection between thinking and willing. The limits of what one can think about seriously – in a sustained, thorough and critical fashion – are set by what one is prepared to do or to countenance. Being willing to think – to think willingly – is not merely to undertake the required commitment of time and concentration. It is to be prepared to absorb what one comes across and to settle for a while in the place of one's arrival, temporary as it may be.

---

12 We recall that the duration allowed to a 'moment' is a function of the process of which it is a hiatus or border.

13 We have examined that route – it leads at best to the faulty idea of the will as an act of inner command, or to an elusive act, as mysterious to the one who wills as it is to those who observe the actions of the one who wills.

14 'Being thoughtful in' is vital. It makes a farce of thought to leave it in another box when it comes time to act. True, faced with the situation, one cannot, in good faith, enact what one had thought of doing. This shows, not that thought should be left aside in action, but that we need continuing thought in what we do.

Though each of the trio – *thinking, willing, judging* – may be made central, casting the other two as mere supporting cast, it is judgment that has arisen latest on the scene and which therefore comes under special scrutiny concerning its aid in moving thinking and willing out of their conflict or stalemate. According to what has been assembled, judging comes to the aid of willing and thinking, and particularly to our understanding of the two and of their inter-relation. In the exercise of judgment we understand better the need of the will for thinking, and the need of thinking for being willing. Simply in willing one has gone beyond thinking. Simply in thinking, inevitably, one has put aside the urgencies of the will. In judging, and in the renewed attention to it we accept the professional preoccupations (*déformation*) of each of them and raise up what lies precisely in the blind spot of each of them.

Cause and effect – one last time

In terms of the different and conflicting moods by which Arendt marks thinking and willing, the appeal to judgment – as achievement and as concept – seems now clear. What of that other principal problem that derives from Kant, and has become central in Arendt's work? The question of how to relate the world of action in its field of cause and effect with that of 'practical' (in the Kantian sense) reason whose sphere is that of a-temporal reasons rather than of causes that bring something about? In the terms transformed by Arendt, how are we to understand how our 'revolutionary' acts of initiation of new lines of events under the emblem of 'birth' go together with the demands of our intellect? That is to say, intellect's demand, its quietly reasonable requirement, is that just like the most mundane repetitions of daily life, the most novel of experiments has its causes and effects.

If it is not a magical judgment that is our hope here and if judgment can offer something, it will be as we know and practise it – an activity remarkable as is thinking and willing and, in the same breath, familiar. We can hope to learn from judgment but the lesson is not that a contradiction can be true – that an event is caused as such and uncaused if considered as an action. As an event in the world an action occurs in a causal system even while it initiates a new series that makes a break with the past. Kant's myth of a 'noumenal' as against a 'phenomenal' world must be ambiguous, even in his own terms, since he means to set a limit to speculative thought, not to construct another, always indeterminable, metaphysical system. Furthermore the division between the worlds is ambiguous since, as he insists rather than merely conceding, the will that operates (non-temporally) in the noumenal, must be the very will that is enacted phenomenally. Otherwise one would not be accountable for one's actual, messy, deeds. We can head towards a 'good' ambiguity, in Merleau-Ponty's terms, only by thinking of the noumenal and the phenomenal as the one event, described in categorically different terms, words that have radically different conceptual and practical milieux.

This last direction towards a solution certainly may sound like the most vapid and familiar of strategies for resolving a philosophical impasse – 'two ways of describing the same thing'. Such a cliché under-describes the solution, built upon the business of judging, that might be fashioned upon Arendt upon Kant. Donald

Davidson (Davis 1983, 58–72) is well known for his neo-Kantian rapprochement between causality and being governed by reasons.[15] An event and its successor *under the concept of causality* are described in terms that may be used in stating a law-like connection between the two events. The same events, however, may be described in terms such as those used in moral justification of what was done. When described in such terms, not surprisingly, there is no law-like connection between event and its successor. The one event is susceptible of various descriptions, as anyone must admit. So we have, here, a model for how events in the 'natural order' are related as cause and effect, while when considered in the moral order, they are not *being so related.* Kant's division of noumenal and phenomenal orders is supplanted by Davidson's distinction of differing descriptive modes – those that support causal laws and those that do not. One understands in terms of moral reasons why the action I took *had to be done* – 'Otherwise I would have perpetrated a manifest injustice.' Also one might understand in terms of cause and effect my considering the moral issue if that process were described in terms of the processes in my brain (presumably) that amount to my thinking about justice. The descriptions of thought as a brain-process relate within a causal law to physical descriptions of my acting justly.

Objections to the success of Davidson's *modus vivendi* for causality and moral (or other) reasons turn around the fact that something different is said about my moral reasoning when it is described, first in terms of brain processes and then in terms of considerations of justice. Some different *property* is attributed by the terms of moral thought that is attributed by the terms of brain processing. Otherwise, nothing seriously different would have been asserted by each mode of discourse. These properties of being 'moral thought' must be different from those of being 'discharges of patterns of electrical current'. Hence, even if Kant's 'noumenal' inhabits the same world as his 'phenomenal' (according to this contemporary up-reading of Kant) there are still two orders of being that inhabit that one world – the merely causal and the morally significant. Kant's problem then returns with full force. Are the properties assigned by the natural, or physical, descriptions the only ones that have any effect on what I do? Then my moral (or immoral) thinking is irrelevant to what I do, and responsibility for what I do cannot be sheeted home to my moral will. Or is it the case that the properties assigned by the terms of moral thinking to (what is in fact) the brain-processing that amounts to that moral thinking do play a role in bringing about the just or unjust action that I commit? In that case, the account of causes as in the 'natural' order is incomplete – contrary to what Kant (and the mainstream of contemporary thought) takes to be required by reason.

Attempts to 'get around' this objection within that way of conceptualising the issue are at best *ingenious*. That is to say, they slip from the mind as quickly as they are promulgated, and produce no rational conviction – only momentary admiration at an academic seminar. One can undercut the whole scheme of the objection, however, by refusing an ontology of properties. Events (or states or processes) produce events (or states or processes). It is not the 'properties' of these things that are efficacious,

---

15 I may refer the reader also to my 'Reasons and Causes' (Deutscher 1976). I argue for a similar position, though in somewhat different terms that do not make the assumption that causality is a matter of law-likeness.

since there are no such things. It is simply ontologically fundamental that events, states and processes[16] are described, truly, in a variety of different ways. This implies nothing about the fact that it is the same event (state, process) that is differently described. It is the event (state, and so on) that is the cause. Hence the many true descriptions of it do not entail a multiplication or division of causes.

That last is the only, effective and adequate interpretation of the solution to the Kant/Arendt problem of intellectual reason's demand for a causal order, and moral reason's demand for a relevant and effective moral (and other evaluative) order. There is, however, a heavy investment of intellectual capital in theories of 'properties that make true the predicates that attribute them'. Such theories exploit the appearance in ordinary language of the causal significance of one's manner of description. You know. 'He was killed because he was shot with a pearl-handled revolver – not that its being pearl-handled had anything to do with it, of course.' Or, alternatively, 'He was killed with a pearl-handled revolver – the pearl-handle was a vital part of the mechanism of that very peculiar revolver, and had it been made of anything but pearl that mechanism would not have operated.' Thus, the 'property of being pearl-handled' can be argued to be causally relevant, or not. If we are to reconcile different orders of true description of causes without multiplying causes and reconstituting the problem we set out to solve then we shall take the problem to require us to recast such a way of portraying events:

> A movement in a certain finely textured low-density material (the pearl handle of the revolver) was linked with the ordinary trigger mechanism so that when the revolver was picked up, the ordinary trigger mechanism would be activated and the revolver would discharge.[17]

This describes the relevance of the pearl handle without invoking a property-entity called 'pearl-handled-ness' that enters into causal relations.

This framework of language does provide a way of describing a possible congruence of simply causal, physical (Kant's 'natural') events and morally (or otherwise) significant thoughts and deeds. And yet the phenomenology of it is unsatisfying. Like its proposed solution, the description of the problem is undertaken from a third-person uncommitted point of view. In Arendt's terms, the vision of mind, the intellect, is being made to predominate over that of the will. As a corollary, the terms of judgment find no proper place in the story. This is part of the cause of dissatisfaction. But also, connected with this lack there is also a missing existential component. The language of 'properties' and 'predicates' speaks from the point of view of one who thinks and theorises, but elides the voice of the one who wills and commits themself.[18] The one who wills and commits themself must actively prefer

16 Objects are not terms in causal relations and so are not mentioned in this list. But of objects, too, it will hold that though there are various different *things to be said about* objects, it is simply fundamental that this is the case, and is not to be referred further back to the existence of *things* that are *said about* objects.

17 Author's illustration of a solution.

18 Kant makes a striking move in this direction in his *Groundwork for a Metaphysics of Morals* (Kant 2002).

one line of action to another. As a requirement of this, they must (given the facts) privilege one view of a situation over another. Look back for a moment at Sartre's re-writing of the Kantian problem and his solution to it.

A slippage of 'nothingness'[19]

For Sartre, cause and effect involve differentiation, and differentiation *already* involves the negativity that only consciousness can establish.[20] This ontological negativity is required for a *nihilating* function. Hence, causality cannot be prior to it. Cause and effect arise only on the ground of nihilation, thus being 'always already' the arena of a possible freedom.[21] The slip between cause and effect is only one manifest expression of the slip between *being* and *negativity* that is engineered by what dwells in an 'exquisite region of Being':

> It is essential therefore that the questioner have the permanent possibility of dissociating himself from the causal series which constitutes being, and which can produce only being (Sartre 1976, 23).

Sartre forestalls the reply that a cause/effect series is a total determinant of every event in every aspect, prior to any interpretation:

> If we admitted that the question is determined in the questioner by universal determinism then *that* the question arises would become … inconceivable (Sartre 1976, 23).[22]

If everything were caused without freedom there would be nothing to choose – no arena for choice, so the motivation of consciousness is not a cause competing with 'natural' causation:

> If we think of prior consciousness as a motivation, we see that nothing has slipped in between that state and the present state (Sartre 1976, 27).

There is no 'indeterminacy' if the slippage is considered as an *absence* and thus an *absence of causation.* It is by an absence vital to causation that the field of cause and effect arises:

> There is no weakening of the motivating force of the prior consciousness. What separates prior from subsequent is exactly nothing (Sartre 1976, 27).

Cause and effect thus appear on the ground of (free) nihilation[23]and to recognise cause and effect is to have accepted freedom. It is the (free) nihilating of a positive

---

19 This section is an adaptation of a section of *Genre and Void* (Deutscher 2003, 71–3).

20 Negativity is no threat to the status of causality if it too is 'ontological'.

21 The world prior to the evolution of free beings must be already such as to permit the evolution of freedom.

22 I have abbreviated and adjusted the standard translation here.

23 Like Kant, Sartre implies no ideality of cause and effect. Like absence, causality appears on the ground of nihilation as real, subject to perceptual judgment.

situation that raised up the positivity of (Kant's general category of) 'effect following upon cause'. I 'caused' there to be causes, as I 'caused' Pierre to be *absent* from the café. The 'film of nothingness' that is enough to separate present state from my past is enough to separate cause from effect in the sense that is required for freedom.

This Sartrean language is closer than Davidson's in mood, affect and ontology to Arendt's reading of Kant's possibility of freedom. In recognising the abyss of freedom before which the mind reels it is Arendt rather than Davidson who draws out the significance of Kant's claim to have discovered in noumenal reason an 'initiation of a new series of events'. For Arendt to properly to register such and idea of 'initiation' requires the figure of being born.

A mood of being free

It may seem strange that one might attempt to catch with a mere 'mood' an ontological difference so pronounced that a Kant would have dared to settle a noumenal order behind what we experience in order to do justice to it. For all that, the conflict persists, every day in the everyday, between the rational demand for explanation of one's own actions and the need to take responsibility for them. Thus Bill Clinton[24] engages in a *bravura* act before an audience of millions, not stooping to totter between practices of apologies for a wrongdoing and explanations of how he could have come to commit it. He explains how, in the context of his childhood with an abusive father he learned to live two 'parallel lives'. This permitted him to succeed in public life though immersed, in a different sense, in a private one whose defects were intransigent to any efforts of his. His simultaneous acceptance of responsibility for having endangered his serious political projects, his marriage and the well-being of a relatively powerless young woman is not precluded by his explanation of some of the causes of his being capable of that endangerment of others.

In fact, when the search for causes of one's actions is taken on as consistent with undertaking responsibility for them, the understanding of those causes can become part of one's responsibility for one's actions. To take responsibility is not just to be sorry, to apologise and to make what reparations are possible. It is to do something about the likelihood of repeating such an offence. It is far from a responsible attitude to refuse, in a moral fervour of undertaking responsibility, the relevance of an understanding of causes. It is part of an error – a capitulation to the myth of willing as an inner act of command that makes of itself both superior commander and obedient servant all at once. We have analysed enough, already, the disintegration of attempts to think – and to live – according to that model.

To undertake responsibility for one's actions within a project of being willing (rather than the Will) is to become responsible for living out a certain kind of being. It is to accept the relevance of medical help, of systematic advice from experts and friends, and of regimes of exercise, of reading, of thought. It is to accept the lesson from causality that one cannot simply 'will' to act constructively rather than destructively, while rejecting the consequence set up within determinism, that once we know all the causes we know that nothing else could have been done. It is not by

24 TV interview broadcast ABC (Australia) 29 June 2004.

access to a power outside the natural causal order but from within the system that we learn to choose the better or more prudent course.

Though we cannot remove ourselves from the field of causes that constitutes the stage for any choice, freedom still exists in our exercise of judgment – in the style with which we meet a situation and confront habits and tendencies. Mostly, we construe these causes *subsequent* to the event, and this limits our control. Nevertheless, a person with mental strength, intelligence and good humour is reliable; they *bear with* remarks and behaviour that drive others to angry authoritarianism. Thus, reasons differ from causes, but as a kind of cause that is handled with judgment – freely. Reasons are causes that I have made my own, evaluating them according to what I (and others) would achieve. We appreciate the causes that bear upon us and turn these to our advantage. Certainly, our *power* to do this has its place in the field of play of factors that influence and modify outcomes but we judge these factors not merely *as* causes. Judgment gives pride of place to the language of cause and effect *qua* power of thought, sense of humour, requirements of justice. Yes, there will be causes for this partial freeing of oneself from causes, too. We may come to know them but in any case, to be free is to judge within them. We establish a degree of freedom when we can at least imagine a field of view outside those factors.

That there exists a field of forces for any judgment need not, therefore, threaten our freedom to choose opinions within reason. We develop a freedom in respect of hitherto unknown causes of freeing, too. Learning something of brain function, we modify its level of serotonin, decrease our intake of alcohol – or simply take a deep breath. In the everyday it is in such ways that, to adapt Kant's language, we create the noumenal within the phenomenal. Though the actions we take in our very freeing of ourselves from causes are themselves caused, still we find paths that lead away from conduct and feeling that is over-determined, unreasoned.[25] In such ways, we can begin to elucidate Kant and Arendt's intuition of judgment as the bridge between natural causes and the will as our freedom of origin.

25 In the last two paragraphs I have drawn upon material in *Genre and Void* (Deutscher 2003, 47–8).

Bibliography

Principal relevant works of Hannah Arendt

(1958), *The Human Condition*, University of Chicago Press, Chicago and London.
(1971), *The Life of the Mind*, Harcourt Brace, New York.
(1992), *Hannah Arendt's Lectures on Kant's Political Philosophy* [delivered in 1970], (with interpretive essay), Beiner, Ronald (ed.), The University of Chicago Press, Chicago.
(2003), *Essays on Understanding* (collected essays 1964–75), Random House, New York.

General and biographical critiques of Arendt

Ettinger, Elzbieta (1995), *Hannah Arendt/Martin Heidegger*, Yale University Press, New Haven.
May, Derwent (1986), *Hannah Arendt*, Penguin, Harmondsworth.
Watson, David (1992), *Arendt*, Fontana, London.
Young-Bruehl, Elizabeth (1982), *For Love of the World*, Yale University Press, New Haven.

Collections of critical papers on Arendt

Garner, Reuben (ed.) (1990), *The Realm of Humanitas: Responses to the Writings of Hannah Arendt*, Lang, New York.
Hill, Melvyn (ed.) (1979), Hannah *Arendt: The Recovery of the Public World*, St. Martin's Press, New York.
Hinchman, Lewis P. and Hinchman, Sandra A. (eds.) (1994), *Hannah Arendt: Critical Essays*, State University of New York Press, Albany.
Kaplan, G. and Kessler, C. (eds.) (1989), *Hannah Arendt: Thinking, Judging, Freedom*, Allen & Unwin, Sydney.
May, Larry and Kohn, Jerome (eds.) (1997), *Hannah Arendt: Twenty Years Later*, MIT Press, Cambridge, Mass.
Villa, Dana (ed.) (2000), *The Cambridge Companion to Hannah Arendt*, Cambridge University Press, Cambridge.

Specialised studies of Arendt's thought

Benhabib, Seyla (1996), *The Reluctant Modernism of Hannah Arendt*, Sage, Thousand Oaks.

Bowen-Moore, Patricia (1989), *Hannah Arendt's Philosophy of Natality*, Macmillan, Basingstoke.
Canovan, Margaret (1974), *The Political Thought of Hannah Arendt*, J.M. Dent, London.
——. (1992), *Hannah Arendt: A Reinterpretation of Her Political Thought*, Cambridge University Press, Cambridge.
Kateb, George (1984), *Hannah Arendt: Politics, Conscience, Evil*, Oxford University Press, Oxford.
Kristeva, Julia (2001), *Hannah Arendt*, Columbia University Press, New York.
Passerin d'Entrèves, Maurizio (1994), *The Political Philosophy of Hannah Arendt*, Routledge, London and New York.
Taminiaux, Jacques (1997), *The Thracian Maid and the Professional Thinker*, Princeton University Press, Princeton.
Tlaba, Gabriel (1987), *Politics and Freedom: Human Will and Action in the Thought of Hannah Arendt*, University Press of America, Lanham, MD.
Villa, Dana (1999), *Politics, Philosophy, Terror: Essays on the Thought of Hannah Arendt*, Princeton University Press, Princeton.

Books containing chapters on Arendt

Bernstein, Richard J. (1986), *Philosophical Profiles*, Polity Press, Cambridge.
Ihde, Don and Silverman, Hugh (eds.) (1985), *Descriptions*, SUNY Press, Albany.
Nye Andrea (1994), *Philosophia: The Thought of Rosa Luxembourg, Simone Weil, and Hannah Arendt*, Routledge, London and New York.
Rosenthal, Abigail (1987), *A Good Look at Evil*, Temple University Press, Philadelphia.

Other works cited

Austin, J.L. (1962), *Sense and Sensibilia*, Oxford University Press, Oxford.
——. (1979), *Philosophical Papers*, Oxford University Press, Oxford.
Cavarero, Adriana (1997), *Relating Narratives*, Routledge, London.
Cox, D, La Caze M. and Levine, M. (2003), *Integrity and the Fragile Self*, Ashgate, Aldershot.
Davis, Steven (1983), *Causal Theories of Mind*, Gruyer, Berlin and New York.
Descartes, René (1954), *Descartes: Philosophical Writings* (trans. Anscombe E. and Geach, P.), Thomas Nelson, Edinburgh.
Deutscher, Max (2003), *Genre and Void: Looking Back at Sartre and Beauvoir*, Ashgate, Aldershot.
——. (ed.) (2000), *Michèle Le Dœuff*, Humanity Books, Amherst.
——. (1984), *Subjecting and Objecting*, Blackwell, Oxford.
——. (1976) 'Conceptual Connection and Causal Relation', *Australasian Journal of Philosophy*, 54, 1, 3–13.
Edwards, Paul (2004), *Heidegger's Confusions*, Prometheus Books, Amherst.

Hegel, G.W.F. (1977), *The Phenomenology of Spirit* (trans. Miller, A.V.), Oxford University Press, Oxford.
Heidegger, Martin (1962), *Being and Time*, Blackwell, Oxford.
——. (1977), *Basic Writings*, Krell, D. (ed.), Routledge, London.
——. (1979–87), *Nietzsche* (trans. Krell, D., Stambaugh, J. and Capuzzi, F.), Harper and Row, San Francisco.
Hume, David (1978), *A Treatise of Human Nature* (ed. Selby-Bigge, L.A., revised Nidditch, P.H.), Oxford University Press.
Husserl, Edmund (1970), *Crisis of European Sciences and Transcendental Phenomenology*, Northwestern, Evanston.
Kant, Immanuel (1987), *Critique of Judgment* (trans. Pluher, W.), Hackett, Indianapolis.
——. (1998), *Critique of Pure Reason* (trans. and ed. Guyer P. and Wood, A.), Cambridge University Press, Cambridge and New York.
——. (2002), *Groundwork for the Metaphysics of Morals* (trans. Wood, A.), Yale University Press, New Haven, London.
Kaplan, Giesela T. and Kessler, Clive S. (eds) (1989), *Arendt: Thinking, Judging, Freedom*, Allen & Unwin, Sydney.
Irigaray, L. (1993), *An Ethics of Sexual Difference* (trans. Burke, C. and Gill, G.), Cornell University Press, Ithaca.
Karpin, Matthew (2004), *The Thesis*, Kardoorair Press, Armidale.
Lacan, J. (1977), *Ecrits: A Selection*, Tavistock, London.
Le Dœuff, Michèle (1986), 'Du Sujet', *Cross-references*, Society for French Studies Supplementary publications, 8.
——. (1991), *Hipparchia's Choice* (trans. Selous, T.), Blackwell, Oxford.
Lewis, David K. (1983), *Philosophical Papers Vol I*, Oxford University Press, Oxford and New York.
Lévy, Bernard-Henri (2003), *Sartre: Philosopher of the Century*, Polity Press, Cambridge.
Merleau-Ponty, Maurice (1962), *The Phenomenology of Perception*, Routledge, London.
——. (1968), *The Visible and the Invisible*, NorthWestern, Evanston.
Nagel, Thomas (1986), *The View from Nowhere*, Oxford University Press, Oxford and New York.
Nietzsche, Friedrich (1967), *The Will to Power* (trans. Kaufmann, W. and Hollingdale R.), Random House, New York.
——. (1984), *Human, All Too Human* (trans. Faber, M. and Lehmann S.), University of Nebraska Press, Lincoln.
——. (1996) *On The Genealogy of Morals* (trans. Smith, D.), Oxford University Press, Oxford and New York.
——. (1998) *Beyond Good and Evil* (trans. Faber, M.), Oxford University Press, London.
Rich, Adrienne (1977), *Of Woman Born*, Virago, London.
Ryle, Gilbert (1949), *The Concept of Mind*, Hutchinson, London and (1963) Penguin, Harmondsworth.
——. (1971), *Collected Papers*, Hutchinson, London.

——. (1973), 'Negative Actions', *Hermathena*, No. 115, (81–93), reprinted in Ryle, 1979.

——. (1979), Kolenda, K. (ed.), *On Thinking*, Blackwell, Oxford.

Sartre, Jean-Paul (1965), *Nausea* (trans. Baldick, R.), Penguin, Harmondsworth.

——. (1976), *Being and Nothingness* (trans. Barnes, H.), Methuen, London.

Scarry, Elaine (1999), *On Beauty and Being Just*, Princeton University Press, Princeton.

Schopenhauer, Arthur (1966), *The World as Will and Representation* (trans. Payne, E.F.J.), Dover, New York.

Small, Robyn (ed.) (2001), *A Hundred Years of Phenomenology*, Ashgate, Aldershot.

Wittgenstein, Ludwig (1953), *Philosophical Investigations* (trans. Anscombe, E.), Blackwell, Oxford.

Woolf, Virginia (1938), *Three Guineas*, Penguin, Harmondsworth.

Index

Page numbers followed by 'f' indicate that the reference is contained in a footnote.

Name Index